Praise for Leora Tanenbaum and *I AM NOT A SLUT*

"This thoroughly researched, galvanizing book will serve as a crucial tool for young women and their families. Tanenbaum navigates the perilous waters young women are swimming in—filled with sexual objectification, double standards, self-exposure, and social censure—and offers them a guide to make it safely to shore."

—Rebecca Traister, author of *Big Girls Don't Cry*

"Girls and young women are inundated with images and messages that teach them sex is the only currency that matters in our culture. But when they follow those cues, they are shamed and excoriated for it. The Internet has made slut-shaming more effective, wide ranging, and deeply damaging. We have a right to own and express our sexuality, on our own terms, without apology or repercussion. I recommend this book to anyone who cares about girls and young women and wants to understand the heartbreaking challenges they face as they grow into their sexuality."

—Aisha Tyler, comedian, actress, and author

"Get out your highlighters: For parents, for educators, and—most important—for girls themselves, *I Am Not a Slut* is an absolutely crucial read. In a time when high school and college are social battlefields for young women, understanding the nuances of sex and shame can literally be a life-or-death project. Tanenbaum's empathetic look at how today's expectations of performative identity can undermine real, healthy sexuality is heartbreaking. With any luck, it will also galvanize a much needed shift, challenging each of us to consider how we participate in creating the world these girls navigate."

—Andi Zeisler, cofounder and editorial director, Bitch Media

"As we see every day at Planned Parenthood health centers across the country, slut-shaming is a harmful—and, at worst, lethal—barrier to sexual health care and information for women and girls. *I Am Not a Slut* offers both a wake-up call about the dangerous impact of the word 'slut' and a path forward to talk about sex and sexuality in an open, positive, and nonjudgmental way."

—Cecile Richards, president, Planned Parenthood Federation of America

"*I Am Not a Slut* is a profoundly eye-opening book about the dangerous world young women are forced to negotiate and the blind eye all too often turned toward it by their peers, adults, and even the media. It should be required reading for anyone who has ever called someone a slut or been called one themselves. It has the power to help young women who are suffering through this kind of shaming to feel less alone and provides a powerful education for those who care about them."

—Elissa Schappell, author of *Blueprints for Building Better Girls*

I AM NOT A SLUT

ALSO BY LEORA TANENBAUM

Bad Shoes and the Women Who Love Them

*Taking Back God: American Women Rising Up for
  Religious Equality*

Catfight: Women and Competition

Slut! Growing Up Female with a Bad Reputation

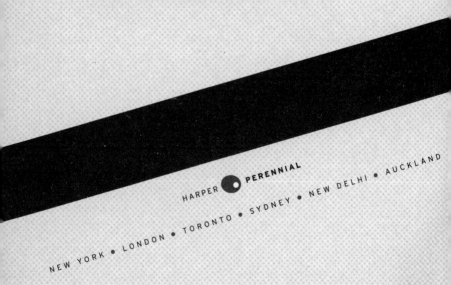

HARPER ● PERENNIAL

NEW YORK ● LONDON ● TORONTO ● SYDNEY ● NEW DELHI ● AUCKLAND

I AM NOT a SLUT

LEORA TANENBAUM

Slut-Shaming in the Age of the Internet

HARPER PERENNIAL

HarperCollins books may be purchased for educational, business, or sales promotional use. For information please e-mail the Special Markets Department at SPsales@harpercollins.com.

FIRST EDITION

Designed by William Ruoto

Library of Congress Cataloging-in-Publication Data has been applied for.

ISBN 978-0-06-228259-0

15 16 17 18 19   OV/RRD   10 9 8 7 6 5 4 3 2 1

CONTENTS

You're a sixteen-year-old girl flopped on the sofa, trying to vaporize anxious thoughts about the SAT prep you're behind on and the classmate who cackled and tweeted the moment she saw your outfit this morning. With one hand, you reach over for the remote and power on the TV. With your other hand, you grab your phone and check your Instagram and Twitter. Whichever screen you look at, you come across images of women acting like stereotypical "sluts" and "hos"—and getting rewarded for their behavior. You pay attention—maybe you could learn a thing or two.

On E!, you see Miley Cyrus twerking at the MTV Video Music Awards. Is this the same girl on your old Hannah Montana *sheets? You marvel over how raunchy and uninhibited she is—what an improvement over her boring, wholesome old Disney identity. Meanwhile, a friend has Instagrammed a pa-*

parazzi shot of Lindsay Lohan getting out of a limo, her short dress exposing the fact that she's not wearing underwear. You wonder if she flashed the photographers on purpose—probably, you figure, because one thing she is wearing is a big smile. And here's another photo—this one's of Rihanna, braless in a see-through dress. She's posing for photographers, looking completely relaxed, so she must know she looks amazing. A text message pops up on your phone; you're invited to a "Pimps and Hos" party on Saturday night. You know the party is just an excuse for the girls to get away with wearing as little as possible, and you can't deal with the pressure of figuring out a hot outfit. But if you don't go, you'll be missing out, so you start thinking about which shoes, top, and skirt will make you look slutty—in a good way.

You roam through the channels on TV, pausing when you find The Bachelor. Several women are sitting in a hot tub in string bikinis, making sexual advances and vying for the attention of a man they barely know. One of these women will "win" a ring on her finger. On another channel, you catch a scene from an old rerun of 30 Rock. Producer Liz Lemon, played by Tina Fey, is far from a slut, yet she calls herself and her colleague Jenna "sluts" in a casual, hip way, as if to show how ironic and witty she is. Finally, you settle on Keeping Up with the Kardashians, even though you can't remember why these sisters are famous—is it because they never tire of showing off their bodies? No matter. You still enjoy watching them ooze sexual confidence.

You compulsively check your Twitter for comments on that girl who got drunk on Friday night and supposedly hooked up with three different boys. OMG—there are photos and videos of her doing a drunken striptease! You can see her face clearly. Classmates are responding: "What a ho! lol!" and "Sloppy slut" and *"Whore deserves to be raped!"* Even though you didn't take off any of your clothes, you also drank too much at the same party, and you don't remember everything that went down. You're terrified that pictures of you will surface, too. So far, you've been safe. Phew! The other girl didn't come to school yesterday, but today she showed up and everyone was horrible to her. The boys kept coming up to her and asking her to send them naked pictures of herself. One of the girls went right up to her and asked why she wore such an ugly leopard-print bra, and then laughed and said maybe it was a good thing after all that she took it off. You were careful not to make eye contact with the girl, even though you feel bad for her. You want to show everyone that you disapprove of the disgusting things she supposedly did—but you don't know exactly what she did, if anything.

All of a sudden your Twitter feed is going crazy. Everyone's tweeting about some guy in California who went on a shooting spree, killing six college students before shooting himself in the head. Turns out he was angry that girls weren't interested in him, and he had vowed to "slaughter every blond slut" he saw. How did he define "slut," anyway? You wonder: Would he have considered me a slut? Would he have murdered me?

Welcome to the homeland of teenage girls and young women, a contradictory landscape in which females are applauded for sexual audacity when they're not being humiliated and disgraced. New ideas about female sexual liberation clash with old stereotypes about "good girls" and "sluts."

In celebrity land, women embrace a "slutty" persona as a conscious marketing strategy. When a private sex tape with an old boyfriend surfaces, it opens up new business opportunities rather than creating a shameful scandal. No skirt for these women is too short; no blouse is too low-cut. On the surface, these women seem to be strong role models, even feminists; they tell the world that women can be as sexually liberated as men always have been.

For teenage girls in real life, "slutty" behavior is an entirely different thing. Girls who dress like Miley Cyrus are mocked and harassed. At best, their names become punch lines. At worst, they become vulnerable to acts of violence. Their reputations can become ruined, and because of the inescapability of Internet chatter, they have nowhere to hide.

What is going on? How can we make sense of this bizarre and jarring contradiction between the behavior sold to girls as good and the very bad consequences for them when they emulate their role models? This contradiction is not simply the result of celebrity culture running amok. *Reality* is running amok. Because it is in reality, not only on some Hollywood set or in the media, that "sluts" are put on a pedestal one moment and then spat upon the next. How has this happened?

The quick, blithe answer is: the Internet. But we have to dig deeper to fully understand the situation in which girls and young women find themselves. The Internet has enabled us to communicate in new ways. But it has also altered face-to-face communication. Even when we aren't connected to any digital gadget or computer, we behave differently from the ways we did fifteen years ago. We all experience and respond to new behavioral norms. It's not incorrect to blame "the Internet," but we have to be clear about what we mean. Blaming "the Internet" is like blaming "culture" or "the patriarchy" for sexist behavioral norms. We need to understand all the dynamics—online and offline—in the new sexual landscape for young females.

I have been researching and tracking the subject of girls' being labeled "sluts" and "hos" for twenty years. In the 1990s, I coined and popularized the term "slut-bashing" to describe a specific form of student-to-student verbal sexual harassment in which a preadolescent or adolescent girl is bullied because of her perceived or actual sexual behavior. The term "slut-bashing" caught on; it is now used as a matter of course by parents, school administrators, academics, and girls and women themselves. My 1999 book about slut-bashing, *Slut! Growing Up Female with a Bad Reputation,* became assigned reading in many sociology and gender or women's studies courses on college campuses nationwide.

Several years ago, I decided to update my research. My plan had been to speak with a new crop of adolescent girls to confirm that slut-bashing is as much of a problem now as it had been then. But the more people I spoke with, the more I came to recognize that the problem is actually much worse today, and that it affects not only adolescent girls but also young women. The new world order of the Internet has upended everything, and I had to completely rethink my arguments. Thus, *I Am Not a Slut* is not simply an update to *Slut!*. It is not merely a report on why girls are slut-bashed and how they respond. This book casts a spotlight of a wider circumference. In these pages, I explore the meanings of "slut" for both adolescent girls and college-age women; the reasons that so many young people today, in the age of the Internet, refer to females as sluts; the methods and strategies girls and women use to respond; and the consequences, sometimes tragic, that result.

I chose to write about slut-bashing because I had been called a slut myself when I was fourteen. I had been the subject of

painful, cruel gossip that began during the spring of my freshman year of high school. Although it ebbed over time, it continued in some form until my high school graduation. Why was
I called a slut? For one thing, I was an early developer. In my
junior high class, I was the first to grow breasts and the first
to menstruate. By ninth grade, I had the physique of an adult
woman. My physical appearance alone marked me as a sexual
being. But my appearance was not the sole trigger. I also did
something profoundly stupid and selfish. I went out on a date
with a boy whom my best female friend liked. Although the two
of them were not dating and in fact barely knew each other (he
attended a different school), I knew that she had her eye on him,
and I should have demurred when he asked me out. We met in
his apartment, with no parents or siblings around, and made out.

Yes, I did something terrible: I broke a basic command-
ment of friendship. However, the punishment I received did
not fit the crime. When my friend found out (the boy called
her and told her everything), she was hurt and enraged. She
decided to get revenge by spreading stories about me. Kids I
had never spoken with, girls as well as guys, came up to me
to tell me off, to look at me with pity or contempt, and to
make jokes at my expense. Strikingly, they did not seem to
care about my betrayal of my friend, which I thought was the
true misdeed. No, the only thing that interested them was
salacious rumors about my sexuality.

At the time, I thought that I was the only girl who had
ever experienced this type of name-calling. I also thought I
deserved to be called a slut, because I felt guilty about my
unethical behavior toward my friend. Therefore it never occurred to me to protest my treatment.

A decade later, a survey conducted by the American Association of University Women found that three-quarters of girls in grades eight through eleven nationwide were sexually harassed in school through name-calling, jokes, gestures, and looks. The *New York Times* reported on the survey during the summer of 1993. I remember eating a muffin in my tiny Brooklyn studio apartment, tiredly flipping through the paper in my precious few minutes of headline-scanning before I began the commute into Manhattan for my job as an editorial assistant. A proverbial lightbulb went on over my head as I read the headline: "School Hallways as Gauntlets of Sexual Taunts."[1] A bar graph accompanying the article broke down the varieties of student-to-student sexual harassment; the graph showed that 42 percent of girls had "had sexual rumors spread about them." At that eureka moment, I realized for the very first time that I too had experienced a form of sexual harassment, and that I was far from alone. My life would never be the same again. Now I had a vocabulary to explain to myself and to others what I had experienced. Now I could make sense of it all.

I resolved to find other girls and women who had been similarly harassed in this manner. During the mid-1990s, I sought out and interviewed fifty girls and women, ages fourteen to sixty-six, Latina, black, and white, from twelve different states, who had been labeled "sluts" or "hos" while they were in school. Working as a freelance journalist, I wrote a series of articles for *Ms.*, *Seventeen*, and other magazines on the subject of slut-bashing. I then expanded my research and wrote *Slut! Growing Up Female with a Bad Reputation*, based on personal testimonies from the girls and women I had interviewed.

The book's main point was that any adolescent girl, even if she had zero sexual experience, could become a target for being labeled a slut or ho. In *Slut!*, I described four groups of girls who were most at risk: early developers and others perceived to be sexually active; girls who were different from their peers in some way; objects of jealousy; and rape victims. I connected slut-bashing with the sexual double standard and explained why this particular form of harassment leads to the sexual policing of all females, whether or not they have been personally targeted. Above all, I showed that a girl called a slut or ho often was targeted not because she was sexually active but because she was socially vulnerable in some way.

Slut! is now recognized as a significant contribution to feminist thought. To date, the book remains the only systematic analysis of slut-bashing. When the book was first published, I was fortunate to be invited to speak about slut-bashing on television programs such as *Oprah*, *Politically Incorrect*, and *The O'Reilly Factor*. Local radio hosts around the country who styled themselves as shock jocks mistakenly thought my book was pornographic and seemed disappointed when I revealed that it was actually about sexual harassment.

Slut-bashing hasn't gone away, but it has taken on different forms over the last two decades. Back in the 1990s, there were no such things as sexting, tweeting, and Facebook drama. Moreover, either a woman was bullied as a slut or she wasn't— period. Today, the Internet and mobile communication have dramatically altered expressions of sexuality for girls and young women. Usage of the words "slut" and "ho" is rampant. Many girls and young women use these words in a casual manner among peers of equal status on social media. In fact, many girls and young women *like* to identify themselves as sluts; to them, this is a *positive* word—but only when used on their terms. When others use "slut" in a negative way, they are said to be guilty of "slut-shaming." The term "slut-shaming" has crept into the feminist vernacular during the last decade to describe a multiplicity of ways in which females are called to task for their real, presumed, or imagined sexuality. "Slut-shaming" is a useful descriptor because today much slut-labeling does not take the form of bullying or harassment. In this book, I distinguish between acts of slut-bashing and acts of slut-shaming. Although both are harmful, they should not be conflated, because, as we will see, they operate quite differently.

In this book, I uncover what girls are thinking and how they rationalize their choices. I reveal the ways in which they navigate mixed sexual messages. I tell girls and adult women that they never deserve to be called sluts or hos—and they never should call themselves sluts or hos—because in the absence of one sexual standard for everyone, the concept of "sluttiness" is grounded in sexist and specious ideas about femininity, even when "slut" or "ho" is used in a seemingly lighthearted or even defiant manner.

If you are a parent of a teenage girl or young woman, you may be desperate to know: Why does your daughter call her friends sluts on social media? Why does she insist on going out in public so scantily clad, to your eye? Why doesn't she try to protect her reputation? You've heard that at high school parties, girls are drinking and then giving boys oral sex. Is your daughter doing this too? If your daughter is in college, you wonder: Is she hooking up? What does "hooking up" even mean exactly?

If you are a girl in high school or a woman in college, you may not be able to articulate the contradiction you are forced to live. You just want to know: How come it's OK for a guy to pressure you day after day to send him a topless photo, and then when you finally break down and do it to get him to stop bugging you, *you're* the one who's labeled a slut and *he* gets a high five from his buddies? And why do people hate "sluts" so much if they also hate "prudes"? How come some girls manage to be "slutty" and get rewarded for it while other girls are "slutty" and get punished for it?

If you are an educator, you certainly recognize the new brutal landscape and the harm it is wreaking, but your hands are tied about what you can do to help. Should you add sexting to the sex-ed curriculum? To what extent can you enforce a dress code without being sexist? What is your responsibility if a girl is slut-shamed on Twitter and Facebook because of activities conducted outside of school, but her harassment spills over into the school environment?

This book will help you to understand the thoughts and behaviors of girls and young women by explaining their motivations. Behaviors that may *appear* counterintuitive in fact make sense when you understand the conflicting pressures that high school girls and college-age women experience. Although their behaviors are rational in the face of mixed sexual messages, they are not necessarily strategic or wise, and very often they end up causing more harm than good. Once you recognize the logic behind their actions, you will be able to help the young females in your life stay safe from physical and emotional harm. You will have the tools to provide the support and understanding they crave. If you are a young woman yourself, this book will help you make sound decisions so that you remain safe.

It's too easy to dismiss slut-bashing or slut-shaming as the product of pathological behavior—that "mean girls" have been socially conditioned to bully, while oversexualized girls are practically asking to be bullied. Attempting to figure out what's "wrong" with either the name-callers or the targets is not productive. Just about every girl and young woman has been on either or both sides of the coin, and clearly not every female is pathological. The problem is not that the name-callers are inherently "mean" or must vent a naturally built-up reserve of "relational aggression"—"mean" and "relational aggression" being fashionable buzzwords among well-intentioned educational administrators trying to stamp out girl-against-girl harassment. And the problem is not that the targets are behaving like out-of-control Lolitas or porn star wannabes. It bears repeating that in many cases the so-called slut's actual sexual behavior is nonexistent or irrelevant.

No, the real problem is the sexual double standard, a bundle of sexist presuppositions that structures the behaviors of many of us in Western society. To understand how the sexual double standard operates in the surveillance-saturated theater in which we now live, I spoke at length and in depth with fifty-five girls and women in North America, primarily between the ages of fourteen and twenty-two. Each admitted to calling others sluts or being labeled a slut herself, or to having witnessed this behavior up close within her peer group. They identify as Latina, black, Asian, white, and biracial. They live within thirteen states and two provinces. They grew up poor, affluent, working-class, and upper-middle-class.[2]

To avoid putting any interviewee at risk for speaking out, I promised everyone anonymity. Thus, I changed the names of all the interviewees—except for academics, journalists, and others who publicly discuss these issues—and I don't name the actual cities and universities in which the interviewees live and attend school. However, all racial identities, ages, and nonidentifying details are left unchanged.

Everyone I spoke with knew I was writing a book on sluttiness and volunteered to participate in my research because he or she wanted to help educate others. In these pages, you will find documented example after documented example of young females labeled as sluts who have suffered harm, as well as testimonies that back up these examples from experts who follow and study the lives of young people. The young women's voices are the most important. They are the most eloquent experts and commentators on their own lives. Their stories are raw, honest, and searing. They speak to the truth in ways that are far more compelling than charts, graphs, polls, and surveys. We cannot make sense of slut-bashing and slut-shaming without their stories.

When I first reported on the phenomenon of slut-bashing in the 1990s, I condemned the behavior of the name-callers, and many people disagreed with my critique. Repeatedly they said to me, "Given the fact that so many teenage girls are having sex and getting pregnant and sexually transmitted diseases, isn't it a *good* thing to shame them? 'Slut' may be an ugly word, and unfortunately there may be some collateral damage, but if it stops girls from having sex at a young age, maybe it's necessary." Putting aside for now the sexism of this mind-set, in which it's not thought necessary to shame sexually active teenage boys because their sexual activity is considered unproblematic, being labeled a slut is not a deterrent to having sex.

First, many girls labeled sluts or hos are not sexually active to begin with. In any event, the overwhelming majority of the girls and women I've interviewed who have been labeled sluts become more, not less, sexually active as a direct result of being so labeled. Not only is the "slut" label an ineffective deterrent, in many cases it hastens rather than delays a girl's sexual activity.

Second, even girls who witness the social downfall of other girls labeled as sluts do not refrain from sexual behavior themselves. Maria, a twenty-one-year-old Latina college student, remembers that in her Miami high school there was a girl in the grade below hers who was "called a lot of names" after she'd had oral sex with a boy from school. "Having seen what happened to her," Maria told me, "I became fearful." And yet Maria herself became sexually active soon after the name-calling began. Slut-shaming does not motivate other girls to remain chaste.

Not a single positive result comes from labeling a girl or woman a slut or ho. An environment in which these labels are acceptable leads only to harmful consequences:

- It suggests to girls and women that their primary value comes from being sexually desirable and available. Yet paradoxically, "slut" also signifies that being sexually desirable and available reduce a female's worth. From every angle, females are evaluated through a sexual prism.

- It props up a rape culture in which many people, men and women alike, believe that coercing a female to perform sexual acts she doesn't want to do, or to which she can't say no, is unproblematic. If a female is sexually assaulted, she is said to deserve it because she's, well, a slut.
- It leads girls and women to engage in self-destructive behaviors such as drug use and abuse, disordered eating, disordered sexual behavior, and suicide attempts.
- It compromises the sexual health of girls and women because they feel inhibited from using contraceptives and even from making an appointment with a health care provider, leading to unwanted pregnancies and sexually transmitted diseases.

Yes, this one little four-letter word is a critical linchpin. To dismantle the severely dysfunctional system of the sexual double standard, we must eliminate the word. Reclaiming "slut" as a positive term, we will see, nearly always backfires. If we want to truly help young women, we need to get rid of the word entirely.

I AM NOT A SLUT

CHAPTER 1

What's the Same, What's Different

At a time when insults travel at warp speed, calling a girl or woman a slut or ho in US youth culture has become prevalent, casual, and normalized. This was not always so. Twenty years ago, the experience of being labeled a slut or ho was not rare, but it also was not ordinary. At that time, just about every middle school and high school seemed to have one, maybe two, girls designated a slut or ho at any given moment. Of course, that was one or two girls too many. The school "slut" was shamed, ostracized, physically harassed, pressured to have sex she didn't want, and raped. Those who mistreated her justified their actions on the grounds that the school "slut" was "too" sexual, and therefore deserved policing or punishment. In fact, in many cases she was not sexually active at all. The "slut" often was singled out because she was an early developer and therefore had the physique of an adult woman; others (classmates as well as adults) assumed that if she *looked* sexual, she must *be* sexual. Even when the school "slut" was sexually active, often she wasn't any more so than her peers.

In many ways, the story is the same as it ever was. Most of the time, the word continues to be used with the intent of shaming a girl or woman. Yet three notable differences mark today's usage of the term.

First, the Internet has made it easier than ever before for any girl or young woman to project and circulate a sexually sophisticated identity that bears no resemblance to her actual sexual experience, which may be nonexistent, and for others to respond by damaging her reputation. A generation ago, a sexually innocent girl who wanted to appear racy went crazy with mascara and eye shadow, or hiked up her skirt after she left home in the morning en route to school. Her parents generally knew who her friends were and when she was going out to see them. Today, however, a girl can take a photo of her naked breasts and email it to a guy she likes, or post a bikini shot on Facebook or Instagram, and her parents will have no idea of her having done so. Meanwhile, bullies of yesteryear had to at least show their faces when they made life miserable for others. Even if they surreptitiously spray-painted "slut" on a girl's front porch or car or school locker, they had to make an effort that carried the risk of exposure. Today, anyone can be an anonymous bully with the touch of a finger on a slim handheld gadget. It doesn't take guts anymore to be a bully, because you don't have to expose yourself and take responsibility for your actions, and it sometimes seems as though almost everyone is a bully. For the girl who is targeted, the experience of being labeled a slut is heightened and sharpened like never before. In today's electronic age, "slut" is an identity with no escape. In the movie *The Social Network*, the character based on Mark Zuckerberg is so angry when his girlfriend rejects him that he goes back to his dorm room and posts nasty comments about her physical appearance on the Internet. Later, when she confronts him, she says, "The Internet's not written in pencil, Mark. It's written in ink."

A second difference is that unlike in previous generations, today the label "slut" snares nearly every young woman at some point. Given the omnipresence of the insult, I believe it's fair to say that every girl in middle school, high school, and even college can expect to be called a slut eventually, if she hasn't been already. When I think back to the situation of two decades ago, when schools had only one or two girls whom others labeled as sluts, I am amazed; we should be so lucky today. Twenty years ago, mistreatment of the school "slut," scary and sexist and sad, was at least not rampant. She stood out precisely because she was somewhat unusual.

But slut-bashing has metastasized. It now goes far beyond bullying. "Slut" is heard frequently today not only in school hallways and cafeterias but also in prime-time television shows of all genres, and in online social media comments. Targets of the insult have expanded to include a wide population of individuals. Today, many girls and women refer to their social equals—in person, online through social media, and via texting and instant messaging—as sluts. Sometimes this usage is casual, even banal, and devoid of an intention to denigrate. Other times the name-caller is motivated to generate "drama"—to whip up public attention, to create excitement, to emulate the dynamics of reality television, in which life isn't worth living unless there's an antagonist to contend with. Sometimes this "drama" is hostile and cruel; it is meant to hurt, and it does.

In this book, I differentiate between "slut-bashing," which is a type of bullying, and "slut-shaming," which is more diffuse. Slut-bashing, I argue, is verbal harassment in which a girl is intentionally targeted because she does not adhere to feminine norms. Slut-shaming, on the other hand, is a casual and often indirect form of judgment. To complicate matters further, sometimes girls and young women engage in a practice I call "reciprocal slut-shaming," in which they take turns calling each other sluts in an apparently friendly manner. However, I will show that regardless of intent, all of these behaviors are absolutely corrosive and wrong. Calling a female a slut even in a seemingly benign context ultimately results in a policing not only of the specific female involved but of all females everywhere.

A third difference is that today many girls and women choose to label *themselves* as sluts—*good sluts*—to assert a positive, even defiant, attitude about their sexuality. As long as they control the label, many adolescent girls say that they enjoy the sexual attention they receive from their peers. To them, "slut" or "slutty" conveys a female who possesses sexual equality with males. If you're around a group of teenage girls or young women, you may hear them call out "Hey slut" to one another. However, it can be hard to know the intention of the speaker for sure. Sometimes in this context, "slut" is meant to be affectionate. But sometimes the intention is to police another girl, to warn her that she's being watched. The speaker herself may not even be clear about her own intent, or she may have dual goals—to be a vivacious friend *and* a guardian of sexual values.

Meanwhile, some adult activists choose to wave the "slut" banner to prove a feminist point. The SlutWalk movement has encouraged women to assert themselves as sex-positive, showing that there's nothing wrong with being a sexual woman. Activists reclaim or "own" the term to disrupt negative associations of femininity with sexuality.

I recognize that some individual girls and women feel empowered when they call themselves and their friends sluts on their own terms. Nevertheless, in the pages that follow I question whether this usage is an effective feminist strategy when employed on a large scale. Repeatedly, girls and women told me that they chose to call themselves sluts but subsequently lost control over the term when others then used the label against them. They used "slut" to mean they were an empowered "good slut," but others turned around the word to mean that they were a shameful, promiscuous "bad slut." Despite its worthwhile intentions, reclaiming the word "slut" may end up causing more harm than good.

Unlike "bitch," which often is turned on its head, becoming a shorthand for "an assertive woman with power" in a positive sense rather than "an aggressive, domineering woman" in a negative sense, "slut" is a more slippery term. "Bitch" refers to a woman's behavior; so as long as her behavior is perceived positively by others, her bitchiness may be considered an asset. "Slut," on the other hand, refers to a woman's essence as a feminine being. Once she is labeled a slut in the pejorative sense, it makes no difference if she changes her behavior or if her behavior becomes well-regarded: she is maligned as a deviant.

In short, the label "slut" is far more common, and utterly more confusing, than ever before. But one thing has not changed: regardless of context, the consequences of being labeled a slut are nearly always damaging. As we'll see, whether the context is slut-bashing, slut-shaming, or even slut-reclaiming, calling a girl or a woman a slut reinforces sexist norms. "Slut" is best regarded as a toxic four-letter word that should be quarantined if not buried.

The "Good Slut"/"Bad Slut" Contradiction

Adolescent girls and college-age women face a profound sexual contradiction. On the one hand, many want to embrace a sex-positive identity as a "good slut" who is free to be sexual on her own terms without judgment. On the other hand, many emphatically do not want to be labeled by others as a slut, because except when used within a tightly contained peer group, the label "slut" indicates that the subject is disgusting and shameful. When someone outside the in-group labels a female a slut, the word becomes evacuated of its positive associations and is left as a container of harsh judgment.

Is it possible to be a "good slut"? Many adolescent girls and college-age women optimistically, naively, say yes. But once they see how "slut" becomes adapted to the presumptions of the sexual double standard—the belief that males can and should be more sexual than females, and therefore that females who are sexually active in ways similar to men are deviant—they come to recognize that the "good slut" identity is ephemeral and tenuous. Ultimately, embracing a "good slut" identity does not serve them well. "Slut" is not an effective or wise organizing principle for expression of sexual freedom, because, as I will demonstrate, this identity makes females unsafe.

This outcome does not mean that females should avoid sexual expression. We *should* be comfortable with our sexual bodies and sexual desire, and we *should* be able to express our sexuality in a developmentally and situationally appropriate manner. But we need to rethink our methods and strategies.

I asked two women, Katie Cappiello and Meg McInerney, who work intensively with teenage girls if it was possible for a young woman to assert her sexuality in a developmentally appropriate and empowering way and *not* be called a slut. They paused for a few beats, unsure. Cappiello is the artistic director and McInerney is the managing director of the Arts Effect, a theater company in New York City for teenagers, which they cofounded. The All-Girl Theater Company, one of the Arts Effect's programs, gives girls leadership tools to initiate social change in their high schools.

"I don't know," McInerney finally responded. "I want it to be possible, more than anything, but I don't know that it is actually possible. If they express their sexuality, every day they have to worry about the consequences. They can't not worry." Cappiello agrees. "The answer is: I don't think so. The only girls we know who are protected from the label are the ones who have never kissed a boy, never wear anything tight, never party, never hook up. Yes, they are protected, but they're also being ignored. They cry about the fact that guys don't know they're alive." There's seemingly no middle ground here: if a young woman does not erase or hide her sexuality, she is at risk of being labeled a slut.

"Slut" is a product of the sexual double standard—the mind-set that males are expected to be sexually active, even in an uncontrolled manner, while females are supposed to police themselves (and other females) to remain minimally sexual. The sexual double standard creates physical and emotional danger for females. Only girls, not boys, are mistreated for being allegedly "too" sexual within a heterosexual context. Yet many people, female and male alike, regard girls and women through a sexual lens. Whether females are sexually active or not, we are seen as beings with sexual potential. Just walking, speaking, and breathing put us at risk for being judged to be "too" sexual.

For at least the last two and a half centuries, white women have been expected to be sexually chaste or monogamous; therefore, their "bad" sluttiness is scandalous because it's a violation of normative behavior. Before the late 1700s, British women were thought to be more sexually desirous than men. As the middle class rose in England and America during the eighteenth and nineteenth centuries, marriage became central to bourgeois society. A shift from the extended family to the nuclear family occurred against the backdrop of evangelical Protestantism and the emerging capitalist and individualistic economy. The family unit became a microcosm of the authoritarian state, and gendered spheres of activity solidified, leading to subordination of women within marriage. The unequal distribution of power within the new romantic marriage led to a new way of thinking of male and female sexuality: men were naturally aggressive while women were inherently passive.[3] Jaclyn Geller, a literature professor and the author of the book *Here Comes the Bride*, a critique of marriage and the wedding industry, notes the significance of the Hardwicke Marriage Act, passed in Britain in 1753. This legislation stipulated that weddings had to be public and ceremonial. Marriages became formalized and regulated by the state. Sexually active women in Britain as well as the colonies who were not wives became regarded as immoral.[4] Wives themselves were also expected to curb their sexual desires. Nancy Cott, a historian, has called this sexual ideology "passionlessness." This dominant view was that white women "lacked sexual aggressiveness, that their sexual appetites contributed a very minor part (if any at all) to their motivations, that lustfulness was simply uncharacteristic."[5] A slut was a white woman who deviated from the ideal.

Women of color, however, have been presumed by white people since at least the 1600s to lack the moral and sexual restraint that white women are thought to possess. The stereotype of white female chastity stands in opposition to a stereotype of black female carnality. As a result, the "bad" sluttiness of women of color reaffirms racist and sexist stereotypes rather than upends them. Thus, Harriet Jacobs, an African American slave, wrote in the 1850s that when her white master sexually assaulted her when she was fifteen years old, her white mistress did not come to her aid. Instead, her white mistress regarded Jacobs as a temptress, and therefore she had "no other feelings towards her but those of jealousy and rage."[6] And still today, when a young woman of color is denigrated by her peers as a slut or a ho, her experience often may not receive the attention it deserves, and she is often left isolated without any support.

Moreover, when females of color attempt, as many of their white cohorts do, to playfully adopt a "good slut" persona, the effort can backfire miserably. Shabiki Crane, a black Canadian woman, recalls that when she attended Catholic school, she and her friends did everything they could to individualize the mandated school uniform. "I, like many girls I knew, chose to wear tight-fitting grey pants as opposed to the ugly, baggy, and shapeless pants from the uniform store," she says.

I remember checking myself numerous times in the mirror; I looked good! Unfortunately, it was not a mutual opinion. The guidance counselor coyly explained to me that I shouldn't wear tight pants because 'people would think badly of me.' He even went as far as to say that Asian and white girls could get away with it because of their shapes, but on me it only looked vulgar. I felt vulgar. . . . It often seemed as if only certain people had the right and privilege to use their sexuality in a manner that was perceived as 'light-hearted' and fun.[7]

Adopting a "good slut" identity is a privilege that many women of color can't access because of racist assumptions about their sexuality.

Queer and heterosexual females also experience slutbashing and slut-shaming in different ways from each other. Some of the women who share their stories in this book are lesbian, bisexual, or sexually questioning. Yet the policing of female sexuality described here is conducted within a heterosexist framework. Regardless of the orientation or gender identity of the girl labeled a slut, she is pushed to conform to heterosexual norms. Slut-bashing and slut-shaming are therefore not only sexist but heterosexist as well.

Different Women, Similar Story

If you are in any doubt as to the violation that girls and women experience from being labeled a slut, listen to their stories.

Jasmine, a twenty-year-old college student on the West Coast, relates how she was slut-bashed in the tenth grade. Jasmine's father is black and her mother is Latina. As a young girl, she lived on an air force base because her dad was in the military, but after her parents divorced, she moved with her mom to a large, gritty inner-city neighborhood. She attended a big urban school whose students were primarily Latino. In describing the various ways in which her school lacked financial resources, she mentions that it offered no honors or AP classes. Four of her friends became pregnant while they were still in high school.

Jasmine is five foot three and curvaceous. An early developer, she became busty at a young age, which led people to assume that she was sexually active, even when she wasn't. In fact, she did not engage in any sexual activity until college; but in high school, "If a boy harassed me, people automatically assumed I was doing things sexually with him." The boys in high school arrived at the conclusion that Jasmine's body somehow belonged to them, not her. She explains,

There was one incident in tenth grade that got me labeled for the rest of high school. I was standing and talking with this boy, Marshall, who is black and was on the football team. He was very popular. Out of nowhere, he shoved his arm down my shirt to try to grab my breasts. I was like, "What the hell is wrong with you? What are you doing?" I pushed him away from me. I was a cheerleader at the time, and some members of my squad saw the whole thing. The next day at practice, all fifteen members of my squad knew about it, and everyone was talking about it. People were saying, "I heard that you let that guy do that." I don't understand why they didn't see me push him away. I guess people see what they want to see.

Because of that one incident, I got labeled a slut. I was not even sexually active, but people *perceived* me as sexual. I knew nothing about sex. I thought "oral sex" meant talking about sex. But I was an early developer, and I was always flirtatious. So people made assumptions. Nobody knew my story. Since that day, people had a sexual portrayal of me. Everyone thought I was screwing half the football team. I told people I was a virgin, and they would not believe me. One person actually told me that I was a liar.

The word they used was "ho." "Oh yeah, she's a ho." "I heard you were a ho." People just came right up to me and said these things to me. One time a guy came up to me and grabbed my wrist hard and said, "You should give me a blowjob before the pep rally." More than once guys would come up to me and say: "Let me get your number." So at first I would think, "Oh, I must look really good today," or

"This guy really likes me." But after he had my number, he would text to say, "Hey, we should have sex."

Jasmine became known as a ho because a boy sexually assaulted her. Then, once she had acquired a reputation, boys assumed she was easy. Jasmine was sexualized even though she'd never had sex. Her body was cheapened even though she treated it with dignity. She was assumed to always say yes even though she repeatedly, consistently said no.

Welcome to the upside-down, mixed-up, warped-mirror world of being a young female in the age of slut-bashing and slut-shaming.

What's even crazier is that, all things considered, Jasmine was *fortunate.* She was not raped—a common consequence of being labeled a slut or a ho. Her reputation did not motivate her to become sexually active when she wasn't ready—another common result of such labeling. She did not develop an eating disorder, become depressed, or turn to drugs or alcohol—all classic coping mechanisms. As awful as her experience was, Jasmine was one of the lucky ones.

A white woman from the Southwest named Jackie, also age twenty, was not as fortunate. "In high school, I was one of those people who wanted to be called a slut because I wanted the attention" is the first thing she wants me to know. "But once I lost my virginity, it backfired." Jasmine's and Jackie's narratives are very different from one another. Yet both are emblematic.

Jackie and I spoke on the phone for an hour. I could hear her three-year-old daughter padding around and giggling; several times Jackie had to put down the phone to tend to her.

When we spoke, she was married and seven months pregnant and living with her grandfather. She volunteered to talk about what happened to her because, she said, she hopes that her story will help other girls learn from her mistakes. Yet her "mistakes" were actions that anyone in her situation could have made.

Jackie grew up poor with her mother, stepfather, and three siblings; the family moved frequently. She was homeschooled until the ninth grade. "My family was very religious, so they kept me home," she says. "So I was kind of shy and introverted." Her high school, the very first school she ever attended, was a big urban public institution with few resources. Forty students were crammed into each classroom. The setting was particularly overwhelming to a quiet, fourteen-year-old homeschooled girl. "I didn't know how to socialize with boys, or with anyone for that matter," she explains. "I was a little behind on that. I really just wanted to be like the girls in school once I went to school. Maybe someone who'd gone to public school her whole life would have acted differently, but I don't know how." Jackie continues,

I made one close girlfriend, who'd had sex at age twelve, or at least she said that she did, and I was kind of jealous. I don't know; I felt I was missing out. All the girls *said* they were sexually active. They liked to call themselves "slutty," but only if *they* called themselves slutty. They thought it was cool if they called themselves that word. If someone else said it, then it wasn't cool anymore. I wanted to be like them. I wanted to lose my virginity to pretty much anybody. So I guess I did kind of act like a slut. My older sister took me to a party, and I got really wasted. The people there were all a few years older than me. Even though I was drunk, I remember what happened. A guy at the party asked me if wanted to have sex, and I said yes. I didn't have to do it, but I wanted to. We did not use a condom. I was scared but excited at the same time.

Jackie told her best girlfriend that she'd lost her virginity, and her friend told a few people. Then, all of a sudden, everyone knew. "Everyone was saying stuff to me. They couldn't believe it. They were like, 'Why did you do that?' My friend joked around with me, saying, 'Oh, you're such a slut, you're a whore.' She would laugh when she said it, but then other people said it and they weren't joking. Everyone started talking bad stuff about me, and guys all of a sudden started coming on to me."

If her friends were also sexually active, or at least claiming to be, why was Jackie singled out as a slut? Jackie has given this question a lot of deep thought. She has concluded that "they sensed that I did it just to be cool. Maybe I seemed desperate, because I had made it clear that I wanted to have sex." This is a common motif: the "slut" identity is more about one's attitude (or perceived attitude) than actual sexual behavior. After all, if a girl has sex with a boyfriend, she is not regarded as a slut. Sexual activity per se does not a slut make.

Jackie became pregnant, which sealed her reputation. After the party, she dated the boy with whom she'd had sex; he is the only sexual partner she's ever had, and he later became her husband. "Everyone at school made me feel really bad about it. To them, I was totally a whore, even though they were sexually active too."

Jackie and her boyfriend did not use contraceptives. "We had no money," she tells me. "I could have gotten condoms for free, but I would have had to go to a clinic near my school, which is also right near the recreation center, which has a pool, and everyone hangs out there. I didn't want the kids from school to see me go in there." She was scared her reputation would intensify if the kids had material evidence—her acquisition of contraceptives—that they could use against her.

Jackie stopped attending school, dropping out after the ninth grade. "Between the pregnancy and being called a slut and a whore, I didn't want to be there," she explains. Her pregnancy miscarried. The next year, she became pregnant again, and she decided that she wanted to return to school. "I was kind of excited about going back. But my mom wouldn't let me. She said, 'Don't go back to school because everyone will think you're a slut.' She would also call me a slut and a tramp. It makes you feel bad when anyone says it, obviously, but especially it makes you feel bad when it's your mom." Jackie gave birth when she had just turned seventeen, and she never returned to school. She now works part-time as a caregiver, although she's not sure how she will continue once her second child is born, which, at the time of my interview with her, would be in two months.

Jackie chose to have sexual intercourse at age fourteen with a boy she didn't know because she thought girls her age were supposed to have casual sex with random guys. She followed a gender script—a set of guidelines that she believed she was supposed to follow to be normal and accepted as a teenage girl—that she inferred from her classmates. Today, she continues to make decisions according to a gender script, but for the first time, she questions whether the script is appropriate for her. I pressed my ear to the phone as Jackie expressed the conflict she faces, the conflict so many females face.

I try to not to ever use the word "slut," because living up to what the word means made me feel pressured to do things I wasn't ready to do. My husband, soon to be my ex-husband, wanted me to dress in a slutty way. I wore short shorts or a short skirt just to please him. Even still, he flirted with other women on chat lines and dating sites. I'm divorcing him and trying to grow up and move past being a slut. When I was with him, I felt that I couldn't just be myself. But I want to be the way *I* want to be. I want to be a good role model for my daughter. It was the same before: I couldn't just behave the way I wanted to or should have. The "slut" word pressured me to be sexually active before I should have been. I wanted to be the slut, but then I couldn't control it. It backfired on me because then I couldn't be the kind of slut I wanted to be.

Jackie's dilemma is that she was told to follow a script that hurts rather than helps her. Many girls and young women face the same problem. They are given one script, a terrible one. They can act out the script faithfully, or they can improvise. Many girls and young women try out a variety of improvisational strategies. Unfortunately, many of their strategies— including slut-bashing and slut-shaming—worsen rather than improve their situation.

The Prude/Slut Contradiction

These girls' and women's experiences illuminate an unstable terrain in which female sexual development is fraught with tricks and traps. It's not an accident, I believe, that the words "slut" and "ho" are popular at the same time that adolescent girls and college-age women face a sexual contradiction of enormous significance. Repeatedly, my interviewees explained that they must prove to their peers that they are sexually sophisticated and knowing. Revealing oneself as a "prude" or sexually ignorant—for girls as well as boys—is the kiss of social death. It means not keeping up, not developing properly, not being normal. Therefore, many girls and young women deliberately construct an identity in which they perform as a sexually empowered female to an audience of their peers, just as many boys and young men feel pressured by norms of masculinity to brag about sexual adventures.

Stephanie, a white fifteen-year-old girl in New York City, relates that she was called a prude when she was in the seventh grade, "when I had braces and everything. I had a really cute boyfriend, and we just hung out and didn't do anything. Kids asked me if we'd kissed, and I said no, and they were like, 'What?' So they said I was a prude. And so I became so irrelevant." (Instead of judging their peers on a scale of popularity and unpopularity, I discovered, teens deem them "relevant" or "irrelevant," also described as being "under the radar.") Stephanie continues, saying, "If you're part of a group that cares about hooking up, and you're not hooking up, then you become irrelevant." Stephanie did not want to be rendered "irrelevant." Who does—especially when you're fifteen years old?

Unlike their male peers, girls have to perform an exquisitely complicated and contradictory sexual role if they want to be regarded as "relevant." Up to a point, they *must* be a little "slutty," however they define the term. But they can't be too much so. Girls and young women report that they constantly must prove that they aren't *too* sexual, *too* promiscuous, *too* far off the grid of feminine normalcy, *too* slutty. As Stephanie's friend Kaitlyn chimed in, "The word 'slut' is the most destructive word you can say about a girl. You feel dirty and you want to go back under the radar." But going back under the radar doesn't help, because the label sticks. "The word is so delicate," Kaitlyn explains. "If you do one thing that pushes the limit, then no matter what you do later, everyone will say, 'See? She's a slut.' You have to put your foot in it, but then if you cross the line everyone will use it against you for years."

This contradiction is a modification of the virgin/whore dichotomy that has plagued women since the third millennium BCE, when the ancient Sumerians divided women into the categories of wife and prostitute. Historically, two mutually exclusive sexual identities—sexually inexperienced wife/ Madonna figure who engages in sexual behavior only to procreate with her husband; and sexually experienced woman/ prostitute who engages in sexual behavior only for personal benefit—were available to women to embrace. This virgin/ whore dichotomy gave women no space to express their sexuality without consequences. Today, the prude/slut contradiction provides two mutually exclusive sexual identities a woman must avoid; again, women have no space to express their sexuality without consequences.

Jill McDevitt, PhD, a sex educator, runs a popular "Virgins and Sluts" workshop with college women. "We talk about the fact that you cannot win," she says. "You act a certain way, which is labeled slut behavior. But you're equally ridiculed for abstaining from sexuality." McDevitt instructs her workshop's participants to fill out two postcards anonymously—one to themselves when they were slut-shamed, and one to themselves when they were virgin-shamed. "Every girl has had both experiences," she explains. "They see that it doesn't matter how you behave; you will be chastised either way. I read the postcards aloud. Girls write things like, 'I wouldn't give him a blow job. He kept asking me, and I kept saying no. He pressured me, and I gave in, and then I was a slut.' And I ask, 'How does this make any sense?'"

The prude/slut contradiction does not make any sense—and yet this tension is central to girls' and young women's lives today. It is present on every page of their gender script. "You're going to get called either a slut or a prude no matter what you do," confirms Kathy, a white twenty-one-year-old college student on the East Coast. Recognizing the trap of the prude/slut contradiction is essential to understanding slut-bashing and slut-shaming. If a girl accidentally crosses the invisible and ever-shifting boundary between "not a prude" and "not a slut," she is written off as a slut who deserves to be policed and shamed. Never mind that being a "slut" is one hair away from performing in a socially acceptable manner. Once a girl is labeled a slut, the show is over: her performance is ruined; her reputation is in tatters.

Girls and young women calling other girls sluts or "hos," I argue, is a logical, even reasonable strategy to rewrite the terrible script that's handed to females. By pointing a finger at another female, the name-caller at least temporarily diverts attention from herself and safeguards her own status. She quite brilliantly in one stroke proves both that she's not a slut (because the other girl, once labeled, is marked as "worse," and when it comes to sluttiness, relativity is everything) and also that she's not a prude (because she's sexually sophisticated enough to be capable of parsing finely observed sexual judgments).

"I've noticed that lots of women call other women sluts and whores," a twenty-two-year-old Latina woman from the West Coast, a recent college graduate who minored in gender and women's studies, tells me. "It's like their way of saying, 'I'm not *that* kind of girl.' It's a way of saying that those girls are less valuable. Before I discovered feminism, I definitely did it too. It's a way to feel closer to guys—not necessarily to get sexual attention but just to get them to think you're a better person than the other girls are."

In a warped way, slut-bashing and slut-shaming may even be seen as forms of safe sex: a girl can preserve her chastity while at the same time shoring up her sexual credentials. These behaviors also position her as more desirable than those belittled as slutty.

Image Control

The prude/slut contradiction is not new. Girls described this impossible tightrope to me twenty years ago, and it wasn't new then either. Why has the response of calling other girls sluts increased in frequency only now?

The answer is that social media have profoundly altered the way people evaluate themselves and others. In particular, social media place girls' and women's physical bodies perpetually on display. Julie Zeilinger, the founder and editor of a feminist blog for teens and young adults called *FBomb*, observes, "Everyone is constantly visible and available—including your body and everything else about you." Moreover, many of us believe today that our bodies *should* always be visible and available. We judge other female bodies, and our female bodies are always judged. Therefore, we worry about our physical selves and our sexual identities in a newly charged way. Performance and surveillance are now central to everyone's lives, and especially so for young females.

Social media tantalize us with the ability to control the way others see us—our image and reputation. We create online profiles, upload photos and videos, and craft an identity we want others to admire. With every keystroke, we imagine that we are shaping our identity to project the best "I" possible.

Yet the promise of controlling our image is false. Others take what we offer online and manipulate the raw material. We don't truly control our digital persona. Our reputations are always at risk. We have to keep up the pace not only with regard to updating our own online identity but also to making sure no one else is tampering with our reputation.

It's no wonder that slut-bashing and slut-shaming have become more commonplace. The stakes are higher than ever before in the performance of everyone's identity, and especially so for young females. If a girl wants to be socially relevant, she can't opt out of the performance (as if opting out really were possible in our digitally connected world). Maneuvering to become the center of attention as one who is neither a prude nor a slut—and pointing fingers at those whose performance is wobbly—is the new normal.

Viewing online photographs of other females, together with leaving comments and "likes," leads to insecurity and competitiveness. Invariably, judgment about girls' "sluttines" comes into play. Cynthia, a white twenty-one-year-old college student from Pennsylvania, explains,

I update my Facebook and check it constantly. I definitely make sure I look good in my photos. And I know it's sad, but I definitely count up how many "likes" I get. It's like a popularity thing, and it becomes a competition over who's popular. You can look up anyone and see what they're doing and what they've posted. You make assumptions of what they're like based on their pictures, not based on their personality. If you stay home one night, you look at everyone's pictures of what they're doing that night, and you see what they're wearing, and you think, "Oh, that person's looking really slutty tonight." So many assumptions go into what people are like based on the photos they're posting, and assumptions about sluttiness are a big part of it.

As appalling as slut-bashing and slut-shaming are, they are sensible responses when one is constantly being judged and judging others. These strategies appear helpful, perhaps even necessary. Therefore, telling girls and women to stop using the label won't work. Why would anyone cease an activity that is logical and reasonable, and seems to get the job done?

We must instead show girls and women the ways in which these strategies are fundamentally misguided. Aside from all the harm we have seen that they cause to others, slut-bashing and slut-shaming also backfire on the name-callers.

- When a girl slut-bashes another girl, she may think she is distancing herself from "bad" sluttiness and proving herself to be a "good slut." In fact, she is setting up herself as a future target. Any girl who calls other girls sluts weakens her own position. If she establishes herself as a judge of sexual values, other girls may come to believe that her credentials are shaky—*Who does she think she is?* They then may decide to reveal her own sexual misdeeds, real or not.

- If she intentionally embraces or owns the "slut" label for herself, she will discover that true ownership is not possible. In this age of social media, "slut" transforms from self-chosen badge of pride to mortifying sign of shame in the time it takes to retweet.

- When a girl or a woman casually refers to another female as a slut or a ho, she reinforces the normalcy of the sexual double standard. As long as the sexual double standard exists, all females are at risk of being judged for their sexuality.

Because the word "slut" has become so accepted and widespread in casual conversation, its sexist sting is undervalued in US youth culture. As the high school teacher played by Tina

Fey memorably told her female students in the 2004 movie *Mean Girls*, "You all have got to stop calling each other sluts and whores. It just makes it OK for guys to call you sluts and whores." The more the word is used, the more it is accepted. When women call each other sluts, even in a lighthearted manner, they lead others to believe it's acceptable to use the term too. When this behavior is normalized, so is sexual assault. As Kaitlyn says, "I pretty much expect to be groped and touched by random guys every time I leave my home in the morning. Girls think it's normal for a guy to grab them at a party. The word 'slut' creates a physically and emotionally dangerous environment for girls."

The only way to end slut-bashing and slut-shaming is to change the environment in which these actions flourish so that the behavior no longer makes sense. This is a far more difficult task than simply instituting zero-tolerance policies for verbal and physical sexual harassment and sexual assault, although such policies are important and necessary. But let's be honest: we are not going to achieve this feminist utopia in which the sexual double standard has been eradicated any time in the near future, although we must continue to work toward it. In the meantime, our wisest move is to demonstrate to girls and women that when they refer to themselves and others as sluts or hos, they are hurting themselves as well as others.

Slut-bashing and slut-shaming inevitably ricochet—on all of us.

CHAPTER 2

Are You a "Good Slut" or a "Bad Slut"?

Recently I attended a forum on feminism at Barnard College. Arriving a few minutes early, I scanned the auditorium, packed with women with book bags, buzzing with the discordance of dozens of simultaneous conversations. My eyes came to rest on a friend of mine, a white longtime feminist activist and writer, sitting in the front row. She was twisted around, talking with someone behind her, and when she saw me she gestured for me to come and take the seat next to her. We hugged and smiled, and she introduced me to the woman, also white, with whom she'd been chatting. The woman, I learned, was also involved in grassroots feminist work.

"This is Leora," my friend said. "She's the author of *Slut!*"

She added, "Leora wrote the book because she had been called a slut when she was in school."

"Oh, you were the school slut?" asked the woman. "Congratulations!"

Congratulations . . . really? Was she being ironic? No: she was offering a genuine compliment.

I smiled politely, but my thoughts swirled in confusion. This woman's affirmation of my reputation was intended, I recognize, as a sly in-joke, a subversive poke at the sexual double standard that denigrates women labeled as sluts. By congratulating me, she was attempting to decrease the power of the sexist belief system that classifies women either as commendable virgins or depraved whores. She was trying to transform "slut," to turn it on its head from a source of shame to a wellspring of pride. She was attempting to suggest that a woman can occupy a category that is neither Madonna nor whore.

But I don't feel proud of having been labeled a slut when I was in the ninth grade. I don't feel ashamed of it either, but at the same time I prefer not to be associated with the word. After all, although I know now that I never deserved to have been called a slut, and that I had been the victim of verbal sexual harassment, the experience profoundly wounded me during a pivotal time in my life. To me, the word "slut" is not funny, and it's not something I want to reclaim. Although this woman good-heartedly meant to connect with me as a fellow traveler on the planet of feminism, I was left feeling that my experiences had been glossed over.

This interaction crystallized that "slut" has no fixed, stable meaning. It can mean "bad slut" or it can mean "good slut." Most of the time, it's the worst insult you can call a woman, signifying that she should feel ashamed of herself for her supposed promiscuity. On the other hand, a woman may embrace the term to prove a feminist point that she is confidently, unapologetically sexual. "Slut is ambiguous because it holds the connotation of being known, sexy and desirable but also excessive, dirty and wrong," observes Jessica Ringrose, a sociologist of gender at the Institute of Education in London.[8] The word is remarkably confusing. And if I find it perplexing to discern its meanings, you can imagine how teenage girls and college-age women—many of whom are plagued by insecurity and the desire to fit in socially—feel.

History of the Word

To grasp how the word "slut" is understood, I began by examining its etymology in Western literature. The first usage of which we know, according to the *Oxford English Dictionary*, is from 1386 in *The Canterbury Tales* by Geoffrey Chaucer. Not yet a noun, the word appears as the Middle English adjective "sluttish" in the "Canon's Yeoman's Prologue." The host of the traveling pilgrims asks the yeoman why his master, who the yeoman has said is very clever and successful, is dressed so poorly: "Why is thy lord so sluttish, I thee preye, / And is of power better cloth to beye, / If that his dede accorde with thy speche?" If your master has the power to buy better clothes, why has he chosen to dress in a "sluttish" manner—in dirty and untidy garments?

In 1402, the English poet Thomas Hoccleve used the

noun "slut" in "The Letter of Cupid" in much the same way Chaucer did, but with regard to a woman—a slovenly woman who did not keep her room clean ("The foulest slutte of al a tovne"). For nearly five hundred years, according to the *Oxford Engligh Dictionary*, "slut" continued to be used as a synonym for a slattern or a woman who is dirty or untidy in her appearance or habits. Shakespeare used the term this way in 1599 in *As You Like It*. Touchstone, the court jester, playfully woos the innocent country girl Audrey, who informs him that she prefers to remain chaste. Touchstone responds, "Truly, and to cast away honesty upon a foul slut were to put good meat into an unclean dish"—meaning, in effect, "It would be as wasteful for a dirty woman to remain chaste as it would be to put good meat in a dirty dish." Audrey, a shepherdess, isn't happy to be called a "slut," but it's clear that the meaning is not connected with her sexuality. She responds, "I am not a slut, though I thank the gods I am foul"—meaning, "Your simile is off base because I keep myself clean, even though I'm a country girl, and therefore I'm not a slut. But I thank the gods I'm not pretty, because not being pretty enables me to remain chaste." Here, "slut" is a derogatory word applied to a woman, but it isn't connected with her sexuality. In the middle of the fifteenth century, "slut" also became a synonym for a kitchen maid, and it also was not used in a derogatory manner.

However, at the same time, another meaning bubbled up; beginning at around 1450, "slut" was used to describe a woman of low or loose character—a woman who was inappropriately sexually forward or bold. Hundreds of years later, Henry Fielding and Charles Dickens still used the term in this manner. As Dickens wrote in *Dombey and Son* in 1848,

"Does that bold-faced slut . . . intend to take her warning, or does she not?" The literal meaning of the word as a woman who didn't restrain her home or appearance by keeping them tidy transformed into a metaphorical meaning of a woman who didn't restrain her sexuality. Being sloppy in matters of cleanliness was akin to being untidy in matters of sexuality. This linguistic transformation occurred at the same time that the sexual ideology of passionlessness for women became ascendant. "Slut" became a judgmental sexual term precisely when women's sexual expression was tightened. The metaphorical meaning is the one with which we are most familiar today—a woman who is sexually promiscuous.

I wonder if our ancestors were confused by these simultaneous, disparate definitions. After all, from the mid-1600s through the mid-1800s, "slut" was used contemporaneously in a playful way, sometimes without negative judgment. John Bunyan, Jonathan Swift, and Samuel Richardson all used the word "slut" in this manner. As Samuel Pepys wrote in his diary in 1664, "Our little girl Susan is a most admirable slut and pleases us mightily." Yet throughout the 1800s, "slut" was also used synonymously with "bitch," meaning a female dog.

Inventive compound nouns, such as "slut's wool" and "slut's pennies," also were coined during this period. "Slut's wool" is what we today call dust bunnies—accumulations of dust found in corners or under beds when a room is in need of a cleaning. "Slut's pennies" are hard knots of dough within a bread loaf caused by imperfect kneading.[9]

These entries in the *Oxford English Dictionary* demonstrate that "slut" is the site of an intersection of gender, class, and race. For over six hundred years, "slut" has referred exclusively to working or poor white women. None of the historical literary usages refers to upper-class or noble white women, or to women of color of any socioeconomic status. Associations were made among white working women and dirt, a lack of control over cleanliness, and a lack of restraint. We may infer that a nonslut was a white woman of financial means with upper-class social status; a shipshape home with floors so clean you could eat off them; a tidy, pulled-together appearance; and a restrained sexual appetite. "Slut" has always implied, perhaps more than anything else, *white low-class vulgarity.*

Why don't we find any Western historical literary examples of black women being called "sluts"? Because femininity was equated with whiteness and sexual restraint. "Slut" had meaning only because it was the opposite of the (white) feminine ideal. Even before white people enslaved black people, they regarded black women as outside the boundaries of femininity. Black women were regarded as *inherently* slutty, unlike white women, whose sluttiness represented a supposed transgression of true femininity. Therefore, black sluttiness did not necessarily trigger a judgmental reaction among white writers.

All women "traditionally have been defined in sexual terms," points out Frances Smith Foster, a scholar of African American literature, because women "alone have a capacity for reproduction and their virtue and value have more often than not been determined by the manner in which it is used."[10] But in Western literature, white women have been categorized as sexually innocent (not sluts) or as temptresses (sluts). Historically, black women were caught in a no-win situation. Under slavery, they were raped by their masters. When ex-slaves wrote about the experience of slavery, Foster notes, they repeatedly stressed that female slaves attempted to remain sexually chaste, yet were forcibly sexually violated through no fault of their own. Unfortunately, despite the attempts of ex-slave narrators to expose this system of sexual brutality, black women became equated with sexuality. White women who were raped were expected to die as a result of their abuse. Their degradation was expected to be totalizing, making postrape life unimaginable. But black female slaves survived their rapes and continued the work they were forced to do—a circumstance used as evidence that they were not properly feminine.[11]

According to Foster, the horrifying irony is that rape victims became associated with wanton sexuality. "The ultimate insult to the image of black women was made not by the narrators, but by their audience"—white readers—"whose concepts of femininity could not allow for inclusion of such creatures as those depicted," she writes. "The black woman's ability to survive such degradation became her defeat."[12] A black rape victim was suspect, because if she were truly feminine she would not be able to survive sexual abuse. Even white abolitionists regarded black women as "so brutalized by slavery that traditional concepts of feminine sensibilities and intellect were not evident."[13] The word "slut" as a shorthand for a woman who fails to live up to the feminine ideals of chastity would not have applied to black women under slavery, who by default were believed by white people to be unfeminine to begin with.

Thus, I found no historical or literary examples of black

women labeled "sluts." The synonym "ho" crept into African American communities much later, only after the civil rights movement, when support for racial equality may have muted the racist belief in black women's essential licentiousness. "Ho" is an alteration of "whore," a synonym for "prostitute" with roots in Late Old English. In the 1960s, according to the *Oxford English Dictionary*, "ho" was used to mean "prostitute." But by the late 1980s, it was used to refer to a sexually promiscuous woman.[14] The hip-hop artist Slick Rick sang in his 1988 song "Treat Her Like a Prostitute": "Now your girl she don't like to have sex a lot / And today she's ready and she's hot hot hot . . . / Next thing you know the ho starts to ill / She says, 'I love you, Harold' and your name is Will."

As "ho" became part of African American vernacular, "slut" was treated as a sort of second-tier four-letter word. It wasn't as crass as other four-letter words, but it also wasn't a word you would utter in your grandmother's presence. When it was used, it was shocking and titillating. In the late 1970s, Dan Aykroyd used "slut" for comic effect in a regular pundit segment on *Saturday Night Live*'s "Weekend Update" called Point/Counterpoint. He and a fellow comedian, Jane Curtin, debated a serious issue; Curtin—conservatively dressed in a blazer and a buttoned-to-the-neck blouse—would offer a reasoned argument, to which Aykroyd always responded, "Jane, you ignorant slut." Aykroyd and Curtin were spoofing people who are unable or unwilling to present evidence to support their argument, and instead resort to ad hominem attacks. (Curtin would respond, "Dan, you pompous ass.") "Slut" in this context was funny because clearly Curtin wasn't a "slut," and it was interjected in a completely inappropriate and vulgar way into a supposedly high-level intellectual debate. Nevertheless, this usage of the word hinted that other women, perhaps less intellectually gifted and less covered up, deserved to be called sluts.

Twenty years later, when my book *Slut!* was published, the word was still inflammatory and off-limits in many newspaper headlines. I was told by a *New York Times* editor that the newspaper probably wouldn't review my book because of the title (it didn't), and other newspapers carefully avoided the term in the headlines of their reviews and features.

There have been several high-profile challenges to "slut" as a derogatory term over the last twenty-five years. In the early 1990s, the Riot Grrrl movement erupted onto the feminist scene from Washington and Oregon. Access to abortion was being eroded through state legislation, and in 1991 the anti-abortion nominee Clarence Thomas was confirmed as a justice of the Supreme Court—despite Anita Hill's accusations of sexual harassment during the Senate Judiciary Committee's hearings. Riot Grrrls were angry. They wanted to raise feminist consciousnesses. They sang about issues such as sexual assault and racism. Kathleen Hanna of the band Bikini Kill scrawled SLUT and WHORE in lipstick on her stomach. "When you take off your shirt [onstage], the guys think, 'Oh, what a slut,' and it's really funny because they think that and then they look at you and it says it," Hanna told Simon Reynolds and Joy Press, the coauthors of *The Sex Revolts*.[15] Hanna upended the ability of slut-hecklers to judge her by beating them to it and embracing the word. Her message was: "OK, you're right; I *am* a slut. I sleep with whomever I want. So what?"

In 1997, Dossie Easton and Janet Hardy published *The Ethical Slut*, a book of advice for people who practice consensual nonmonogamy, also known as polyamory. Since then, "slut" has been used by polyamorous people in an approving way to mean someone who openly expresses his or her choice to have multiple sexual partners. The authors define the term as "a person of any gender who has the courage to lead life according to the radical proposition that sex is nice and pleasure is good for you."[16]

In 2002, Jessica Crispin, a book critic, founded the literary blog *Bookslut*. The cheeky title implies that reading promiscuously (excessively and across genres) is good. "Sluttiness" in this context is a state to which book lovers should aspire.

In the early 2000s, the New York women's networking group SLUTS—Successful Ladies Under Tremendous Stress—formed as part of a savvy "new girls' network" of high-powered women in the world of business. The humorous name adds a dash of frivolity to the serious ambitiousness of the women.[17]

In 2011, a feminist movement called SlutWalk began holding demonstrations across North America and then around the globe. Marchers protest the acceptance or rationalization of sexual assault on the grounds that, by wearing revealing clothing or behaving in any way that could be considered "slutty," the victims were "asking for it." In reclaiming the word "slut," protesters raise awareness that nothing a woman does ever invites or excuses sexual assault. (See chapter 8 for further discussion of the SlutWalk movement.)

So is the word "slut" finally rehabilitated?

Not in most corners of the United States, where the pejorative meanings of "slut" and "ho" predominate. Since the 1990s, parties known as "Pimps and Hos" began springing up on college campuses. Guys dress up like pimps, women wear outfits to look like sex workers, and the understanding is that the guys have permission to treat the women like sexual objects. Simultaneously rewarding and policing "sluts" is the unspoken theme of these parties. This agenda was clearly articulated in 2009 in the first episode of the reality show *Jersey Shore*, in which the female cast members sexualized themselves with heavy makeup, high heels, and long hair while simultaneously insulting other women who behaved similarly; one of the women asserted that "sluts need to be abused."[18]

In 2007, after the Rutgers University women's basketball team lost a national championship game, the nationally syndicated white radio host Don Imus referred to the students as a bunch of "nappy-headed hos." The women's athletic success had nothing whatsoever to do with sexuality. Apparently the sight of physically strong, confident black women confused Imus, who could make sense of them only by maligning them based on racist and sexist assumptions that black women are inherently slutty.

Slut-bashing continues within middle schools and high schools across the country. Since 2008, there has been a drumbeat of names of girls who have killed themselves after having been harassed and repeatedly called a slut by their classmates, either in person or online. Jessica Logan, eighteen, from Cincinnati, Ohio. Hope Witsell, thirteen, from Ruskin, Florida. Phoebe Prince, fifteen, from South Hadley, Massachusetts. Alexis Pilkington, seventeen, from Long Island, New York. Rachel Ehmke, thirteen, from Mantorville,

Minnesota. Audrie Pott, fifteen, from Saratoga, California. Felicia Garcia, fifteen, from Staten Island, New York. Amanda Todd, fifteen, from British Columbia, Canada. Jessica Laney, sixteen, from Hudson, New York. Rehtaeh Parsons, seventeen, from Nova Scotia, Canada. Gabrielle Molina, twelve, from Queens, New York. Preadolescent and adolescent kids know that when they want to wound a girl they dislike for any or no reason, "slut" is the most effective weapon.

In 2012, the conservative radio host Rush Limbaugh proved that he behaves just like a schoolyard bully himself. Limbaugh called Sandra Fluke, then a Georgetown law student, a "slut" and a "prostitute" after she testified about her law school's health insurance policy on birth control coverage during an unofficial Congressional hearing. Fluke argued that the co-pay for birth control should be covered by health insurance companies. Women, Fluke testified, should not have to foot the bill—which easily can climb to six hundred dollars or more a year.

Limbaugh asked the fourteen million listeners of his radio program, "What does that make her? It makes her a slut, right? It makes her a prostitute. She wants to be paid to have sex. She's having so much sex she can't afford the contraception." Even for Limbaugh, these comments crossed a line of decency. After several sponsors withdrew their advertising from his show and President Barack Obama weighed in, calling Fluke to thank her for speaking out on women's health care concerns, Limbaugh apologized—sort of. He wrote on his website, "My choice of words was not the best, and in the attempt to be humorous, I created a national stir. I sincerely apologize to Ms. Fluke for the insulting word choices."[19] He expressed regret that he had used the words "slut" and "prostitute," but he didn't retract his argument that Fluke was an immoral woman because she believes that birth control is basic health care.

In the spring of 2012, President Obama announced that he would give a commencement speech at Barnard College rather than at Columbia College, his alma mater. Barnard is the all-female sister school of Columbia University, whose campus is across the street in Morningside Heights in New York City. Hundreds of resentful Columbia students slut-shamed Barnard students so viciously on Columbia's student-run blog that even the *New York Times* reported on it.[20] Anonymous students complained that because admission to Columbia is more selective than admission to Barnard, the women at Barnard are therefore less intelligent and more sexually promiscuous than the women at Columbia. According to Ravenna Koenig, a Barnard student, "slut" was "one of the tamer words used" on the blog.[21] Columbia students wrote,

"While you guys were perfecting your deepthroating techniques and experimenting with scissoring and anal play, we were learning Calculus (usually by sophomore year of high school)."

"Barnard is full of academically inferior students that are able to use OUR campus, take OUR classes, and are stereotypically easy to get in bed. We feel like we worked our asses off to get here, and it's annoying as fuck that Barnard can get the milk for free, so to speak."

"That is why we hate you cum dumpsters."

"Moral of the story is that ugly, feeble Barnard women

need to shut their jizz holes and just be happy that Columbia let Barnyard pretend it was affiliated for this long."[22]

Why did resentment against Barnard focus on the sexuality of its students? Because when you want to put down or undermine a woman, accusing her of being slutty works every time.

Later in 2012, the YouTube entertainer Jenna Mourey, known as Jenna Marbles, released a video titled "Things I Don't Understand About Girls Part 2: Slut Edition," in which she railed against "sluts." She defined a slut as: "someone that has a lot of casual sex," who has one-night stands with random guys, and who has sex with other girls' boyfriends. As of this writing, the video has had more than five million views. Like Limbaugh, Mourey was forced to reevaluate her stance on "sluts" after dozens of disgusted fans created their own YouTube videos critiquing her. She told the *New York Times* that she "doesn't regret the video, but plans on avoiding similar topics for now."[23]

In March 2013, two teenage football players were convicted of publicly and repeatedly raping a girl in Steubenville, Ohio, who was so drunk she had passed out. For approximately six hours, the two boys took the unconscious girl from one location to another, assaulting her in a car on the way. No one tried to intervene. In fact, over a dozen peers photographed the naked girl and documented the assaults, as well as the mocking reactions of the rapists, on Twitter, Facebook, Instagram, and YouTube. The victim was widely blamed for being raped on the grounds that she chose to drink to excess and because she was supposedly slutty. After the two teenage boys were found guilty of rape, reactions on Twitter included comments such as "she's the town [————] anyways. She's hasn't stop drinking yet. just pray. cause God's gonna get her worse then anyone can."[24]

Even the tennis superstar Serena Williams raised the issue of the victim's supposed sluttiness during an interview with *Rolling Stone* magazine:

> **D**o you think it was fair, what they got? They did something stupid, but I don't know. I'm not blaming the girl, but if you're a 16-year-old and you're drunk like that, your parents should teach you: Don't take drinks from other people. She's 16, why was she that drunk where she doesn't remember? It could have been much worse. She's lucky. Obviously, I don't know, maybe she wasn't a virgin, but she shouldn't have put herself in that position, unless they slipped her something, then that's different.[25]

Williams echoed the commonly held belief that a slut is a sexually active girl who drinks to excess and therefore did something wrong that caused her own sexual assault.

A slut or ho is not only someone to be judged; she is also someone to be disbelieved. She has no credibility. As a result, when she's gang-raped, her friends are more likely to snap photos of her assault than to snap away the rapists.

Contemporary Definitions

What is the essence of "bad" sluttiness? What ingredients transform an empowered "good slut" like the one envisioned by Kathleen Hanna and SlutWalk feminists into a shameful "bad slut"?

In the summer of 2013, I led a workshop on slut-shaming for counselors of a Jewish summer sleepaway camp in the Northeast. The counselors were primarily (though not exclusively) white, educated, college-age men and women, gay and heterosexual. I asked them to write down the definition of "slut" that comes to mind when they hear campers or their peers use it. Making it clear to me that they do not endorse these associations, they scribbled:

> "A girl who is known to hook up with a critical mass of people within a given timeframe."

> "A girl who dresses or behaves in a promiscuous way."

> "A person, generally female, who is overtly promiscuous through her clothes or actions or speech."

> "A female who has more sexual interactions than her peers do."

> "A woman who gets with a lot of guys or is very flirty or wears inappropriate clothing."

> "A girl or woman who does many sexual activities with many partners in a brief period of time."

> "An older teenager or young woman who wears provocative clothes and doesn't think about the consequences."

> "A girl who has sex with a lot of boys or dresses provocatively or is not afraid to express her sexuality."

> "Someone who doesn't respect her body and allows others to disrespect it."

"A girl who does inappropriate things with a boy or boys outside of a relationship."

"A girl who gets around, who hooks up a lot but with no emotional attachment."

"A girl who's sexually active in some way, or who has a reputation of having multiple partners in a short time span, whatever that means."

At first glance, these definitions appear extraordinarily vague. What does "a critical mass of people within a given timeframe" actually convey? What does it truly mean to do "inappropriate things"? Many of the counselors hedged their definitions with the word "or"—a slut does this *or* she does that *or* she does this other thing. They seemed to have difficulty pinning down a specific definition. Clearly there is no one definition. "Slut" is in the eye of the beholder. Similar to how Supreme Court Justice Potter Stewart said in 1964 that he couldn't define hard-core pornography but "I know it when I see it," the definition of sluttiness is likewise slippery yet identifiable. Young people simply know it when they see it.

But take a closer look. There is one common element, one telltale sign: agency. The "bad slut" actively *does something* to earn her reputation. She is never passive or in the wrong place at the wrong time. She has put effort into her sexuality—and for that reason, she has been condemned.

The same dynamic is captured by *Urban Dictionary*, an online reader-created slang dictionary. "Slut" is the second most popular "S" word on the site. It is sandwiched between "sex" and "shit." Readers of the site submit definitions; once a definition is posted, other readers determine its popularity by voting it up or down. Of the 360 posted definitions for "slut," the most popular one is "A woman with the morals of a man." Is this definition positive, negative, or neutral? Impossible to say. Of the twenty most popular entries, most are negative and female-specific; of those definitions, all involve agency:

> "A derogatory term. Refers to a sexually promiscuous person, usually female. One who engages in sexual activity with a large number of persons, occasionally simultaneously. Also refers to one who engages in sexual activity outside of a long-term relationship within the duration of said relationship. . . . In some cases, used to refer to a woman who is wearing 'skimpy' or tasteless clothing."
>
> "a girl thats fucked so many guys she cant close her legs anymore."
>
> "Slut: a girl who will sleep with anyone."
>
> "A female who will screw anyone who asks her to."
>
> "A chick that will spread her legs for anything of the male species. They also use their looks to get what they want . . . and if a guy wont do what they want they are then labeled 'gay' by the slut."
>
> "A female, who's legs are open like 7-11. (Community Pussy.)"
>
> "A female, who's vagina is like a car park, guys can 'park their car' anytime."
>
> "Scum of the earth."

Some of the definitions are presented neutrally:

"A female who has multiple sexual partners without engaging in any relationships."
"A female who enjoys performing sexual acts with multiple partners."

Several contributors expressed empathy for "sluts" even
while they derided them:

"an unintelligent girl with low self-esteem that will do
anything for attention and the approval of others.
They start having sex with guys left and right to
make them (the guys) happy and then they start
to get used to the sexual lifestyle and actually start
depending on it. Sluts are great people deep down
inside they are just caught up in a downward spi-
ral of a dirty lifestyle created by scumbag guys who
claimed they loved them but all they really wanted
was to stick it in and get it out. Sluts are NOT just
good for sex, they are people just like you and me
and they can love too, just give them a chance."
"girl who will fuck/suck anyone because she has no self
esteem, not to be confused with a girl who loves to
have sex. Sometimes fucks to get guys to like her,
never works."

One contributor extolled the "slut"—sarcastically:

"Someone who provides a very needed service for the
community and sleeps with everyone, even the guy
that has no shot at getting laid and everyone knows

it. She will give him a sympathy fuck either because someone asked her to or she just has to fuck everyone she knows. These are great people, and without them sex crimes would definitely increase. Thank you slut, where ever you are."[26]

So the components of a slut's sluttiness include:

- Displaying agency; being active rather than passive; choosing her actions (even when she is a victim of manipulative men).
- Deviating from the sexual behaviors of her peers.
- "Having sex" (heterosexual intercourse) or "hooking up" (engaging in any sort of sexual activity, which may or may not include intercourse) with more than one partner outside a romantic relationship, with little to no time in between partners.
- Not being choosy with her sexual partners.
- Giving the appearance of any or all of the above, even if she's not actually sexually active.
- Wearing clothes that her peers determine are too sexually revealing.
- Expressing sexual confidence.

As a result of her characteristics, these corollary statements are regarded as valid:

- Because she doesn't treat herself with respect, others don't have to, either.
- If a guy sexually assaults her, she has no one to blame

but herself. If she weren't slutty, she wouldn't be assaulted.

- Despite her low status, she may be praised for providing a service in the way that a prostitute does.
- Her reprehensible behavior is the result of her upbringing; therefore she is someone to be pitied.
- Alternately, she should be praised for asserting herself in the face of the sexual double standard.

Being a Slut Can Be Good. . . . Except When It's Bad

We know what "slut" has meant historically, and we know what most people today are trying to convey when they use the word. But what does "slut" mean to the teenage girl or young woman who is herself so labeled? How does she make sense of this word to herself? How does she understand the term, especially if she's not sexually active or not more so than her peers are?

I went directly to the most knowledgeable, reliable source: straight-talking New York City high school students, ages fourteen, fifteen, and sixteen. I asked a group of seven girls what the word means exactly among their peers. Members of an acclaimed theater group called the Arts Effect that draws students from several different private and public schools, they sat in a semicircle on the floor of a downtown studio, wearing jeans, tank tops, and hooded sweatshirts. Although the Arts Effect is multiracial, the girls who showed up on this particular day all were white. At first they seemed eager to decode their language for me. But as our conversation progressed, it became clear that they were mostly eager to decode their language for themselves. Articulate, thoughtful, and poised, the girls wanted so much to talk about the word "slut" that they found it difficult to contain their thoughts. Their sentences galloped over each other.

The first thing they wanted me to know was that sometimes, if they're able to control the circumstances, girls enjoy being known as sluts because the label indicates that they are being talked about. In the age of social media and reality television, being talked about is a baseline requirement of being someone who matters. If you're not talked about, you're not "relevant," or you're "under the radar." Teenagers emphatically want to be relevant and on the radar.

Nicole, sixteen, offered the example of a girl in her school who had "hooked up" (in her definition: engaged in kissing or sexual acts without crossing the threshold to penetrative intercourse) "with multiple guys" at a party.

"It gave her power and status," Nicole explained to me.

"Wasn't she worried about being called a slut?" I asked.

"Well, people were talking about her. Yes, there was negative attention, but there was also good attention. This was the first party of high school. She was literally posting on her Facebook status things like '27 guys!'"

Confused, I asked, "Isn't that really risky?"

Nicole patiently explained, "Yeah, it's risky. But everyone gets called a slut. It's just normal. Everyone's sort of a slut. You get called a slut for pretty much anything. In middle school there is the experience where just one girl is the slut—and it was me for a little while—but, like, in New York City my experience is that pretty much everyone gets called a slut for something that they've done."

"The word is used as justification," explains Stephanie, the fifteen-year-old girl who had explained that girls don't want to be seen as prudes. "It's so easy to label a girl—positively and negatively. It's not always bad. It's not always, 'Oh, she's a slut, don't talk with her.' Sometimes it's"—Stephanie switches to a perky, upbeat tone—" 'Oh, she's so slutty!' It can be used differently in a positive way"

"In the sixth grade," chimed in Rachel, "I literally hadn't even started wearing a bra yet, and my friend said, 'All the boys think you're a slut.' I took so much offense to that! I didn't know what it meant. I had never gone out with a boy. I had never kissed a boy. It's really murky."

"My sister's twelve," Jocelyn, fifteen, told us, "and it's like, if she even talks to a boy at recess, she gets called a slut."

Nicole continued where she had left off a moment earlier. "It brings you power, and it gives you social status. That's all really true. But no girl goes to a guy thinking, 'Oh, hooking up with him is going to get me power.' It's a very blurred line between good and bad results from being called a slut. A girl kind of weighs the odds."

"OK," I said. "I understand that on the one hand, you need to prove to everyone that you're sexually sophisticated, but on the other hand, you can't be seen as *too* sexual So you have to do *something* to prove that you're sexy and desirable, but you have to be careful about what you do."

"Right!" exclaimed Nicole, brushing away a lock of hair that kept falling into her face. "But there's a blurred line, and you take one step too far and it's like, 'Wow, that was insanely slutty of you to do that.' And it's not clear what the line is until it's crossed. If you're at a party, you can't figure out where the line is, but the next day you're looking back and you think, 'Oh, that was a bad idea,' but you didn't know that when you were doing it. You know what I mean? Because I mean, if the night's not finished yet, how could you know if what you're doing is the worst thing that will happen? So you're a slut if you go farther than you were supposed to, not because you did something that's specifically slutty."

"What if you're really popular?" I asked. "Does that make you immune from being called a slut in a bad way?"

"Not necessarily," said Nicole, and the others agreed. Jocelyn elaborated, saying, "Well, slutty behavior might seem more normal if you're very popular. The word means something different depending on so many different things. If everyone hooks up with three guys, and one girl hooks up with six guys, she's the slut even though everyone else should be too."

But, I pointed out, she was talking mostly about girls who were known to hook up with boys. What about girls like Rachel, who was called a slut when she had never kissed a boy? Or Jocelyn's twelve-year-old sister, who gets slapped with the label simply for talking with a boy? Wasn't it true that you can be called a slut even if you're not doing anything sexual at all?

All the girls agreed, and I asked them to explain how the same word could be used in such vastly different circumstances—to describe the not-yet-sexual twelve-year-old and the older teenage girl who flaunted her sexual exploits—and how it could also be used alternately as a hurtful insult or as a badge of honor. For the first time, they were silent.

I checked in with Katie Cappiello and Meg McInerney, the two dynamic women who run the Arts Effect, at a café in Manhattan's Greenwich Village to talk about the group interview. Although she hadn't mentioned it during the interview, one of the girls, Cappiello told me, had recently decided to have sex.

She came over to my apartment crying one night. She said, "This was what I wanted to do, so I did it. I wanted to have sex with him, yes, and I also wanted to start dating his best friend not long after that. So what? I told myself, 'I'm a feminist, damn it, and I should be allowed to do these things and make these choices for myself.'" But now she realizes she had been trying to convince herself that it would be OK. The right to make decisions for yourself is almost a lie. It's not that simple. Those guys told their friends, and now her life is miserable. The girls in school call her a slut. They say to her, "Hey, you're walking funny today; are you sore from all the action you're getting?" She thought she had made an empowering choice, and now look what's happening.

The girl now recognizes that sexual equality does not in fact yet exist in practice. When a girl and boy are identically sexually active, only the girl is treated punitively.

For some high school girls, then:

- Being a "slut" is good—but only when the girl herself is orchestrating her own reputation and maintains control over it.

- In some social circles, it is compulsory to achieve "good slut" status. A girl must behave like a "good slut" whether she wants to or not.
- Once a girl achieves "good slut" status, she is always at risk of losing control and becoming known as a "bad slut."
- The boundary between "good" and "bad slut" status, which is determined by one's peers, is fluid.
- If her peers determine that she has descended into "bad slut" status, she loses social status and becomes the object of harassment and ostracism.

A girl's compulsion to achieve "good slut" status is the result of the prude/slut contradiction. Not wanting to be perceived as a prude, girls perform an act of sexual bravado—whether they want to or not. "There's nothing wrong with these girls wanting to explore their sexuality," Cappiello points out. She and McInerney not only work with girls to hone their acting skills; they also provide opportunities for the girls to talk about the issues that concern them—and the slut-prude tightrope is the number one issue on their minds. "Their curiosity is totally normal, and we want to encourage them in that way," Cappiello continued. "But it becomes so hard. How can they explore their sexuality when they don't even know what their actual desire is?"

"That's exactly right," affirmed McInerney. She continued,

We often talk openly with the girls about where their desire to explore their sexuality comes from. Why do they feel the need to be sexual in the first place? Are they engaging in certain sexual acts because they have a genuine desire to explore their sexuality in a particular way? Or is it because the boys they like are encouraging them to do so? Do they want to kiss or make out with another girl, for example, because they like the girl, or because they like and want the male attention that goes with doing so? If a girl told us, "This particular sexual activity is something I really want, this is something I want to do," we would say, "Great!" But that's not what they are telling us. Usually it is not clear what they really want. Usually what they say is, "I want him to like me" or "I may as well do this now and get it over with." We never hear them say anything like, "I want this." These girls are not doing sexual things for themselves. We believe that girls should be sexually empowered. But what exactly are their motivations? They say, "I own my sexuality." But do they really?

The reason it's impossible for girls to untangle their motivations, Cappiello adds, is that "they don't want to be a prude." When avoiding prudery is a priority, how does one know when a girl is being sexual because she really wants to be? "They don't know what they really want," she says. "And there are drastic consequences for the decisions they make, and now those decisions are permanent because there's an online record."

The "Bad Slut" Violates Feminine Norms

I wondered if college-age women who are labeled "sluts" agree with their younger cohort about the contradictory meanings of the term. I theorized that women ages eighteen to twenty-two may feel less pressure to prove they're not prudes, since 71 percent of nineteen-year-olds have had sex, according to the Guttmacher Institute, with seventeen being about the average age of first sexual intercourse.[27] Therefore, I guessed, college-age women may not feel as compelled as younger teenage girls to behave like a "good slut." I figured that they might have less to prove.

It turns out that women between the ages of eighteen and twenty-two narrate slut stories that contain similar tensions between proving oneself to be not a prude and presenting oneself as a "good slut." However, these young women express the tension with different language. They talk about sluttiness within a discourse of sexual freedom. They told me that being sexually active, especially outside a romantic relationship, is perceived as an issue of "pride." It is "liberating." But is liberation really liberating when it's compulsory?

"Women at my college are very comfortable sexualizing themselves," reports Min, nineteen, an Asian American woman who grew up in New York City and now attends an elite university in the Northeast. "They see being sexual as a feminist statement. To them, being liberated is being sexual. So they do sexual things even if they don't want to in the name of feminism." Echoing the high school girls, Min continues, "The women here sexualize themselves but not necessarily to please themselves. Often it's just to please the guys." Is this what feminism today looks like to college-age women—mandatory sexualization? I believe it's fair to say that the positive connotation of "slut" has led at least some young women to embrace a warped vision of feminist sexual liberation. Certainly many young women actively choose to be sexually active because they want sex. It's simply not true that every sexually active female is coerced into being sexually active. But either way, the "slut" label wreaks havoc.

Maria, twenty-one, tells me that she had sexual intercourse for the first time when she was a freshman in college. In her sophomore year, she says, "I was single and became sexually active with more than one person. I also realized that I was bisexual. It was the first time that I recognized that my desires were not dirty, and since my relationship with my boyfriend had ended, I wanted to act on my desires. But I noticed that other women did not accept me and did not want to invite me to parties because they thought I would sleep with boys they liked. I started to notice jealousy. In high school, it was the girls with confidence who were called sluts regardless of their sexual activity. I started to see the same thing here at college too. This was hard for me because I was in the process of figuring out that I needed to have pride over my sexuality."

As Maria notices, sluttiness is more about attitude than behavior—a key element that holds true for both teenage girls and young adult women. I asked Maria why she thinks the other women find her threatening. "I ask myself this question all the time," she responds. "Partly it's because of my bisexuality. Being bi is not taken seriously. People think it means you're easy, that you could be with anyone. There's a stereotype that you're not discriminating. But another reason is that I make it clear that I'm not looking for romance. A lot of women hook up with guys with the hope that the hookup will become a relationship. Even when they're hooking up casually, they try to do it with the same person again and again. And I'm not doing that."

"Normal" females are supposed to want romance, not sex for its own sake. Choosing to be sexual purely for the sake of the sex—being a sexual agent—is not considered naturally feminine. It is an expression of pure confidence, and stereotypical femininity at some level is supposed to encompass neediness. Renee Engeln, the director of the Body and Media Lab at Northwestern University, told the *New York Times* that "we have complicated reactions to confident women in general, and particularly to women who are confident about their bodies. Women sometimes see them as arrogant."[28] I would add that we also have complicated reactions to women who are confident about their sexual selves.

Vanessa, a white twenty-one-year-old student, shares her "slut story," which took place at a summer camp when she was nineteen and working as a counselor. One of the other counselors, she said, "was hitting on me, but I pushed him away and told him I wasn't interested. One of the girls, who liked him, was very angry with me even though I had pushed him away. I told her, 'If I wanted to hook up with him I would, but I don't want to.' That statement got me in trouble. Later, I hooked up with a different guy that no one had a claim on. Somehow I became known as the girl who slept with different guys. I think it's because I made it clear that I wasn't interested in a romantic relationship and I was, like, really unapologetic about it. I recognize the way hooking up works, and I didn't expect a hookup to continue into a relationship. I saw it for what it was. Every summer there's a counselor who's the slut, the summer slut. That summer I was known as the summer slut, even though I had done nothing wrong."

Maria and Vanessa were labeled sluts because they violated

two central rules of femininity. To be sure, there are countless unspoken rules governing women's appearance and behavior that girls infer and internalize as they come of age. But to avoid "bad" sluttiness, they must adhere to two rules in particular:

RULE 1 Females must attract the sexual attention of many unattached guys, but they may have sexual activity only with one guy, who is a boyfriend or potential boyfriend.

"Marriage is still the goal and norm of most young women—look at the lionization of Kate Middleton, Duchess of Cambridge," notes Jaclyn Geller, author of the book *Here Comes the Bride*, alluding to the fact that the Duchess of Cambridge has a university degree, yet she is lauded for spending all her time fulfilling the roles of wife and mother. "The ultimate expression of sexuality is still supposed to be with one's husband, and that's what society rewards us for." Girls and young women are preferably expected to seek out sexual relationships within a romantic framework. But girls recognize that boyfriends can be scarce or undesirable. Therefore, depending on the values of her peer group, a girl or woman might be able to hook up occasionally with different partners, so long as she allows some time to lapse in between each encounter.

RULE 2 Females must never act as if they are trying too hard.

They must hide the tracks of their performance of femininity. They can't expose their effort. The girl or woman perceived to be "trying too hard" to capture male sexual attention is a potential target for slut-bashing. To avoid this fate, she must display her sexuality in a low-key, understudied way—the way a "good slut" is supposed to.

The combination of rules 1 and 2 results in this principle:

You will do everything you can to invite unattached males to think you're sexy, but only because you're looking for a boyfriend. You may not have sex with anyone except with a boyfriend. All the while, you will pretend that you aren't really trying, and that you don't really care.

Min admits that when she was in the eighth grade, she called several girls "sluts" to her friends. "Those girls wore shirts that were low-cut, and everything was tight. Actually, it took me a while to realize it, but I was jealous of them. I actually wanted to be their friend. They were pretty, they went out to parties, and they dressed well. I would make fun of their profile pictures because to me, they seemed attention-seeking and flirtatious."

"What made you choose the word 'slut' when you were putting them down?" I asked Min.

"To me, sluttiness is trying too hard to get attention. It's not necessarily about having lots of sex. It's just considered bad to be too attention-seeking if you're a girl. I'm a feminist now, and I know it was wrong for me to use the word. I also think that there's nothing wrong with having sex. But the problem is that the word is used to describe an attitude. Being slutty is about being unfeminine in an amplified way. People also put an adjective in front of 'slut.' They say 'fat slut'— that's a prevalent one. It means that a girl's too fat to wear revealing clothes, that she shouldn't be wearing what she's wearing. So again it's connected with her attitude."

"'Slut' portrays a woman who gains attention by throwing herself at men," agrees twenty-two-year-old Diana, a white college senior in California. "It makes you seem disgusting. With Instagram and Facebook, a slutty girl is the one uploading photos to compete with other girls for male attention. She's uploading photos to steal your boyfriend."

The notion that sluttiness is about agency or an attitude extends beyond the college years. Daniela, a thirty-two-year-old Latina bartender in Texas, says that the slut is "the girl who gets on the bar dancing, even if she's in a monogamous romantic relationship. And she's probably wearing a short skirt. Or every night a different guy walks her home from the bar, and everyone sees, and even though she's not having sex with any of them, she looks kind of skanky."

Parents today raise their daughters to take ownership of their actions—to be assertive, to go after what they want. In short, parents teach their daughters agency, an essential ingredient for equality. But often agency is mistranslated and misunderstood. Today, girls in financially comfortable communities grow up hearing endlessly that they have "girl power," that they can "do anything they set their minds to." This bland message of empowerment is often understood as: Girls *must* do it all. Although no one can possibly be high-achieving in every area—academics, sports, student government, community service, the arts—the girls who try and then stumble feel like failures. To save face, they pretend they aren't trying. They absorb the lesson that they must hide how hard they are working to do it all.

"The first message" teenage girls get in Newtown, Massachusetts, reports Sara Rimer of the *New York Times,* is: "Bring home A's. Do everything. Get into a top college." The second message is: "Don't work too hard."[29] Well, of course doing "everything" requires hard work. How could it not? The second message isn't really "Don't work too hard"; it is actually "Never let them see you sweat."

Femininity entails, in the words of a Duke University sophomore, "effortless perfection." In 2002, Duke undertook a large-scale research project called the Women's Initiative to evaluate the status of women on its campus. For undergraduate women, the study revealed, the goal of "effortless perfection" was oppressive. Women reported that they faced a constant burden of proving themselves academically successful, ambitious, thin, pretty, well-dressed, and fashionable—all simultaneously, all without visible effort.[30] Meeting this goal is simply not possible. As Jessica Ringrose puts it, the demands of femininity establish the concept of femininity "as a site of perpetual failure."[31] No one can avoid failure.

"It used to be that people said, 'You look pretty' or 'You look beautiful,'" observes Elizabeth Semmelhack, the chief curator of the Bata Shoe Museum in Toronto. "Now it's 'You look hot' or 'You look sexy.'"[32] Being "pretty" or "beautiful" is a passive stance. If you don't have at least some genetic luck, all the makeup and hair dye in the world won't make you gorgeous. But being "hot" or "sexy" can be achieved through effort—the right clothes, makeup, hair, posture, attitude. Being "hot" or "sexy" is the product of effort, and all females know it. Yet as one Newtown student, who scored a perfect 2400 on her SAT, told Rimer, "It is more important to be hot than smart. Effortlessly hot."[33]

The "bad slut" is the girl or woman who exposes the effort behind being hot. She ruins the charade for everyone else. She turns inside out the farce of femininity. *Of course* being feminine requires effort! Helena Rubinstein famously said, "There are no ugly women, only lazy ones."[34] But being feminine also requires *pretending* that it doesn't require effort. Many females despise the "slut" for revealing their secret.

We have seen that "slut" is used in myriad ways—positive and negative; about sexually active females and not sexually active females; to describe those who have "too much sex" and with "too many partners" and those with clothes that are "too revealing"; to refer to females who are confident and unapologetic about their sexual desires and those who reek of desperate neediness for male attention. What is the bottom line?

A "good slut" is sexy yet not oversexualized. Preferably she has only one sexual partner, although her peers reserve the right to set a standard allowing her more than one, or none at all, provided that she's low-key about it. She knows how to present herself as sexually knowing, yet she does not appear needy or desperate.

On the other hand, a "bad slut" violates expectations of feminine norms. She exercises sexual agency. She has sex outside the permitted boundaries established by her peers. She actively provokes male sexual attention, including that of guys with other girlfriends or hookup partners. She exposes the reality that being sexy is a deliberate performance that is unnatural, difficult, and requires serious effort.

For her sins, she must be punished.

CHAPTER 3

Slut-Bashing: Face-to-Face and in Cyberspace

"My best friend had a slut reputation in high school," Sharon, a twenty-year-old Italian American woman who grew up in Queens, New York, is telling me. We are in the lounge of her college's student center, sunk into club chairs. It's Martin Luther King Jr. Day; the new semester begins a few days later, and we are the only people in the lounge. Still, Sharon has lowered her voice. I lean forward so that I don't miss a word.

"How did it start?" I ask. Every slut narrative has an identifiable beginning.

"She liked a guy, but the problem was that he had a girlfriend," Sharon remembers. She's wearing green pants, the color bouncing off her hazel eyes, and a black knit scoop-neck top and black Converse sneakers. "But he liked my friend too," she continues. "He broke up with his girlfriend so that he could start dating my friend. He didn't cheat on her. The girlfriend did not take it very well. She seemed to think that my friend had 'stolen' her boyfriend, and she wanted revenge. So she and her friends started spreading stories that my friend had slept with ten guys that year. They never said anything bad about the guy. That's what was flying around Facebook."

"Was the name-calling only online, or was it in person too?" I asked.

"Both," Sharon said. "On Facebook, people wrote that she was a whore, a slut, a boyfriend-stealer. But she didn't steal anything and she didn't do anything wrong. The boy liked her and they ended up dating for two years."

One day in the middle of class, Sharon's cell phone vibrated in her jeans pocket. As soon as she could sneak a peak, she pulled it out. "Where R U?" her friend had texted. "I need U 2 wlk w me 2 class. Grls thretnd 2 thro me dn strs."

"Would they really have done it though?" I asked, wondering if the girls were making an empty threat just to prove a point. But Sharon is insistent. "They really would have done it if they could have. I definitely think they would have. But since they didn't go through with it, when my friend went to the school administration the school didn't do anything about it."

Another school day, another act of slut-bashing. Sharon's friend was targeted because she was believed to have been an oversexed slut who had stolen another girl's boyfriend. But we know that although sluttiness is seemingly about sex, it's really about something else. "In my high school," says Sharon, "you were a whore or a slut if you ate too much and didn't gain a pound. You were a whore or a slut if you bought the same prom dress as the head cheerleader. You were a whore or a slut if I don't like the way you look in that shirt, or I think your boobs are too big."

Sharon's friend was called a slut because she was believed to be a girl with *agency*—the capability of exerting power over a situation. Framed in this way, Sharon's friend appeared to violate the rule of effortless perfection. Instead of radiating an aura of effortlessness, she emitted a smoke signal of desire. According to the girls who slut-bashed her, she *chose* to do something wrong and therefore *deserved* her slutty reputation. The boyfriend's sexuality, meanwhile, was never questioned or maligned.

Agency is a critical element of the sexual double standard, in which only girls, never boys, are called to task for their real or presumed sexual aggression. In both rounds of my research, I found that not all girls so targeted are chosen because of sexual behavior. In fact, many of my interviewees—those from two decades ago as well as today—had no sexual experience at all, or no more than their peers did, at the onset of the name-calling. Nevertheless, the sexual double standard lurks in every slut-bashing story. The sexual double standard is a necessary ingredient that justifies the targeting of specific girls, and the perception of the presence of agency on the part of a female is what triggers the sexual double standard.

In schools, a girl is singled out as a slut because she deviates in some aspect from feminine norms, and she is believed to have actively caused this deviation. In addition to the girl considered to be too sexual, other categories of "sluts" are:

- The girl regarded as "other" or different from her peers in some way.
- The girl envied by other girls because she's perceived to have an unfair advantage with boys.
- The survivor of sexual assault.

Since every girl may fall into at least one of these categories, even transiently, every girl is a walking potential target.

The paradox of slut-bashing is that a girl's sexual history or lack thereof becomes irrelevant from the moment she is labeled a slut. Once she becomes known as a slut, a girl is sexualized evermore. The narrative of the hypersexual girl takes off, becoming embroidered and bedazzled as it passes from locker room to Twitter to Instagram.

What does it feel like when the kids you see every day in school are making jokes at your expense, often right in your face; calling you vulgar names on social media sites so that everyone can see; and shunning you socially at athletic games and after-school club meetings? "All I wanted to do was go home and cry," reports a twenty-two-year-old white woman from California, remembering her reputation when she was eighteen. "It's degrading," is the way a white sixteen-year-old girl describes the experience. "And the most upsetting part is that it's not even about sex. Calling a girl a slut is about making her feel bad about herself."

"The general perception in my high school," adds Sharon, "is that you don't associate with any girl labeled a slut or a whore. You avoid that person."

"'Slut' is a label that falls on you and then it's so hard to get rid of it," comments a white twenty-one-year-old student in Pennsylvania. "It's not fair to label someone, because then they are stuck with it forever, and if they were having sex with lots of people before, maybe they're not even doing that anymore. But it follows you forever anyway."

"I don't want my little brother or little sister to hear that I'm a slut," confesses Diana, a white twenty-two-year-old college senior in California. "That is my biggest fear. I want to be a role model to them, and I'm scared that I'll be tarnished in their opinion."

Calling a girl a slut in school often is an act of bullying that may be characterized as abuse. According to the American Association of University Women, nearly half of all girls (46 percent) in grades seven through twelve experience sexual harassment in some form, mostly verbal harassment (unwelcome sexual comments, jokes, or gestures) that takes place either in person or by text, email, Facebook, or other electronic media.[35] When these acts fulfill certain criteria, they may be classified as "bullying." According to Dan Olweus, the Swedish psychologist who pioneered research on bullying in the 1970s and 1980s, bullying is a form of abuse that encompasses three characteristics:

1. The acts are intentionally aggressive and negative. They may include physical contact, words, gestures, faces, or intentional social exclusion.
2. They are carried out repeatedly and over time.
3. There is an imbalance of power in the relationship between the victim and the bully or bullies. Because of this power imbalance, the student who is bullied has difficulty defending herself or himself.[36]

New research shows that victims of bullying are not necessarily socially isolated and completely unprotected at the very bottom of the social pecking order, and bullies are not generally at the very top. Rather, "most victimization is occurring in the middle to upper ranges of status," according to Robert Faris, an assistant professor of sociology at the University of California, Davis, who led a research study on aggressive behavior among high school students. Many teenage bullies, Faris found, go after those whom they consider to be social rivals.[37] Almost anyone can be a bully, and almost anyone can be a victim. Whether or not this was always the case, it certainly is so today in the cyber world. To Olweus, bullying always includes a differential in social status between the bully and the bullied. To Faris, that distinction is not a necessary component.

With regard to slut-bashing, I observe a differential in adherence to feminine norms. Therefore, I advance a slightly different way of looking at bullying through the lens of the "slut" label: *Slut-bashing is a particular form of bullying, I argue, because it is verbal harassment conducted repeatedly over time in which a girl is intentionally targeted because she does not adhere to feminine norms.* Thus, slut-bashing is less about social status and social power and more about *gendered* status and *gendered* power. From afar, the slut-basher and her victim may appear to occupy a similar rung on the social ladder, but the girl labeled a slut is vulnerable as a result of her botched performance of femininity.

Bullying is a hot topic of conversation—among adults. Spam lands in our in-boxes asking, "Is Bullying on Social Networks a Problem?" We were transfixed in May 2012 when a Rutgers student, Dharun Ravi, was convicted for bullying his gay roommate, Tyler Clementi, through social media. When a Republican candidate for president, Mitt Romney, was accused of having bullied a gay classmate in high school, the news landed on the front page of the *New York Times*. School social workers email parents with updates on professional development workshops they've attended on bullying intervention techniques.

But the discourse is quite different among teenagers. They tend to be loath to describe acts of bullying with the term "bullying," which they perceive to be a problem limited to younger kids in elementary or middle school. In part this may be the result of the implementation of antibullying programs within elementary and middle schools; when students graduate and move on to high school, they may associate bullying as a phenomenon from their past and not of their present. But in large part, teenagers want and need to regard themselves as agents with control over their lives. They don't want to be told that they are powerless in the face of a phenomenon greater than they are. "Admitting that they're being bullied, or worse, that they are bullies, slots them into a narrative that's disempowering and makes them feel weak and childish," explain danah boyd and Alice Marwick, researchers at Microsoft Research whose work focuses on teenagers' use of social media.[38]

Instead, teenagers—particularly girls—refer not to "bullying" but to "drama." "Drama" can mean gossiping about another girl, joking about her, or calling her names, explain boyd and Marwick.[39] Different from the conventional understandings of bullying, drama is performed exclusively by girls; it is reciprocal; and it is performed in public online. Drama is a way to get attention. It is a public performance. "'Drama' allows teens to distance themselves from practices which adults may conceptualize as bullying," write boyd and Marwick. "As such, they can retain agency—and save face— rather than positioning themselves in a victim narrative. Drama is a gendered process that perpetuates conventional gender norms. . . . Dismissing conflict as drama lets teens frame the social dynamics and emotional impact as inconsequential, allowing them to 'save face' rather than taking on the mantle of bully or victim."[40]

My interviewees repeatedly preferred the word "drama" when describing acts of slut-bashing. "Drama" is a concept they understand, and it helps them organize their thoughts about what has occurred to them. Oksana, a white twenty-two-year-old college senior in New York State, shared with me that when she was in the ninth grade, "there was all this drama after I had a sexual experience with my boyfriend." Girls who were friendly with the boyfriend started calling Oksana a slut. They wrote comments on her friends' Facebook pages such as "Don't hang out with Oksana." She says, "It was bad because everybody's network is connected, so everybody sees it right away." But she was careful never to use the words "bullying" or "slut-bashing" or any term that would imply that the girls were behaving inappropriately, and that she might have needed protection. "They just tried to create drama," she insisted. Oksana used the word "drama" to demonstrate simultaneously that she was slut-bashed and that she's a tough girl. "Drama" is a vehicle for taking agency or ownership over a horrible situation. Downplaying the events as drama shows that a girl is not a blubbering victim. She is confident; she can handle the situation. But regardless of the language they use to describe slut-bashing, the reality is that most girls can't handle it.

Slut-bashing isn't new, but the Internet and mobile communication have enabled it to envelop girls' lives. Unlike for previous generations of girls, slut-bashing now is inescapable, anonymous, and eternal. A girl may be called a slut or a ho everywhere and at any time—not just when she's in the school cafeteria or gathering books from her locker. She can't hide, rushing to her bedroom and slamming the door behind her; she can't even transfer to a different school and get a clean start. If she's being slut-bashed, hurtful messages appear the moment she turns on her phone, tablet, or computer. Disconnecting from the Internet isn't a viable solution, since that means disconnecting from social life completely. Besides, with teachers increasingly integrating technology into their classroom and homework assignments, disconnecting is not even a choice a girl is permitted to make. Diane, a white twenty-six-year-old marriage and family therapist in California, tells me that when she was seventeen, a "gang of girls" attacked her on MySpace. "They called me a bitch to make me fearful and to threaten me. It was easy for them to reach out to me, to find me, with the technology, which was pretty new at that time. They could see that I had posted pictures of myself with a guy I had hooked up with, and they decided that that meant I was having sex with guys and therefore I was deserving of being attacked."

Slut-bashers are also strengthened by the Internet and mobile communication. Hiding behind the anonymity of the technology, their impulse to bully is fueled by the knowledge that no matter how coarse and abusive they are, they can't be tracked down. They may regret their actions after the fact; but once comments are sent, they can be endlessly mass-forwarded, posted online, and linked to multiple sites. Completely scrubbing away the names, photos, and comments about an individual girl may become impossible. Even when an online comment is deleted, it's never really eliminated.

Not only young females are vulnerable: any person's professional or social reputation can be discredited because of untrue reports posted online. We are all vulnerable in the digital world. But many adults can move on, fight back, enlist professional support, or post their own narratives. Typically, young people possess far fewer resources and far less savvy.

The addictive nature of the Internet can make its effects unbearably corrosive. Psychologists treat patients who have been diagnosed with Internet Addiction Disorder. When a girl today is labeled a slut, her bullies are in her bedroom with her, one click away. As much as she may not want to, she can't quite help clicking and reading the most recent remarks posted about her online for all to comment upon.

Who ever thought that we could be nostalgic for the odious comments carved into bathroom walls? The ephemeral nature of that graffiti posed an advantage. A freshly painted wall after summer break indicated that what was written last year was dead and buried. A new year meant a new start for both the bullied and the bullies. However, unless the wall was photographed, there was no evidence of the abusive comments. If a girl was abused year after year, she lacked a compilation of evidence over time. Today, a girl can create a record of screenshots and printouts to bolster her position that she's being bullied.

To explain the viciousness of anonymous bullying, I need to say only one word: Formspring. A social media site created in 2009 that has since waned in popularity, Formspring quickly became the online destination for mean, crude, anonymous comments and questions. It was, according to the *New York Times*, "the online version of the bathroom wall in school, the place to scrawl raw, anonymous gossip."[41] Sharon broke it down for me: "You create an account, and then people can anonymously ask you any question about anything. Since they know you'll never know who they are, they ask crazy things. They can search your name, or they find you because your profile is connected to your Facebook or your Twitter or Tumblr. They ask things like, 'What size bra do you wear? Your boobs are huge.' Or 'Why are you acting like a slut and whore?' Some people actually expect you to answer. Then you post their question with an answer, so everyone sees it." At that point, the identity of the person questioned becomes public, but the questioner still remains anonymous.

I stopped scribbling notes on my legal pad, flabbergasted. "Why on earth would anyone *choose* to have a Formspring?" I asked. Yet Sharon was the one dumbfounded by my middle-aged obtuseness. "The entire high school was involved in it!" she replied. "How can you *not* be curious to see what it was all about?"

In her insightful exploration of bullying, *Sticks and Stones: Defeating the Culture of Bullying and Rediscovering the Power of Character and Empathy*, the author Emily Bazelon notes that a million people joined Formspring in the six weeks after the site went live; over the next few years, it had en-listed twenty-five million users, one-third of them seventeen or younger. "The whole point of Formspring," she observes, "seemed to be that it was risky and public—like walking on a tightrope." One fourteen-year-old girl told her, "It's like an interview where you find out how other people really see you. It's just honest. Even if what you find out about yourself is bad, you think you want to know."[42]

Sharon echoed this obsessive desire to know what every-one is saying about you, even if it's abusive. "Does anyone ask neutral or nice questions, or is it all mean stuff?" I wondered.

"All mean stuff," Sharon answered, "because that's more fun."

"And why does anyone answer and post mean questions?" Sharon looked me right in the eye. "Girls want attention," she replied. She paused. "But we have to start playing smarter."

Abusive comments on Formspring have preceded—and even followed—a number of teens' suicides. In fact, Form-spring ceased being a well-known secret among teens when the word got out in March 2010 that it was linked with the suicide of a seventeen-year-old girl, Alexis Pilkington from Long Island. Although her parents did not believe that abu-sive online messages caused her to take her own life, Suffolk County police officers investigated graphic, lewd images that were posted *after* news had spread about her death. On Formspring and Facebook, people posted photos of Pilking-ton doctored to look as though she had a noose around her neck.[43]

Since Pilkington's suicide, Formspring has been replaced in popularity among teenagers by Ask.fm, founded in 2010.

The company says it has fifty-seven million users in 150 countries, with half its users under the age of eighteen. The site adds an additional two hundred thousand new users each day. The average visitor spends one hundred minutes a month on the site.[44] In 2013, a fourteen-year-old British girl committed suicide after receiving abusive messages from Ask.fm users such as "drink bleach," "go get cancer," and "go die." A mother of a teenage girl from Irvine, California, who was bullied on the site told the *Los Angeles Times*, "For teens, this is a feeding frenzy in shark-infested waters without a cage."[45] A twelve-year-old girl from central Florida, Rebecca Sedwick, also killed herself after receiving hate-filled messages from fifteen middle school children on Ask.fm as well as the messaging apps Kik and Voxer. The harassers wrote, "Why are you still alive?" and "Can you die please?"[46]

Stephanie, the fifteen-year-old girl from New York City, explains, "People can ask you questions anonymously—really personal questions. You can post video responses also. People feel obligated to answer what other people ask you. You could ignore the questions, but then people will give you a hard time: 'Why are you on Ask.fm if you're not going to answer the questions?' Then you're not relevant. People won't go to your page anymore, and no one will ask you questions anymore."

Kaitlyn adds, "If you're a girl, the questions are 100 percent are about sex. 'How many guys have you hooked up with?' 'How far have you gone?' 'How many blow jobs have you given?' These questions start in the seventh grade."

"What do guys get asked?" I wondered.

"Their questions are also about sex, but the tone is more

playful with guys. It's not judgmental," Katilyn explains. "The guys ask each other questions to get advice, like 'How far did that girl go with you, and would you do it again?' It's not about judging the guy."

But the girls are always judged on the basis of their sexuality. Sometimes they are lumped together into a group of interchangeable "sluts" via "slut lists." These compilations of girls rated "hottest" to "ugliest," sometimes listing phone numbers next to full names, were shocking in the early 2000s but now are as common as a celebrity sex tape. Certainly you don't need the Internet to create a "slut list": At New Jersey's top-ranked high school, Millburn High, senior girls every year for a decade used paper and pens—the old-fashioned, quaint method of bullying. The list included incoming freshman by name and was circulated on the first day of school as a hazing ritual.[47] But in this day and age, who needs notebook paper? How last century. Online "slut lists" are not only faster and easier, they're harder to attribute to any individual slut-basher.

In one of the more well-publicized online incidents, in 2011 a list of over a hundred girls from seven high schools in Westchester, New York, and Greenwich, Connecticut, was forwarded so many times that one teen decided that it would be easier for everyone involved to post the list on Facebook. To avoid being flagged on Facebook as abusive, the boy called it a "smut list" rather than a "slut list." The girls, some as young as fourteen, were ranked according to the sexual encounters they allegedly had engaged in and were willing to do, and the list included anonymous commentary. Their first and last names were included, but all boys' names were omitted. The "smut list" group received over seven thousand likes overnight. Facebook removed it two days later after parents and school administrators appealed to the site to take it down, but the damage already had been done.[48]

The Sexual Double Standard

Why do teenagers appear to have a relentless desire to categorize girls sexually? Because they (as we all do) live and breathe under the regime of the sexual double standard.

Yes, the sexual double standard exists even today. On the face of it, this claim may seem ludicrous. After all, many women are exceedingly open about their sexuality, and from afar it may appear that they face no consequences for doing so. Many willingly and inexplicably have bared their breasts for Girls Gone Wild videos and during halftime at football games.[49] Girls' and women's tops have cutouts in the most unexpected places, forcing the wearer to expose her bra or forego it altogether. When Madonna and Beyoncé performed at the Super Bowl, their outfits and shoes made them look as if they had walked off a porn set. Girls and women have flooded Facebook with so many photos of themselves in bikinis that a new iPhone app, Pikinis, automatically finds swimsuit photos of your friends or even strangers based on their proximity to your city or your campus. Brides routinely celebrate at their bachelorette parties by eating penis-shaped cake.

But it is a misunderstanding to conclude that these acts are the result of sexual equality. The opposite holds true: Some women sexualize themselves inappropriately as a result of sexual *inequality*. A great deal of the time, women's sexuality is stomped over. In fact, many Americans can't handle hearing the word "vagina" and therefore censor it. In 2007, a public high school in Cross River, New York, suspended three sixteen-year-old girls who said the word "vagina" during a reading from Eve Ensler's play *The Vagina Monologues*.[50] In 2012, Michigan State Representative Lisa Brown was barred from speaking on the House floor after she used the word "vagina" during a speech against a bill seeking to ban abortions. A fellow legislator said, "What she said was so offensive. It was so offensive, I don't even want to say it in front of women. I would not say that in mixed company."[51] In 2013, an Idaho science teacher was investigated for using the word "vagina" with his tenth-grade students in biology class.[52] In multiple separate incidents, Facebook has removed photos of mothers breastfeeding, saying that they violated the company's rules of decency, even though paid advertisements on the site displayed topless women.[53]

Often, boys and men sexualize females in an aggressive manner with an implicit understanding that it's acceptable to force a girl or woman to have sex even if she says no. At the top-tier Piedmont High School in the San Francisco Bay Area, a "Fantasy Slut League" of male athletes amassed points for sexual activity with female students in an online competition that lasted for five to six years.[54] At California State University, Long Beach, a weekly student newspaper ran an article titled "How to Get Laid: A Girl's Guide for Guys," which included this nugget of advice: "When you get to her place just get to the fucking no dilly dallying, you don't want to give her time to really think about it. Don't be afraid to be aggressive."[55]

In sum, female body parts are regarded as offensive, female sexual activity is mocked as a competitive sport for guys or preyed upon as an opportunity for coercion, and girls are reduced to sexual playthings. If *you* were caught in this messed-up milieu, isn't it possible that you might respond, at least sometimes, in less than healthy ways? Maybe you too might internalize your own objectification. Perhaps you also would flaunt your body, sometimes aggressively, sometimes in inappropriate times and places. Maybe this is the only way you know to get attention and have a good time; after all, no one has shown you anything different. If women's bodies and sexual desires were perceived as utterly normal and mundane, if they could consent to or refuse offers without fear of repercussions, perhaps women wouldn't feel compelled to objectify themselves (or men; don't forget that penis cake) because they would have nothing to prove.

But in the meanwhile, no matter what a female does sexually, she is judged in a way that males are not. Boys will be boys . . . and girls will be "sluts." And now we even have the research to prove it.

A University of Michigan psychologist, Terri Conley, designed a study with her colleagues in 2012 showing that heterosexual women who accept offers of casual sex are judged more harshly than men are. She further demonstrated that women are less likely than men to accept such offers, and that this gender difference is at least partially caused by anticipatory negative judgment. Women themselves also told Conley and her research partners that they expect to be perceived more negatively than men are for accepting an offer of casual sex.[56]

Conley and her colleagues conducted several experiments as part of their study, encompassing nearly three thousand participants, ranging in age from eighteen to seventy-four. In the first experiment, college student volunteers read about one random student approaching another, introducing himself or herself, and asking if they could have sex that night. The second student agrees. Half the participants read a version in which the second student who accepted the casual sex offer was named Lisa, while the other participants were told that the accepter was named Mark. Both male and female participants rated Lisa more negatively than Mark. "Overall," write Conley and her colleagues, "our results were consistent with the existence of a sexual double standard for casual sex. Participants perceived Lisa to be less intelligent, less mentally healthy, more promiscuous, less competent, and more risky than Mark— even though Mark and Lisa both accepted the sexual offer."[57]

In a second experiment, Conley and her colleagues wanted the participants to situate themselves in the scenario. How would they expect to be perceived if they themselves accepted or rejected an offer of casual sex? The female participants who imagined agreeing to the sexual offer reported that they expected to be perceived, relative to the men, as more promiscuous, socially inappropriate, and sexually desperate. They also reported that if they turned down the sexual offer, they would expect to be regarded, relative to the men, as more intelligent, mentally healthy, physically attractive, socially appropriate, and sexually well-adjusted. In short, women assumed that accepting a casual sex offer would cause others to perceive them negatively and that rejecting a sexual proposal would cause others to think of them positively.[58]

Finally, heterosexual participants recalled the most recent time they experienced a casual sex offer. Overwhelmingly, men were more likely to accept the offer (63 percent) than to reject it, while women were far more likely to reject the offer (70 percent) than to accept it. The women reported that they were less likely to accept the offer because they perceived they would have been evaluated more negatively had they accepted it.[59]

Based on these results, Conley and her colleagues see evidence not only of a stigma for women who engage in casual heterosexual sex, but also of a "backlash effect"—conforming to sexual norms because of the fear of stigma. In other words, the fear of a stigma associated with accepting an offer of casual sex leads women to refuse such offers. Conley and her colleagues write, "Our results strongly support the existence of a sexual double standard, at least regarding casual sexuality."[60] Their findings are consistent with the sexual double standard because they suggest that men are granted more sexual freedom to engage in sexual activity than women are.

But isn't it possible that women are less likely to accept an offer of casual sex not because they are afraid of stigma but because they just don't like casual sex as much as men do? Maybe they are just biologically different. Maybe women's and men's hormones and chromosomes render them essentially dissimilar from one another. This could be true in theory, but in practice it isn't. Under the right circumstances, Conley shows, women are just as interested as men are in casual sex.

Jumping off from a widely cited 1989 study by two psychologists, Russell Clark and Elaine Hatfield, which demonstrated that men are fairly likely to agree to sex with a stranger while women are exceptionally unlikely to do so, Conley in a separate study sought to show that this gender difference is not biologically determined.[61] She theorized that in the Clark and Hatfield paradigm, a casual sexual proposal "is uniquely repulsive to women . . . because of what it conveys about the male proposer's sexual capabilities and safety."[62] She warned that "to generalize from this situation to make judgments about women's attitudes toward casual sexual encounters in general is not justified"[63] and that "existing research suggests that concerns about danger and pleasure are prominent for women in a variety of casual sexual encounters."[64]

In fact, Conley demonstrated that women avoid casual sexual encounters of the type described by Clark and Hatfield only when they believe that the sexual encounter will be unpleasant or risky. They are more likely to participate in sexual encounters if they have good reason to believe that the experience will be pleasant and safe. "In that way," Conley wrote, "women are a lot like men."[65] If the circumstances are favorable to women—including being free of stigma—women and men behave similarly. Thus the sexual double standard should cease, because it is built on the assumption that males want sex more than females as a result of biological differences.

I spoke with Conley on the phone, asking her to help me make sense of her research. I wanted to know: If it's not in fact true, why did the Clark and Hatfield study perpetuate the idea that males want sex more than females do because of biological gender differences? The sexual double standard, Conley responded, is a "fundamental attribution error—

when you make attributions to individuals instead of to the situations they are in." When you take into account stigma and backlash, females do not differ from males in their sexual desire. Thus, a female who expresses sexual desire is not deviant; there is zero biological basis for the concept of a slut.

Furthermore, Conley's research also suggests, she told me, "that the reasons casual sex may be 'bad' for women are fixable. For example, we know that in casual sexual situations, men believe that women are not as entitled to pleasure. And we also know that there is a stigma for women. If we could change those things, then the sexual situation would become a more equal and even playing ground." In such a scenario, the idea of a slut would make no sense from any angle— biological or social—because female sexual agency would be considered yawningly normal.

The Sexual Girl: "It's Like It's All Her Fault"

The sexual double standard at its core is a narrative about agency: Girls are supposed to hide the fact that they are going after what they want, especially if what they want is sexual pleasure. "The summer between my sophomore and junior year of high school, I hooked up with a football player," twenty-two-year-old Gloria shares with me in a Skype interview. Gloria is a Latina college student on the West Coast. It's 7:30 a.m. Pacific time, but she's an early riser and she's ready to talk. Her brown hair is pulled back with an athletic headband, and her large brown eyes are looking directly into her computer's camera. "He wasn't the first person I had sex with, but he was the first person I had casual sex with. We were on his mom's couch," she continues, "and I started to bleed. My blood seeped into the fabric of the couch. I found out later that I had an inflamed cervix"—it turned out to be nothing serious, just an infection that was easily treated with medication—"but I didn't know it at the time. Immediately I felt ashamed and worried." Was Gloria worried about the fact that she was bleeding? Did she think maybe she had a sexually transmitted disease or something precancerous in her cervix? No, she was worried for an entirely different reason: "I knew that he was going to tell people, which he did."

How was she so certain he would tell people? I ask.

"I just had this sense about it. He was on the football team, and a girl bleeding on his mom's couch was too good a story to not tell everyone. And I was right."

Kids at school started coming up to Gloria, even people she thought were her friends, saying to her, "Oh, she does that" and "I heard what happened." They didn't just say it in her ear. "They said it to me when other people were around, trying to be funny. But it was ostracizing because they were trying to be funny but not to me. It was at my expense. They didn't care about my feelings."

Even though Gloria and I are looking at each other through cameras, her eyes appear so sorrowful that I feel as if we are facing each other in person. "The story was never about him, even though he hooked up with a lot of girls," she continues. "There were no repercussions for him, just for me. He stopped talking to me because he never really cared about me; he just wanted to hook up with me. He continued hooking up with other girls."

Gloria's fourteen-year-old sister, Christina, is itching to get on the Skype interview too. She wants to tell me about her friend, who had sex in the sixth grade with an eighth-grade boy. "He pressured her into it," Christina explains. "She's, like, really, really pretty, and the boys were always asking her for sex. After she had sex with him, everyone found out, and she's been called a slut ever since then. The boy is not called any names. It's like it's all her fault. I think it's stupid. It sucks to get pressured to have sex, and then to get labeled when you do."

Are you seeing a pattern here? Girl and boy engage in a sexual act; girl is harassed, her life is worsened; boy's life continues as before, if not improved.

Here's another tale of the sexual double standard: Sasha is a white forty-four-year-old single mother, but she too can't get out of her head her own experience with slut-bashing three decades ago in a small town on Long Island. "I got a huge crush on someone on the football team—he was a senior and really cute," she tells me, sounding just like the teenager she was back then. "But I did something horrible! I gave him a blow job in the back of his car. Oh my god—it was horrible!" Sasha is clearly embarrassed, and she doesn't know quite how to express the fact that she never finished the act. "It wasn't even a whole blow job!" is how she finally puts it. "We were in the back of a car after a party, and there was another couple in the front, and they told people, and everyone found out. So I was the dumb tenth-grade girl who was the talk of the locker room. And I hated giving him the blow job, actually. I didn't get any pleasure from it. It wasn't something I enjoyed at all. I was more like, 'Can we be done now?' And he didn't do anything for me [sexually]; it was just an ego trip for him to have me do this to him."

Sasha needs a moment to collect her thoughts. She clearly remembers everything, but the humiliation of it all is washing over her. After a pause, she continues. "So everybody knew me, but there were two specific girls who gave me trouble. Maybe they were mean to me because they were burnouts who smoked cigarettes, and even though I was a cheerleader and hung out with the jocks I also smoked and would hang out with the burnouts. So maybe they felt I was encroaching on their turf?" she asks rhetorically, and then answers her own question. "I think they felt they had some claim on the guy. They called me a slut, and I was horrified. When someone calls you that, you don't want to go to school. You don't want to show your face. You want to disappear."

But Sasha did continue to attend school, and she was scared. The two girls threatened her physically, and Sasha had reason to believe that they would actually fight her. "They were tough bullies. They got into fights all the time. One of them got on my school bus one day and gave me the finger and threatened me by saying, 'Something's going to go on.' I was shaking. I would never have hit anyone, and I had never been in a fight."

In the end, the girls never did pick a physical fight with Sasha, and after a few months they stopped slut-bashing her. "Even though it didn't last for a very long time, to me it felt like the end of the world," Sasha recalls. "One day seemed like a year."

And what happened with the guy? "I was a silly, naive girl," Sasha says ruefully. "I thought he was cute and that if

I did that act for him, he would then like me and talk with me and maybe even want to hang out with me. What was I thinking? He never even said hi to me again afterwards. I felt really crappy. I felt, like, I don't know—tainted. You know what I mean?"

A generation later, the same story repeats. Just as with teenagers yesterday, when teens today sense that a girl is being sexually active out of a desperate desire to be liked—and giving a boy she barely knows oral sex can certainly appear desperate—they pounce on her. The act is too aggressive in a needy way. The girl is expressing sexuality but not sexual confidence, which leads her peers to conclude that she has crossed a line. Remember, a successful performance of femininity requires acting as if everything is effortless—especially sex.

Vicki, a twenty-two-year-old white lanky college senior wearing a chunky southwestern-style knit cardigan over a loose shirt, meets me at a diner near her campus. The second the menus are handed over to the waiter, she is launching into her slut story.

"I never talk about this because I really just want to forget it happened. But here goes. I was popular; people liked me. I was in the ninth grade, and there was a boy in the tenth grade. He wouldn't talk to me in person, but we started instant messaging on AOL Instant Messenger. He was sexy and he told me I was pretty. We arranged to meet up after school one day before I had basketball practice, and we went into the private handicapped bathroom with the lock. I tried to give him a blow job for, like two seconds, but I had no idea what I was doing. I was wearing braces! So I stopped and that was the end of it. Then I went to practice. I thought the whole incident was kind of funny, so I told my friends about it. But they didn't think it was funny at all! They thought I was disgusting. Nobody said that the boy was disgusting. He just kept on living his life."

Vicki has several theories to explain her friends' response. First, she was the first among them to do anything sexual, "and they didn't understand." Second, "they thought I was too aggressive." Third, they thought the location—the handicapped bathroom—"was too racy, too scandalous."

The girls told other people what Vicki had done, and "I'm sure they exaggerated it," Vicki believes. "From that point on, I was a social outcast. I was iced out. People said I was disgusting. There were five hundred kids in my grade, and everyone knew. After that I wasn't popular anymore. Even two years later, some random boy stopped me in the hallway and said, 'Wanna go in the bathroom again?'"

Vicki's story is just another tale of the sexual double standard in play, but it has a twist. Her sister, who's two years older and was in the eleventh grade at the time, was very popular—and also known to be sexually active. She was able to get away with it. In fact, the name on her powder-puff football jersey was "Tulsa"—"a slut" spelled backward. "Everybody knew and thought it was so funny, and she didn't mind," Vicki marvels. "She went about it with confidence. She went around owning her sexuality in a way that I didn't. It was so different for me. I wasn't willing to stand up for myself. And my friends looked down on me and wouldn't support me."

At first, what jumps out from this story is how arbitrary slut-bashing can appear. If both girls were known to be sexually active, why was Vicki, and not her sister, targeted? Is slut-bashing mercurial? In fact, there is a logic behind it. Vicki was targeted because she came across as desperate while her sister appeared calm, cool, confident, and controlled. Vicki's sexual agency was suspect because she was perceived to have overplayed her hand. She appeared insecure, and her agency was too visible.

The "Other" Girl: "I Didn't Do Anything; It Just Happened, I Guess"

You don't have to be sexually active to be perceived as a slut who has crossed boundaries of gendered norms. Any girl who's regarded as "other" can become the next "slut." If she's a new student, overweight, an early developer, a member of an economic or ethnic minority, or just different in any way, her femininity and sexuality can be called to task.

Jessica, twenty-three, is getting ready to graduate from college in two weeks, but she carves out the time to speak with me in between finals and job interviews. She is Latina, as well as a fluent Spanish speaker. In her freshman year at her California high school, she fell into a habit of speaking Spanish with a Latino boy who was in band class with her. "He was just being flirty with me," she explains apologetically. "I just liked him as a friend. It really wasn't a big deal." But it was a big deal for the boy's white girlfriend, who didn't speak Spanish and didn't understand what Jessica and the boy were saying. Jessica theorizes that the girlfriend came to believe that Jessica and the boy were speaking romantically to each other.

"So she spread a rumor about me. She got her friends to come right up to me and say 'home wrecker' and 'slut.' She should have blamed her boyfriend, but it's easier to blame the girl; they never blame the guy. I didn't feel comfortable going to band class after that, and as soon as class was over I would leave and not hang around with the other kids in the class."

The role of agency is important in this story: the white girl was threatened by Jessica's active communication with the boyfriend. Since the white girl didn't understand what they were talking about, she imagined that Jessica was behaving aggressively. Girls regarded as "other" are regarded as provocateurs, even when they have done nothing active to provoke anyone.

Sharon, the woman whose best friend was threatened with being thrown down a flight of stairs, was herself called a slut despite her having zero sexual experience. Sharon is differently abled. She is both visually and physically impaired; in high school, a paraprofessional helped her walk from class to class. It was obvious that she had special needs. "When you stand out, you get labels," she theorizes, "and 90 percent of the time, the label for me was 'slut' or 'whore.'" Her huge high school had a number of differently abled students with special needs, so she wasn't the only one. But Sharon says that she never fit in seamlessly with either the nondisabled kids or the differently abled kids. "Many of the kids in the disabled community had more severe disabilities than I did. Overall, I'm considered to be in pretty good shape, so there was some jealousy of me." In addition, Sharon was a very early developer who began menstruating at the age of eight and who was wearing a double D bra by the ninth grade.

"There was one girl I'd been in school with since kindergarten all the way through twelfth grade. She and I had totally different disabilities, and she was more limited than I. She would say to me, 'You're a fucking whore, you're a fucking slut, your boobs are too big, no guy would ever date you, you don't dress the right way.' She was always trying to bring me down emotionally. I wasn't having sex, and I never gave any indication that I was."

It's possible that Sharon might have been singled out even had she been flat-chested, but being an early developer definitely added to her disadvantage. I asked Sharon if she ever reported the girl's harassment to a school administrator, or even to her paraprofessional. She never did; it never occurred to her. "You know," she answered, "I thought it was normal to have people make fun of me. For me, it was a normal occurrence."

Like Sharon, Molly, a twenty-year-old white woman who grew up in Kentucky, didn't do anything yet was perceived to have provoked her reputation. She was also called a slut in high school despite the fact that she was completely sexually uninvolved with others. She was the new girl who had just moved from a medium-sized city to a small city in her junior year. There were a hundred students in her grade at her new school. It was November, and Molly was at a football game when a girl she had befriended revealed that many girls were calling her a slut behind her back. "It came out of nowhere," Molly recalls. "I still don't understand it. I didn't do anything; it just happened, I guess. Maybe it was the way I was dressing? I'm not sure. I didn't think I was wearing anything unusual. I felt horrible. I barely knew anyone and no one knew anything about me. I was not a slut. I had no sexual experience."

The only thing that might explain her reputation, Molly says, is that she was "the new girl from the city. They might have thought I was snobby and uptight. I asked my one new friend to talk to the other girls and get them to realize that I wasn't that way." By senior year, the reputation had fizzled. "I was in a relationship with a guy, so that probably put down my label because everyone could see that I was in a relationship." Ironically, having sex (with a boyfriend) made Molly less likely to be considered slutty because she was doing what girls are "supposed" to do.

The Pretty Girl: "They Saw Me as a Threat"

Sometimes a girl is targeted because other girls are jealous of her. They may regard her as exceptionally pretty, or as someone who's getting too much attention from boys, or who seems to have some undefinable unfair advantage as a girl. Erica, a twenty-one-year-old sophomore at a New England college, falls into this category. We are speaking to each other via Skype. Erica is white with shoulder-length light brown hair. She's put on a touch of makeup today—I detect a bit of eye shadow beneath her strong, groomed eyebrows. She comes across as a natural- and wholesome-looking young woman who is pretty in a subtle, laid-back way.

"In the eighth grade, the kids called me a cocktease because even though I had girl friends, I also had several close male friends, and that was considered weird," she recalls. "It was like they thought I was looking for male attention, and that that was a problem. When I got to the ninth grade, I was hanging out with the friends of my older brother, who was in the tenth grade. There was this one girl in the tenth grade who wanted to cut me down. I think she thought, 'Who is this ninth-grade girl hanging out with these older boys?' She wanted to make me look bad, and she started going around saying that I was a slut and having all this sex." She then got other girls to do it.

Erica had never even kissed a boy. "I was just comfortable with guys. People didn't get it. It was like they couldn't imagine that I *wasn't* being sexual with them." The name-calling was in person, online, and through AOL Instant Messenger. "One day a group of five girls pulled me aside and said to me, 'Jeff is off-limits. You're not allowed to talk to him.' But Jeff was my friend! They didn't want me hanging around with guys at all." Erica believes that the girls were insecure about their own status with guys. Fabricating a story that she was a slut was a strategy to isolate her from the guys, to sabotage her status and poison her popularity.

Diana, a white twenty-two-year-old woman in California, was also positioned in the center of a false slut narrative. When she was eighteen, during the summer between her graduation from high school and the beginning of college, she began working at a restaurant as a hostess. She became friendly with the chef, who was twenty-six. "Someone started stories that we were hooking up late at night in the kitchen. There were lots of crazy stories that were not true. We were not hooking up at all! He was more like an older brother to me. But there was this server who was hooking up with him, and I guess she saw me as a threat. All of a sudden she got all these other people at the restaurant to say that I was a slut. I felt like I was constantly being watched and judged; it was like being in high school all over again—all this drama. But it wasn't high school; it was my workplace, and I had to put on a smile the whole time and make it seem like everything was OK even though it wasn't."

I asked Diana why she thought the server refused to believe that there was nothing sexual going on with the chef. She doesn't want to answer me, but I press her. "I guess it's because I'm considered pretty," she finally says sheepishly. Diana is thin and blond with a small nose. "It's possible that the women thought I was more attractive than they are. I feel really bad saying this, but really I think that they were just jealous."

In Erica's and Diana's case, why didn't the guys stand up for them? Because a guy's status is enhanced if everyone thinks he's having sex with another girl, even if in reality the two are nonromantic friends. It's not in his interest to set the record straight. At Diana's restaurant, "any time a new girl comes in [as an employee], the guys all look her over to decide if they want to hook up with her. They try to one-up each other over how many girls at the restaurant they've slept with." So the girl or woman in this situation is left on her own, no one defending her or explaining that the stories are in fact not true.

The Raped Girl: "She Believed Him, Not Me"

When I began my original research on slut-bashing two decades ago, I was ignorant of the prevalence of sexual assault.

As I interviewed more and more girls and women in the 1990s about being labeled sluts, however, I was repeatedly told stories about sexual assault—at the hands of strangers, dates, acquaintances, and family members. I wondered: How was it possible that so many of these girls and women had been assaulted? I came to understand how widespread sexual assault truly is, and how often it is minimized or denied, especially when a girl or woman believes that she has done something to deserve it. Because so many girls and women who are sexually assaulted are labeled as sluts, many believe that they were not truly assaulted. After all, the thinking goes, a slut isn't entitled to say no and if she does, why would anyone listen or care?

This is what the "slut" label does at its very worst: it convinces girls and women who have been victimized that they are the ones who have done something wrong. This dynamic is experienced in two ways. First, if a girl is already labeled a slut and then is assaulted, she may blame herself for having the reputation in the first place; if her assaulter knew about her reputation, he may have reasoned that she was not entitled to refuse a sexual encounter with him and that he was entitled to force her. Second, if a girl is not already labeled a slut and is assaulted, she may then become labeled as a result of her assault; when others find out that she was involved in a coerced sexual encounter, they very often side with the guy who assaulted her and blame the victim for having been victimized. A nonslut, a sickeningly high proportion of people believe, knows how to avoid being raped. It is the female's responsibility to not get raped rather than the rapist's responsibility to not rape.

Samantha, a white thirty-one-year-old waitress on the West Coast, was labeled a slut after she was raped. She was fifteen and drunk at a high school party. She knew the guy who raped her; he was twenty-three and the party was at his house. He was dating a senior girl, whom Samantha knew. He was not drunk. "He took me into his room," Samantha remembers. "I was in and out of consciousness. He was a big guy, and he penetrated me. Other people at the party must have known what was happening because someone tried to get me out of the room, although it's possible that they thought we were just having sex."

The next day, she told her rapist's girlfriend. "I said, 'I got drunk and your boyfriend took advantage of me.' But she believed him, not me. Then she and another girl ganged up on me and called me names. The other girl was angry with me because I was dating her ex-boyfriend. I was real confused because I thought I had done the right thing by telling her, even though I felt that I was at fault because I had been drunk. But these two girls had their own reasons for telling everyone I was a slut. Then there was sort of a joke about the rape. It was like, 'Don't leave Ted alone with your girlfriend because he'll rape her,' so people did know the truth, but he never got a bad reputation the way I did because of it."

"I'm guilty of having done the same thing myself," Allison confesses to me. An acclaimed actor who has performed on HBO and onstage, Allison is a thirty-nine-year-old white woman who also made a choice to believe the rapist rather than the rape victim. When she was in college, her fiancé sexually assaulted her best friend. "If I believed her," Allison explains, "I would have been losing my future. So I stayed with him and didn't speak with her. The truth is that I knew it had happened. I did believe her. Half of me looked at him as a rapist, but the other half worried what would happen if we broke up." Allison married the man who raped her best friend. They divorced after three years when Allison realized that she could be alone and also be OK. At that point, she could no longer justify to herself remaining in a relationship with someone she knew had done a terrible thing.

Samantha tells me that after she was raped, "I was messed up sexually for a very long time. At first I deliberately didn't sleep with anyone. I thought the rape was my fault, and I just wanted to get away from anything having to do with sex. Then, when I was older and I did start having sex, I would get triggered and just start crying, sometimes in the middle. I've been to counseling, but this is something I just have to live with."

I ask Samantha if the rape or the "slut" reputation in the wake of the rape is the cause of her distress. "It's both. It's the two events together. But they are also separate. Being raped is being abused by a man. Being called a slut is being abused by a woman."

When Boys Slut-Bash

Although I have found that most slut-bashers in schools are girls, boys also participate. Sometimes a boy threatens to spread a "slut" reputation if a girl breaks up with him. That is what happened to Sarah, a white twenty-one-year-old lesbian from the East Coast. Before she came out, she had a boyfriend in her junior and senior years of high school, "but he really didn't want me to break up with him," she recalls. "It was a bad relationship. I wasn't sure where my sexuality was going, and I probably shouldn't have been with him in the first place. I knew from the beginning that it wasn't working out. He was not the nicest person, and he was possessive."

Then he started using slut-bashing as a form of blackmail. When Sarah told him that she had doubts about their relationship, "he threatened to tell everyone at school I was a slut and he said he would make up lies about me. I was terrified that I would lose my reputation and my friends. When I look back on it now, I realize that probably wouldn't have happened, but at the time I didn't know that. Plus, I had really low self-esteem, and I thought bad things about myself, so I thought that everything he said must be true." Sarah stayed in the relationship for a year and a half even though she wanted out after a few weeks.

Other times, boys slut-bash for the usual reason—to put a girl in her place. Maria, the twenty-one-year-old Latina, tells me that just two months ago she was called a slut to her face by two guys who go to her college. Maria is bisexual and openly sexually active with multiple partners. Until now, no one had ever called her a slut before. But she was at a party, and a guy approached her, saying, "I've heard about you. I heard you get around a lot." He said it in a flirtatious way, leading Maria to believe that he was interested in her. As he approached her again, another guy whom she recognized but didn't know walked over to the two of them and said to the first guy, right in front of Maria, "She's a slut." Then the two guys laughed.

"Right in front of me," Maria adds bitterly. "I had never experienced that before. I felt humiliated. Before this incident, I never felt that I had to apologize for my sexuality, but now I was being judged. It doesn't feel good to be judged. They laughed at me like I'm a joke."

To these college boys, there is something wrong with Maria's femininity. But if she's not behaving in an appropriately feminine way, does that mean that she's masculine? No: the "slut" is a gendered category unto itself, neither completely feminine yet also not masculine. When boys slut-bash, they position themselves in relation to the "slut" to prop up their own masculinity just as slut-bashing girls position themselves to prop up their own femininity.

Michael Bamberg, a psychologist at Clark University, has demonstrated that adolescent boys make sense of themselves as masculine through ridicule of a "slut." In a fascinating 2004 journal article, he analyzes the way five fifteen-year-old boys described a girl in their school as a slut.[66] They told the adult moderator about the girl during a three-minute digression within a two-hour group discussion. The boys had been talking about friendships with boys when the moderator shifted the topic to girls. Two boys then began to describe the female classmate, saying that she was sexually promiscuous and may have been pregnant. They went on to relate that she apparently had written a letter in which she discussed her pregnancy. One of the boys, Ted, claimed that he had access to the letter. The boys' word choices are pivotal in understanding how this girl functioned as a symbol of femininity gone wrong. The digression started out like this:

TED   Actually, a girl, a girl in our class . . . last year she was like, she was always a little bit crazy, she always wanted a lot of attention and she didn't get it, she didn't get the attention she needed, and so this year she's had a lot of sex with boys in order to . . . gain attention of others around her.

FRED   And not just sex but everything. She's got—earned—the reputation . . . she's earned the reputation of being . . . a slut, that's how everyone knows her.

MODERATOR   . . . How does she feel?

TED   She likes it.

FRED   I think she likes it.

TED   She needs the attention, she likes the attention. I think she enjoys the attention so much that I think she is worthless . . . she's horrible . . .

FRED   She . . . most girls are not like that but for some reason you know how they say negative attention is better than no attention at all. She really likes the attention she's getting.

TED   Yeah . . . and also . . .

FRED   Now everyone knows who she is . . . I know it may sound mean to say this but we couldn't really care less about her anyway.[67]

Ted introduced the topic of the girl and ascribed to her full agency. As Ted told it, the girl wanted attention from her peers, and in full control of her actions, chose to have "a lot of sex with boys" so that she could "gain attention of others around her." As a result, Fred pointed out, the girl now had a reputation of being a slut. But notice that Fred started to say that she "got" a reputation and then changed his word to "earned." Bamberg points out that this linguistic slippage is not an accident. Fred indicated to his peers and to the moderator that the girl deserved to be called a slut. In these boys' minds, Bamberg writes, "What she did led to what she got; it was deserved. She earned this reputation; this is a fair deal."[68] Agency was placed completely on the shoulders of the girl. The agency of the boys and other classmates who had labeled her a slut was now erased from the narrative, because in this telling, it was inevitable and natural that such a girl would be called a slut.

The boys were most interested in the girl's motives. She was a "slut" because she wanted attention. Later in this conversation they also discussed the fact that the girl wanted everyone to read her letter. They positioned her as a girl who was irresponsible; she cared too much and tried too hard—in opposition to Fred, who said that "we couldn't really care less about her anyway." By situating himself as someone who didn't care about her, in contrast with the girl who cared too much, Fred suggested that he is impartial, trustworthy, and moral. After all, he doesn't gossip; he's just providing information that may be useful to the moderator. He doesn't care too much; he couldn't care less about her anyway. Fred—and the other boys—are fundamentally different from this "slut," who herself is different from other girls because "most girls are not like that."

Bamberg notes,

The category of girls—in general, "good girls"—is established as a middle ground, in between "sluts" and "us," depicting a space distinctly separate from the space the boys claim for themselves. And girls, who traditionally or "naturally" engage in "popularity work," run the risk of overdoing it and becoming victims of their own desire to be popular. They may end up as sluts. Thus, to run the risk of becoming a slut is only possible for those who occupy that middle ground: One has to be a girl to engage in popularity work, in contrast to us, as boys, who could never slide into this, because we do not need to engage in this type of work.[69]

The boys' masculine identity was not threatened because, they implied, they would never engage in the type of attention-seeking behavior that girls do. They are rational, mature, and able "to make justifiable claims about their moral standing the way adults do to police children."[70] Those who do not "overdo" it—those who don't exercise agency inappropriately—are permitted to police those who do.

Brittany, a nineteen-year-old white college student from the East Coast, tells me about a high school boy who rounded up other boys and orchestrated a slut-bashing campaign against her. She thinks that his insecurity "as a guy" led him to harass her in this way. The boy, Jason, was her second boyfriend; they started dating in the middle of sophomore year. Before Jason she had dated another boy with whom she was not sexually active; as a result, he had called her a prude, and other kids in school had, too. "It's not that I think that girls shouldn't have sex," she explains to me, "but I just personally didn't want to. But I also didn't want the weight of that label, 'prude,' on me."

So when she started dating Jason, she figured she could shed the "prude" reputation. She says,

He started pressuring me to do sexual things I didn't want to do and I didn't feel comfortable doing, but I did them anyway. The summer before junior year, when I was sixteen, he wanted me to masturbate for him, and it kept escalating. He started sending me pictures of his penis. He wanted me to send him pictures of me naked, including my face, even though he cropped out his face. I never did send him any pictures because my mom had always told me never to send naked pictures of myself, and I figured she had said it for a good reason. But I did send him texts with sexual words.

He also wanted me to wear certain clothes. I remember one time I wore a certain skirt for me, because I thought it looked nice. But he treated me like I was an object. He called me 'bangable,' which disturbed me, even though I think he was trying to compliment me. He thought I was wearing the skirt to get his attention, which led him to think it was OK to touch me even if I didn't want him to.

I didn't want to lose him, so at first I gave him hand jobs, but he kept pressuring me for more, so then I gave him blow jobs. Finally I gave in and had sex with him. The first time I was in the eleventh grade, the week before I turned seventeen. With each stage [of the progression toward intercourse], I felt dirty. I felt like I was less and less desirable to other people, like I was more used up. I know that's a horrible way to put it, but that's the way I felt.

At first, I was a little glad because now I wasn't a prude anymore. But then I started to feel ashamed. He was all happy about it, but at that point I'd rather have been called a prude.

He never forced me to have sex. I always said OK, even though I didn't really want to. I said OK to get him to stop bugging me, because he bugged me every day. He tried to have oral sex with me, but he didn't know what he was doing, so I told him to stop. [*Laughs.*]

It's not that I didn't want to have sex. I wanted to do sexual things too. But I didn't think he was the right person to do them with. I just didn't feel right about doing them with him.

I think a lot of his bugging me was because of the pressures he felt as a guy. He was a little short, just an inch taller than me, and people picked on him for that reason, so maybe he felt this was a way to be a guy.

During their senior year, Brittany broke up with him. She wanted to date someone else, but she waited until after she and Jason were completely through. Jason enlisted "a lot of guys" to walk up to Brittany and call her a slut and a ho. "They did it mostly in the hallway, and they did it loudly so that everyone could hear. This went on every day for a month." Brittany went to the school's security office to complain. "I was embarrassed and angry," she says. "I knew I wasn't a whore. He also got this one girl to call me a bitch and a ho on Facebook, but mostly it was just guys saying it to me in the hallway."

Brittany doesn't know how to explain Jason's behavior. "It

was ironic and ridiculous," she fumes. "*He* was the one who pressured *me* to do all that stuff, and then he was getting people to call *me* a slut! How come *I* was the slut?"

Brittany was the "slut" so that Jason could salvage his own reputation in the face of being rejected by his girlfriend. Jason degraded her to elevate himself. That is what slut-bashing is all about: making the slut-basher feel secure in his or her own masculinity or femininity. Slut-bashing reveals the tenuousness of gender identities. If femininity and masculinity require slut-bashing to be bolstered, how stable can these identities really be?

CHAPTER 4

Reciprocal Slut-Shaming: Sexual Identity in an Online World

Before social media, there was no ambiguity when someone called a girl a slut. She knew she was being insulted, bullied, harassed, or abused. But today, "slut" is often a casual, recip-rocated greeting among peers. "It's like saying hi in passing," reports a white twenty-year-old college student. "Girls calling girls sluts is really prevalent. It's become normal to do it." Daniela, the Latina bartender in Texas, says, "Around here, girls basically call out 'slut' as a sort of compliment to any female who looks good. Basically, you say it to any female." Sarah, the twenty-one-year-old white student whose high school boyfriend used slut-bashing as a form of blackmail, tells me, "On my campus, girls say to each other, 'Hey, you're such a slut' or 'You're such a whore,' and I've never heard anyone get upset about it. It's just a way for girls to acknowledge each other."

"Slut" is also commonly used on social network sites. Georgiana, a twenty-two-year-old white doctoral student in comparative literature, reports that her peers routinely call each other "slut" on Facebook as a complimentary greeting. She tells me that the women in her program sexualize themselves in their Facebook photos to attract attention from both females and males. Even doctoral candidates in their twenties and thirties, who presumably would be most likely to gain status from their academic work or job prospects rather than from their bikini shots, are chasing status from their sexuality. In response to their profile photos, their peers offer sexual validation.

A lot of girls [and women in their twenties] think that showing their bodies on Facebook is the best way to get attention. In the comments section, people tell them that they're hot and they give them "likes". Girls use the word "slut" all the time when they're "liking" a photo. They write, "I love you, you slut." They mean it to be positive. So then a girl thinks, How many likes can I get? Because if she posts a picture of herself wearing a cropped shirt and short shorts, she'll get a million likes. And that is very rewarding. And then the other girls who are paying attention see that this is a way to get attention, so they do it, too. So then everyone starts to do it. You even see girls who are fourteen, fifteen, doing the same thing.

Guys also like to show off their bodies. They post pictures of their abs and their tattoos. But guys don't have to post pictures of their bodies unless they want to. That's their choice. All a guy really has to do is "like" a girl's picture or comment on it, and that's enough for him to get status because it shows everyone that he's in the game and that he's friends with hot girls. It's more important for him to "like" hot girls than to be hot himself.

It's different for girls. Facebook, Twitter, and Instagram teach them that they will get status and be rewarded if they sexualize themselves and get called sluts.

Note that images of female bodies offer validation not only for girls and women, who are judged on the basis of their own appearance and sexiness, but also for boys and men, who are judged on the basis of their *appreciation* of female bodies. Images of sexy females have currency for everyone, females and males, while images of sexy males have limited currency. Within this framework, casual usages of "slut" are like trading cards. The more a girl receives positive affirmation for being "slutty," the more her status is strengthened.

But at what cost? Girls and women are saying that they "love" the "slut" in question. Do they really? After all, we have seen that "slut" is an infinitely confusing term. Its meanings are not always obvious. How is a girl or woman supposed to know if she's being complimented or insulted? "I've been called a slut in a joking way by my roommate," says Jasmine, the twenty-year-old black and Latina student in California. "She's like, 'God, you're such a slut!' She said it three times over the last year. I laughed it off the first time, and after that

I ignored her. She totally was judging me for hooking up with guys. She wanted to insult me, but under the cover of a joke."

Because "slut" has become an acceptable label among close friends, it can be used to frame an insult inside a term of endearment. "To me," explains Sarah, "it's like, 'Hey, maybe you've done some crazy things over the weekend, so I'm going to call you a slut, but I'm not trying to be derogatory.'" Translation: You are sexual, which is to be admired as long as you don't go too far, in which case it's bad—really bad. I'm calling you a slut, and I'm leaving my meaning deliberately ambiguous. I have my eye on you. But I'm being very casual about it, and I'm not putting in any real effort here, and if you accuse me of shaming you, I will deny it.

Unlike slut-bashing, which is an overt form of bullying, *slut-shaming is a casual method of judgment. It may be indirect and conducted only one time, and its intention may not be clear. Like slut-bashing, slut-shaming is a method of policing a girl or woman for being inappropriately sexual and deviating from normative femininity. Reciprocal slut-shaming is a two-way communication system in which two girls or young women alternately police and affirm each other's femininity.*

Even when used in a casual, reciprocal way among peers, in person or online, "slut" remains a hammer to nail down the sexual double standard. Do not be fooled by outer layers of friendliness. Beneath lies a judgmental and sexist core. Reciprocal greetings of "Hey, slut" constitute slut-shaming in camouflage. Because it's performed covertly, slut-shaming is easy to deny and dismiss—even when it's damaging girls' and women's reputations.

It's not an accident that of all the informal salutations

females have at their disposal to acknowledge each other—
"girlfriend," "sista"—"slut" is now ascendant. Young females
are creating a sense of identity, even a sense of community,
through recognition of each other as sexualized people. They
are "not prudes"; they are "sluts"—*good* sluts"—the kind
that are acceptable and valued. This is the way young females
perform femininity.

Achieving "good slut" status depends primarily on the
judgment of other girls and women; guys' opinions carry
some, but not as much as girls', weight in this arena. After all,
"good slut" status is ultimately an affirmation of femininity
and reputation, which have meaning only within a community of girls and women who determine the extent to which
each member conforms to or violates a series of rules. We
are "good sluts" only if members of our peer group say that
we are after we have proved that we fulfill the criteria they
have established. We need their affirmation to maintain our
status. In turn, they require our validation to maintain their
own status. But a girl's validation counts only as long as she is
in good standing, so the platform for validation is weak and
could crash at any given moment.

In the era of online social media, girls and young women
have turned to new technologies to prove their credentials as
"good sluts," which authenticate their offline performance as
normatively feminine. Almost all teenagers in America use
social media, according to the advocacy organization Common Sense Media. Although Facebook is falling out of fashion, it remains the dominant social networking site.[71] Calling
a fellow female a slut within a social media platform seals the
deal: two females recognize each other as "good sluts." Each

enters into this exchange to elevate her own status as sexually attractive. But because "slut" can also potentially mean "shameful, disgusting, sexually out-of-control female," greeting another female with "Hey, slut" is a sly wink that says, "I'm watching you, and I'm policing you." The exchange is empowering and disempowering at the same time.

Discipline and Punish

Reciprocal slut-shaming among peers is a new phenomenon. When I was harassed as a "slut" in the 1980s, the idea of "Hey, slut" being a friendly greeting was absurd. Trying to make sense of this fast-moving twenty-first-century behavior, I first turned to the works of several twentieth-century philosophers of critical theory for whom the power structures implicit in the acts of performance and surveillance play a big role. I wanted to comprehend the psychology of reciprocal slut-shaming. Why has exchanging insults become acceptable, expected, and even desired behavior among young women?

Louis Althusser, the French Marxist philosopher, argued that capitalist states require an ideology—a system of ideas and representations that are understood as natural yet in fact are manufactured by the state to exercise power so that individuals (or "subjects") accept the state's authority. Althusser called this process "interpellation" or "hailing." He offered the example of a police officer calling out to a passerby, "Hey, you there . . ." When the hailed individual turns to acknowledge the police officer, he transforms from an autonomous person into a subject willing to accept the authority of the state.[72] He accepts that the police officer holds power over him. The passerby accepts as natural and unremarkable that there exists a power imbalance between himself and the officer.

Through the "slut" greeting, girls and young women hail each other the way the police officer hails the citizen. In this verbal exchange, however, each female takes a turn acting as police officer *and* passerby. Femininity is an ideology, and slut-shaming is a hailing mechanism that transforms females into both disciplinary agents *as well as* feminine subjects. When woman A posts a sexually revealing photo on a social networking site, and woman B comments, "You're such a slut!" woman A recognizes herself as a "slut"—either a "good" or "bad" one depending on whether or not woman B "liked" the photo—and also affirms the fact that she is being judged and policed. Woman B is policing woman A. When woman A reciprocates on woman B's post, the roles are reversed.

Sexual policing is enormously easy today because women's bodies are photographed, tracked, and monitored overtly and covertly within social media. Boys' and men's bodies are photographed, tracked, and monitored as well, but not nearly as often as girls' and women's are. The social news site Reddit, along with Tumblr, Twitter, Flickr, and other sites such as Creepshots.com, has encouraged users to post "creepshots"— nonconsensual pictures of women taken in public spaces. The Reddit forum Creepshots (now shut down) stated on its introductory page, "When you are in public, you do not have a reasonable expectation of privacy. We kindly ask women to respect our right to admire your bodies and stop complaining."[73]

"My students describe a suffocation," says Shira Tarrant, PhD, a professor of women, gender, and sexuality studies at California State University, Long Beach, and the author of *Men and Feminism* and *When Sex Became Gender*. "They feel a relentless pressure to put themselves on display. They are constantly under surveillance, not only with the ATM cameras and other surveillance cameras that are on streets and in stores and in national parks, but also with the photos they and their friends take for Facebook and Instagram and Snapchat. They have to perform for the cameras constantly."

In a sense, young women are living within a surveillance prison—a "panopticon." We all are. The panopticon was a prison designed by Jeremy Bentham, the British philosopher of utilitarianism, in the late eighteenth century (although it was never built), that enabled a watchman to observe prisoners without their knowledge. The panopticon consisted of a courtyard with a circular tower in the center. Surrounding the tower were buildings divided into cells; each cell had two windows. One window faced the tower, and the other faced the outside to bring in light. One gaze, like a Facebook news feed, saw everything.

Michel Foucault, another French philosopher, expanded on the concept of the panopticon. He noted that the cells become "small theaters, in which each actor is alone, perfectly individualized and constantly visible."[74] The prisoner can't see if the watchman is in the tower; he never knows if he's being observed within his "theater." Therefore, he must always assume that he's being observed and perform the way he would if he knew that the watchman were eyeing him. In effect, he becomes his own jailer. Meanwhile, the watchman is himself also being observed and therefore must regulate his own behavior as well.[75] Observation becomes a mechanism of discipline and coercion. Self-surveillance—the result of having to assume you are always being watched—assures that at all times, individuals discipline themselves.

Self-surveillance also underlies the fictional totalitarian society depicted in George Orwell's novel *1984*, in which the leader known as Big Brother and his Thought Police spy on all citizens through hidden microphones and cameras. Orwell wrote in 1949,

There was of course no way of knowing whether you were being watched at any given moment. How often, or on what system, the Thought Police plugged in on any individual wire was guesswork. It was even conceivable that they watched everybody all the time. But at any rate they could plug in your wire whenever they wanted to. You had to live—did live, from habit that became instinct—in the assumption that every sound you made was overheard, and, except in darkness, every movement scrutinized.[76]

Orwell's description of self-disciplining as a result of surveillance was prescient. Whether or not the National Security Agency is a Big Brother monitoring US citizens, in our digitally networked age we are all monitored by people we know and do not know: friends, family, colleagues, acquaintances, and everyone within each of their social orbits.

The feminist philosopher Sandra Lee Bartky expanded on Foucault's understanding of disciplinary practices with regard to women.[77] "We are born male or female, but not masculine or feminine," she notes. Femininity is a performance requiring "disciplinary practices that produce a body which in gesture and appearance is recognizably feminine."[78] Bartky points out that to conform to femininity, a woman must always remember that her body is meant to be seen by others. Therefore she must discipline her body, which must be the "right" size and shape; she must submit to regimes to control her skin, hair, makeup, fingernails, and toenails; and she must select an appropriate wardrobe. Bartky locates the source of discipline within a "system of sexual subordination" to which women voluntarily seek initiation. "No one is marched off for electrolysis at the end of a rifle," she points out, "nor can we fail to appreciate the initiative and ingenuity displayed by countless women in an attempt to master the rituals of beauty." But women do risk social and romantic censure, even ostracism, if they don't conform to societal norms of beauty, and therefore they may become compliant within the regime of femininity "just as surely as the army aims to turn its raw recruits into soldiers."[79] Femininity as an ideology serves as a prison guard, and because women are rewarded for compliance, they police themselves as if they lived within a supervised prison.

Motherhood had long been the central feature of normative femininity, according to Bartky, but in the 1980s, when she wrote her analysis, she argued that motherhood had given way to the sexualized body as that which defines femininity.[80] Three decades later, the self-regulation of women's bodies has become truly oppressive in the mirrored hallways of social media. Today, the aesthetic of pornography determines the ideal of sexiness; achieving a sexy appearance involves mimicking the grooming habits of women who work in pornography. Women involved in sex work have become mainstream stars, even role models. When Jenna Jameson promoted her book *How to Make Love Like a Porn Star*, thirteen-year-old girls came to readings to tell her she was their role model. Although Jameson's book relates a story of resilience—Jameson overcame rape, drug abuse, and alcoholism to become hugely successful in the adult film industry—her teenage fans seemed to have overlooked, or been unaware of, the book's message. Jameson told the *Los Angeles Times* she was bothered by the fact that her young fans looked up to her as a porn star and not as a three-dimensional person.[81] When Tracy Quan, a prostitute who also wrote a book, shared a meet the author event at a Barnes & Noble with Chief Justice William Rehnquist, she told the *New York Times*, "If that's not being part of the Establishment, I don't know what is."[82] Since so many heterosexual boys and men fantasize about women who look like Jameson and Quan, many girls and women come to believe that they should look like Jameson and Quan themselves.

Jennifer Keishin Armstrong and Heather Wood Rudúlph, the authors of the book *Sexy Feminism*, point out that because of pornography, "huge breasts, platinum hair, and hairless vaginas seem standard,"[83] and with the popularity of so-called Brazilian bikini waxes, it is now "a routine occurrence to pick your legs up over your head, approaching yoga's plow position, and/or turn over on your side and spread your cheeks for the nice lady making you pretty."[84] To be sure, bikini line maintenance is not necessarily a form of pornographic grooming. Many women want to wear a bathing suit in public without displaying errant pubic hairs, and a normal bikini wax, which strips away the hairs at the top of the inner thighs, is the least uncomfortable method of removing those pesky hairs. Brazilian waxes are different not in degree but in kind. In a Brazilian, every single pubic hair is ripped out. Hairlessness is popular because porn stars are hairless; many ordinary women and men associate sexiness with hairlessness. As pornography has gone mainstream, so has the porn aesthetic.

Pornographic grooming practices are not just for adult women. Preadolescent girls are now going to spas to get bikini waxes. "For waxing, 12 years old is the 'new normal,'" Melanie Engle, a Philadelphia aesthetician, told the *Today* show's website. Armstrong and Rudúlph note that one New York salon advertises special rates for "virgin" waxing of "virgin hair" (prepubescent traces of hair from pubic hair follicles). "Virgin hair can be waxed so successfully that growth can be permanently stopped in just two to six sessions," explains the website for Wanda's European Skin Care Center. "Save your child a lifetime of waxing . . . and put the money in the bank for her college education instead!" The owner told the *New York Post* she'd seen two hundred child clients in 2007 and advised girls to begin waxing at the age of six.[85]

Teenage girls, meanwhile, are turning to breast augmentation; in 2012, over 3,500 girls eighteen and younger underwent this procedure.[86] If an adult woman contemplates having her breasts enlarged, she is capable of taking into account the medical risks involved to arrive at a sound decision. Such a procedure may not be risk-free, but at least she's able to assess the costs and the benefits for herself. But girls who are still physically developing are not always capable of arriving at the best decision. Diana Zuckerman, the president of the National Center for Health Research, told the *Washington Post* that she has "concerns about teens undergoing plastic surgery at a time when they are psychologically vulnerable." While the increases in surgery on noses and ears among children and teens under eighteen are not dramatic, the "increases in breast implants and liposuction are very dramatic. In fact, the number of girls 18 and younger getting implants has tripled in the last few years," she says. The distinction between surgeries like rhinoplasty (nose reshaping) and otoplasty (pinning back protruding ears) versus breast implants is that the latter have a high complication rate, she adds. "Having something implanted in your body causes more problems as the implant ages," she explains.[87] Breast augmentation also implants an idea in a girl's head: that her body should conform to a narrow ideal of sexiness.

Even before they menstruate, girls develop an awareness of themselves as sexual objects meant to pleasure guys. Shira Tarrant observes to me that for females, performance means looking sexy for the benefit of other people. Young women always have to think of themselves as sexualized objects to be consumed. "It's not '*I* think I'm sexy' but 'Do *you* think I'm sexy?'" Rosalind Gill, a British cultural theorist, points out that there has been "a shift from sexual objectification to sexual subjectification in construction of femininity." There has been "a move from an external male judging gaze to a self-policing narcissistic gaze."[88] This dynamic probably was always present to some extent, but it is amplified now in the age of surveillance. With the phone in her pocket acting as a GPS tracking device, a woman today may be surrounded by people who can photograph or record her with their own phones or with Google Glass. A woman today knows that her image may be broadcast at any moment to others near and far—prompting her to be hyper-self-aware of her appearance at all times. Men experience the same thing, but men are not judged by their appearance in the way that women are. To Gill, the new internal gaze is particularly exploitative because many women today actively choose to sexualize themselves in the name of liberation, but in the end they are really choosing to be regarded as sexual objects.[89] Girls and women "choose" to represent themselves as "good sluts," yet their "choice" is made within a regime of surveillance, policing, and self-discipline.

A girl or woman who successfully conforms to "good slut" ideals finds herself trapped: The better her performance, the more evidence exists that can prove she's really a "bad slut." "You have evidence that you can use against a girl," says Stephanie, the fifteen-year-old New York City student. "Everyone has profile pictures of themselves in bikinis. It's so easy to label any girl a slut because you have all this evidence. All you have to do is go to her Facebook." If you're not slutty enough in the good way, or if you're slutty in a bad way, the news is all over the Internet, leading to slut-bashing or other forms of gendered social ostracism such as being rejected by a sorority or a club because of sexual reputation, or losing professional opportunities.

Women objectified and policed themselves long before the Internet, as Sandra Lee Bartky demonstrates. They have long been the watchman in the panopticon's tower, who himself is being watched. These processes are not new. Women in previous generations took diet pills during pregnancy to avoid excessive weight gain, wore breathing-constricting girdles to give the illusion of a wasp waist, vacuumed their homes in dresses and high heels, did aerobic exercise to look sleek like Jane Fonda, and slept with painful hard curlers in their hair—all in the name of feminine beauty.

What's new is that surveillance and self-surveillance have become inescapable and relentless. For women previously, the sidewalk was not a catwalk with paparazzi snapping photos of them against their will. "It's like you can't go anywhere without people keeping track of you," says Jessica, a twenty-three-year-old Latina. "You'll be talking to someone, and they'll be like, 'Oh, you were at that party the other night,' and it's like, 'How do you know? I never told you.' Or they'll say, 'You looked good at that party the other night.' People really pay attention to where you are and what you're doing. It's kind of scary, but I've kind of accepted it."

Observes Julie Zeilinger, the *FBomb* editor, "You can't be invisible, and you need to look perfect all the time. And you're always being compared with everyone else. You have to worry about the way you look every single moment of every day. I know that body image was an issue for women of previous generations too, but for my generation it's just constant." The inescapability and relentlessness of surveillance, combined with the sexual double standard and the need to perform femininity, have collided to lay the foundation for reciprocal slut-shaming. When I call another woman a slut in a casual way, I am entering into a tacit agreement with her. I am affirming her sexual attractiveness, and I expect her to affirm mine. I am colluding with her in the understanding that I live in a time of economic uncertainty, when top grades in school may not lead to a good job, or any job, and my parents may be under- or unemployed at any moment; therefore, my sexuality may be the only ticket I have to any semblance of success. But I also am policing her sexuality, which is all too easy with social media, and I know that she will feel entitled to police mine as well. But what else can I do? I recognize that I am sharpening both ends of the stick, and that someone, perhaps myself, will get hurt . . . but this is the way femininity is performed, and if I want to perform femininity, this is how the show goes.

Posing for Evidence

The early days of the Internet offered the promise of identity reinvention. Women and men alike could experiment with their online identities, and this was acceptable and normal behavior in the playhouse of Multi-User Domains, or MUDs. Users constructed selves that had no connection with their offline lives. In 1995, Sherry Turkle, a visionary in contemplating the intersection of personal identity and technology, wrote joyfully about this promise in *Life on the Screen: Identity in the Age of the Internet*. Back then, as a famous *New Yorker* cartoon put it, an animal could be online without worrying that his identity would be found out: "On the Internet, nobody knows you're a dog."[90] People logged online and assumed multiple fake identities, knowing that everyone else online was playing a role too. Turkle's book teemed with optimism and hope about a "decentered self" on the Internet, a lively space where we are "encouraged to think of ourselves as fluid, emergent, decentralized, multiplicitous, flexible and ever in process."[91]

By 2011, the year she published *Alone Together: Why We Expect More From Technology and Less From Each Other*, Turkle had thrown in the towel. The self had changed—and not for the better. Anonymity was over. Privacy had evaporated. The world now is one of "rapid response" in which there is never enough time "to sit and think uninterrupted."[92] Turkle's primary concern now is that people become depersonalized in the flood of emails, texts, messages, posts, photos, and videos. We now treat those we meet online as objects, and we treat ourselves as objects that need to be "branded" to gain recognition.

Teenagers are most vulnerable because they are developing their sense of self within an environment without privacy or personal space, and because they're forced to work overtime to keep their social media image "sleek" like a "gym-toned body."[93] Turkle offers the example of a fourteen-year-old girl who has just joined Facebook. The girl is fraught with anxiety over her profile. She keeps tweaking it. Should she list herself as single if she has a boyfriend? What if she and her friends post their status as being in relationships, but their boyfriends don't? Even the act of confirming or ignoring a friend request makes her nervous. Another girl tells Turkle that her preference is to include only her "cool friends" and not the "more unpopular ones," but she can't because she's "nice to a lot of other kids at school." So she decides to include everyone who asks on her friend list, but she's unhappy about it because this isn't the identity she wants to project.[94]

All the high school students Turkle spoke with told her

that they update their Facebook profiles incessantly. They post comments multiple times a day because if they don't, and someone sees that they're not communicating all the time, they fear they will look like a loser. Therefore, they write on other kids' walls so that those kids respond on their own walls. They must reveal information about themselves because the more they post, the more attention they'll receive online.[95] Now with the app Klout, the stakes are even higher: Klout ranks users with a numerical value based on their level of social media engagement. Communicating online often and with many is the ticket to appearing popular. "Comments are not simply a dialogue between two interlocutors," notes danah boyd, "but a performance of social connection before a broader audience."[96] As Katherine Losse, an early Facebook employee, observed about her colleagues' socializing techniques, commenting on someone's post "was better than speaking to them, because everyone saw it. Everyone wanted to see everything. This was all justified under the company's corporate buzzword, *transparency*."[97]

Teenagers know that even when they're alone, they're not really alone. Because of "transparency," other people are stalking them online by looking at their photos and comments without making their presence known. Their lives are not dissimilar to those of celebrities. If a teenager gets drunk at a party, someone will snap a photo with her phone, upload it to the Internet, and tag (publicly identify) it, so that other people will see it and comment on it. Any time they go out in public to do anything at all, teenagers are at risk of being photographed and tagged. They can never relax in public. They must always be on guard. They are always being watched.

Online identity is no longer fluid as it had been fifteen years ago. To the contrary: identity is constrained—often into something that does not resemble the image we want. Femininity is also a constraining performance. And femininity in the age of social media is the most constraining performance ever.

In this environment, girls and young women are doing something rational and understandable. "All they want is evidence to prove that they're sexually empowered without crossing the line into being sluts," says Katie Cappiello, the artistic director of the Arts Effect in New York City. "One girl told us that the reason she goes to parties is so that she can be documented being at parties. Girls' sexuality is just another thing to document."

For the people who create and control social media, girls' sexuality is also just another thing to exploit. Social media would collapse, it seems, without images of sexualized females. According to Katherine Losse, "women's images drive" Facebook. Losse worked at Facebook from 2005 to 2010 in a series of jobs culminating as Mark Zuckerberg's speechwriter and is the author of a memoir, *The Boy Kings*, about the company's work culture. On Facebook, she writes, "the most popular content has always been intimate, personal photographs of women."[98] Mikolaj Piskorski, a professor at Harvard Business School, confirms Losse's observation. He has found that women receive two-thirds of all page views on Twitter, Facebook, and MySpace. "People just love to look at pictures," he says. "That's the killer app of all online social networks. Seventy percent of all actions are related to viewing pictures or viewing other people's profiles." Most photo viewing is done by men looking at women they don't know, followed by men looking at women they do know, followed by women looking at other women they know.[99]

Posting photos of oneself is excessively popular, Piskorski speculates, because it's a way to represent yourself as a well-liked, high-status person without having to boast outright. I would add that for females, it's also a way to perform femininity without demonstrating a lot of effort. Posting a photo of oneself looking amazing in a killer dress (especially if you can tell that someone else snapped the photo) is a way to enact the femininity rule of "effortless perfection." Even so-called selfies have become so casual they appear effortless. Ironically, these photos of oneself are rarely candid shots; they are nearly always posed, and it's obvious that the subject is striking a sexy pose because she's aware of the photographer or at least of the camera. She is working very hard in her performance, but she tries to make it seem as though she's phoning it in (which she's literally doing with her smartphone). It's crucial to pretend that it's all effortless, that she doesn't really care. That way, if she fails at femininity, at least everyone will think she never really tried all that hard. If she succeeds at exaggerating her sexiness without crossing the invisible line into sexual excess, she is then complimented by her peers on her sexiness. Grateful, she returns the favor.

Of course, all this image control does require effort. It requires shrewd manipulation. According to a survey conducted by the late Stanford professor Clifford Nass, teenage girls sometimes digitally alter the photos of themselves they post online to make themselves appear thinner than they really are.[100] Girls also ask their friends to post positive comments about their Facebook photos with the hope that these comments will spur others to post similar compliments.[101]

Julie Zeilinger meets me at an Upper West Side café in Manhattan. A twenty-year-old student at Barnard College, she has come of age with social media and has never known anything else. She remembers vividly when she and her friends excitedly discovered MySpace in the sixth grade. "Finally, a way to know how popular we *really* were!" she writes in her book *A Little F'd Up*. "We could actually *count* our friends and compare them to other people's. We could flaunt our inside jokes by writing on our friends' profiles for all to see. We could post a profile picture that captured our cuteness at its ultimate peak, and flaunt it to all! Rejoice! O, happy day!"[102]

But first, everyone needed an amazing profile photo. So they set up a photo shoot during their lunch period and practiced their poses. "We asked each other, 'Should I pose like this?'" she tells me. "Our photo became synonymous with our identity and personality." But she and her friends realized that that as flattering as their profile photos were, one was never enough. They needed a new picture *every day*. So they started skipping lunch and heading to the girls' bathroom, "our little preteen bodies positioned on top of toilets, blowing kisses to a friend who stood below with a camera."[103]

To make themselves look sexy, Julie and her friends perfected what is called the "duck face." You have no doubt seen the duck face, even if you didn't realize that it had a name. "To perfect the duck face, you must make your eyes as big as possible." Zeilinger explains. "Your lips must resemble, as the name implies, a duck. You must purse them and then shove them away from your face as far as you possibly can. . . . I think this is supposed to emphasize one's cheekbones, and admittedly, it does."[104] It also makes the lips appear pouty in a sexually charged way. The duck face is supposed to look authentic, but it is entirely manufactured, the way models pose in front of a fan so that their hair looks naturally windswept. But at least every once in a while in real life, the wind does sweep our hair back in a pleasingly attractive way. When was the last time you saw an unposed teenage girl and thought she resembled a duck—and that this was a good thing?

Celebrities—They're Just Like Us!

The duck face is an example of how girls and young women attempt to control their image through the emulation of celebrities, who have to manipulate their faces in unnatural poses because that's part of their job. Regular girls and young women have come to believe that the perfection of celebrities' images is attainable—if they discipline their bodies, purchase the right clothes and shoes and bags, and carry the right attitude. Since the performers on reality television are not professional actors, ordinary people are greatly influenced by them. Michael Stefanone, who studies the social psychology of technology use at the University at Buffalo, and his colleagues Derek Lackaff and Devan Rosen argue that the boundary between the celebrity world and the everyday world of ordinary people has been eroded. "Taken together, reality television and [social media] set the stage for a major shift in the way individuals perceive their role in the media environment. Rather than simply being the target of mediated messages, they see themselves as protagonists of mediated narratives and can integrate themselves into a complex media ecosystem. The media tools and strategies employed by celebrities and their handlers—airbrushed photos, carefully coordinated social interactions, strategic selection and maintenance of the entourage—are now in a sense available to everyone." Stefanone and his colleagues conclude, "Results suggest that social behaviors commonly associated with mediated celebrity are now being enacted by noncelebrities in an increasingly mediated social environment."[105]

Regular people mimic reality television performers not only in appearance but also in behavior. The reality television genre requires performers to reveal their private thoughts and emotions to their entire viewing audience. Similarly, blogs, photo sharing, and video sharing are methods of disclosing private items to a large public audience. Young people, growing up with reality television, produce online content to be like the celebrities who are rewarded for doing the same thing. Many feel pressured that they *must* blog, they must *publicize* photos and videos, they *must* create collages of other people's material in order to be rewarded with high social status.

But at what cost for girls? Erica, a twenty-one-year-old white woman who attended an elite New England high school on full scholarship—her father is unemployed and her mother works in retail—remembers that in her school,

Some girls became sort of celebrities because of the Facebook personalities they had made. They took pictures of every single thing they did. The other kids had a double perception about them. On the one hand, they were seen as glamorous, but at the same time, they were considered insubstantial. There was one girl, fourteen, who was very wealthy and had to be hospitalized because of cocaine abuse. She actually posted pictures of herself getting wasted, wearing very little. And the other kids just loved talking about her. They would say, "She's a disgusting slut," but they couldn't stop looking at her Facebook. But nobody ever said, "Wait a minute, this girl needs help." Instead, it was just like, "Can you believe that she did that?" It was like she was an object to watch and follow. It was like she wasn't even a real person.

Cappiello adds, "Kids are photographing reality instead of experiencing it. That's why when a girl is raped, like in Steubenville, the reaction is, 'This is something to document, not something to stop.'" In an effort to be like the reality television stars they look up to as role models, girls and young women are distancing themselves from appropriate *real* behavior. Their peers are transformed into objects to watch and document, not people to interact with and protect when necessary.

Used properly, social media can boost a girl's confidence, especially if she's shy or awkward. Amanda Marcotte, a feminist blogger, points out to me, "Social networking can be a relief because you do have control. When you're an awkward teenager, it can be hard to respond to people on your feet. But online, you can slow down and edit your responses. You have the advantage of time, even though there is pressure to respond right away. You can choose photos that are the most flattering ones. There's a lot of power in that aspect.

You have immediate control over how you're perceived in the world."

But your power extends only so far. For one thing, anyone can tag unflattering or private photos of you at any time. Even if you untag yourself, you might be too late if the photo has been seen by others, and it remains online even if your name isn't associated with it. Jasmine, the twenty-year-old black and Latina student who, you may recall, was called a slut after a football player at her large urban high school tried to grab her breasts, tells me that on Halloween of her senior year of high school, someone uploaded a picture of her without her consent. "I was blacked-out drunk and dressed kind of scandalously," she says. "They took the picture with my phone and then uploaded it to my Facebook." Jasmine explains to me that on Facebook, when you upload a photo from your phone, you don't receive a notification, so she had no idea what had happened. "I found out because my mom came into my room and said very coldly, 'Your friends uploaded a picture of you on Facebook.' I didn't know what she was talking about. I deleted it from my profile page and all I can hope is that it's not out there."

For girls, the ability to manipulate their image becomes a mandatory compulsion to do so. Jenna Wortham, a *New York Times* technology reporter, explains that the "feedback loop of positive reinforcement is the most addictive element of social media. All those retweets, likes and favorites give us a little jolt, a little boost that pushes us to keep coming back for more."[106] Girls in particular "feel all this pressure to represent themselves as sexually attractive, but then when they do, they become the target of vicious criticisms," notes Amanda Marcotte. She continues,

The girls are made to feel ashamed for posting sexy poses. They cannot win. And meanwhile, no one worries about the way boys represent themselves sexually. Besides, it's not easy looking sexy. Most girls are kind of inept at it. They make the "duck face" and everyone mocks them, but what else are they supposed to do? *You* try making yourself look sexy, and you'll see that the whole exercise is ridiculous. We did the same thing when I was a teenager, the only difference being that we did it on film, and there was only one copy of our ridiculous sexy poses.

Everyone knows that the reality depicted on social media is as artificial as the reality portrayed on reality television. And yet, we can't help but wonder if perhaps a drop or two of authenticity is included. After all, things that are filmed or otherwise documented can sometimes seem more real than real life. "People emphasize certain things to portray themselves in a certain way," says Jasmine. "I know girls who post photos with people who are supposed to be their friends, but I know they hate those girls. So you see these photos of people who appear to be friends even though in reality they hate each other. So many people have a fake Facebook persona. Nobody ever posts anything that makes them look bad. People live in a fantasy world that gets expressed on Facebook."

But then why do people keep returning to Facebook to see what their peers are doing? "Because there are some genuine relationships and photos," answers Jasmine. "But I don't think you can trust it. You look at someone's Facebook and you think, 'Oh, her life is so great!' But it's all so fake."

Adds Zeilinger, "Body image is the number one issue

girls write about on the *FBomb*. It's the topic I'm most often asked to speak about. It's a huge issue. Girls tell me, 'I know that photos are photoshopped, and I'm a feminist so I know I shouldn't feel this way, but I *still* feel bad about my body because these photos are everywhere."

The world portrayed in social media is artificial and manipulated, yet it can feel so very real—just like femininity. In both, females stitch together an image of themselves as sexually alluring while hiding the seams of their effort. In both activity on social media and in the performance of femininity, females put on a performance that can backfire at any moment.

"Because of social media, there's no room for mistakes," observes Katie Cappiello. "Girls can't make real sexual choices. Once you're branded a slut, you can't back away from that. It's part of your permanent record. And if you try to make a shift from being sexually active to not being sexually active, you're called out for being a fake or a phony or a poser. If you've cultivated a slut identity online, now you're expected to own it in the real world."

If You're Female, You're Being Rated and Judged

Behind every act of reciprocal slut-shaming lingers an unspoken question: Which female is sexier? Who has more status? Competitiveness is in the DNA of social media. When he was a Harvard undergraduate in 2003, Mark Zuckerberg came up with the idea of Facebook after first creating a hot-or-not site called Facemash. According to Claire Hoffman of *Rolling*

Stone, Zuckerberg had just been jilted and went to his dorm room to think up a vindictive plot. He revealed his plans for Facemash on his blog, writing, "Jessica A—— is a bitch. I need to think of something to take my mind off her. I need to think of something to occupy my mind. Easy enough, now I just need an idea." He hacked into Harvard's private online directories of student photos, downloaded photos of his classmates, and posted them online next to farm animals. Students could rate who was more desirable. (Contrary to the depiction in the movie *The Social Network*, Zuckerberg included both males and females.) By 11:09 p.m. that night, the site was up. Over 450 students signed up with twenty-two thousand page views. In a matter of hours, Harvard administrators shut down Zuckerberg's web access. He was accused of violating student privacy and downloading property without permission. But the accusation didn't hurt his reputation, and he wasn't expelled. He went back to his dorm and celebrated with champagne with his roommates. He wrote later in a deposition that people "are more voyeuristic than I would have thought."[107]

Several years later, Facebook's engineers revisited the Facemash concept—this time for rating only females. Katherine Losse recalls that one day, one of the engineers showed her an application he was working on called Judgebook, whose purpose was for Facebook users to rate female users on their appearance. Two women's Facebook profile photos appeared side by side with a space for the viewer to input a score for each one. Writes Losse, "This was a way for men on Facebook to explicitly judge women's looks and assign them a score. To host the application, the engineer purchased two domain names: Judgebook.com and Prettyorwitty.com. "You could either be pretty or you could be witty and, in either case, you would definitely be judged and scored and rated." (The application never went live.) "Facebook made it possible for men to have endless photographs of women available for judging, like so many swimsuit models at a Miss America pageant," Losse observes. "Because, with Judgebook, like all Facebook platform applications, women did not have to consent to have their photographs used by the application."[108]

Young male social media programmers just can't get Facemash out of their heads. Ranking women according to their appearance, they seem to believe, is every man's right, and every male programmer has a social obligation to help his fellow men fulfill their destinies. In 2010, a Boston University sophomore named Justin Doody ripped off the Facemash concept, creating RateBU.com. He claims he was inspired after seeing the movie *The Social Network*. "Me and some friends just saw it and were like 'Wow, we could make this,'" he said.[109] Users upload photos from Facebook. Photographs of two women are placed on a page side by side and the user votes on who is the "hottest." As with Judgebook, the women themselves do not upload their own photos and do not consent to participate in the competition. But while Judgebook thankfully never moved forward, RateBU.com, I'm sorry to say, is an actual live, popular site. In the comments section following an article about RateBU.com that appeared on a Boston website, one student wrote,

The women who appear on Doody's site aren't asked permission to use their photos and names. A lot of the women featured are shocked and hurt that their privacy is being affected. . . . While Doody and his friends may find his site "entertaining" and all in good fun, most people on campus DO NOT. . . . A lot of women on campus no longer feel safe on campus and it is all thanks to Doody and this ridiculous site.

Doody claims that he's not doing anything illegal, since the women have already posted their photos on Facebook.[110]

But men are not alone in this judging behavior. Many women deliberately position themselves as "hotter" than their peers. One in four women admits to deliberately tagging unflattering photos of her Facebook friends. In a survey of 1,512 women over eighteen, two-fifths also admitted to purposely posting pictures of friends not wearing makeup, and one-fifth refused to remove an unflattering photo when asked to do so, in an act of "photo sabotage."[111] What better way to shore up your own attractiveness than by surrounding yourself with unattractive women? If this attitude is shockingly callous and superficial, it may be the logical consequence of social media meeting feminine performance. In a study of 3,500 girls ages eight through twelve, Clifford Nass found that the girls who used social media heavily had fewer positive feelings about their friends than did other girls their age. They also were more likely to have friends whom their parents considered to be a bad influence. Girls who had more face-to-face communication with friends and less online communication were more likely to have healthy emotional interactions.[112]

Zeilinger sums up the anxieties of girls who automatically regard their peers as adversaries:

Who is this person, this perfect teenage girl? Well, she's beautiful . . . but approachable. She's thin but not "scary" thin. She's funny but not funnier than guys, who all adore her. She doesn't let people walk all over her, but she's not strong-willed or opinionated. She's smart, but she's not a brainiac or a geek—and if she is, her other qualities (like beauty and willingness to party) must be pretty excellent to overcome that severe pitfall. . . . We're all competing to be a person who doesn't have deep, meaningful life experiences. . . . We're competing to play her, to perform the role, because, really, nobody is that perfect girl.[113]

Notice all the "buts" in Zeilinger's description of the "perfect teenage girl." She is this but not that, that but not this. She has to be extraordinary without being threatening to other girls. This description is reminiscent of the definition of a "good slut"—a female who is sexual but not too much so. No wonder there's so much competition to embody this girl: no one even really knows what she's supposed to look like.

Since performing femininity requires some measure of competition, many girls and young women possess a desire to make other females jealous. Social media enable them to get the job done. Georgiana, the doctoral student, remarks that "there's this passive-aggressive behavior where people post pictures with the intent of making other people jealous. And look, I've certainly done it too. You read about all these great things your friends are doing, or you find out that they just got into a good college or graduate school, and you think, 'Everything is going better for them; what am I doing with my life?'" She admits that when she's hanging out with friends, "and I know that there's a girl who maybe should have been invited and wasn't, and I'm glad she wasn't invited and I want to make her feel bad, I will post a picture of us with the intent of hurting her."

But doesn't posting photos vindictively make Georgiana look like a vindictive person? "No, it doesn't, actually," she replies. "I can always deny it. Twitter and Facebook are really good for this sort of thing. It's so easy to make other people jealous, and from my observation it's girls who are doing this. You would think that it stops after high school, but it doesn't. In my graduate program, some of the girls are twenty-seven, twenty-eight years old, and they do it all the time. They deliberately post things to hurt other people."

Immature online competitiveness spills over onto real-world interactions. Sharon, the twenty-year-old who was slut-bashed within the community of differently abled students at her high school, was on her high school's volleyball team. In her sophomore year, she was about to start the game with a serve. "I was really focused and I was a decent server, and there was dead silence because it was the very start of the game," she tells me dramatically. "And a mom stood up and screamed, 'Number seventeen is a fucking slut!' I lost my focus and I lost the serve."

"Did she call you a slut because she could tell, or she knew, about your disabilities?" I aked Sharon.

"I doubt it. I don't think she knew anything about me, and at that point there was no way to discern that I was differently abled. My best guess as to why she did that is that it was a competitive game. She wanted her daughter's team to win, so why not make the girls on the other team feel bad? She didn't know who I was; she just knew that I was on the other team and she could see my last name and the number seventeen from my jersey. I couldn't believe that an adult would do that." When reciprocal slut-shaming is normalized—even to the point at which parents are taking part in it—it's a short step toward harassment and bullying.

Reciprocal slut-shaming boils down to the fact that young females get the quickest and the most validation from sexual attention—not from grades, sports, community service, leadership roles, or participation in the arts. Sexual attention, for many girls and young women, trumps all of those achievements. As a result, they compete with each other on the field of sexuality. "A lot of girls don't like it when another girl gets sexual attention because it makes them feel worse about themselves because that's what they value for themselves," fifteen-year-old Stephanie explains. "They value the way they look and the way that boys feel about them. So the way they can make themselves feel better about not having guys want to have sex with them is by saying that the girls who are getting the sexual attention are doing something wrong. There's a group of girls in my school that are very pretty, and the other girls say they're sluts and that the only reason the junior and senior boys like them is because they will give it to anyone."

The young woman who says "Hey, slut" is doing the only thing a young woman can actively do to potentially elevate herself when she's being sexually monitored, sexually policed, and sexually rated in comparison with her peers every moment of every day. But this behavior wreaks havoc not only on oneself and on one's friends but on every female within one's social milieu, including those in the generation to follow. Twenty-one-year-old Erica tells me that on Facebook, she used to regularly write comments such as "What's up, bitch? What's up, slut?" She also began to refer to herself as a bitch and a slut. To Erica, there was nothing wrong with doing this. But one day her mother saw her Facebook and scolded her, saying, "You shouldn't call yourself that." Erica told her that it was OK because it was just with her girlfriends.

But during my senior year, my feelings changed. The little sister of my boyfriend, who was in the seventh grade, asked one of her friends who went to my school if she knew me. And the other girl, who was also in seventh grade and didn't know me at all, said, "Oh yeah, she's one of the sluts of the school." I felt bad that I was projecting this image to younger girls who didn't know me. This girl had an image of a slut that looked like me! That's when I started to think, "What image was I projecting?"

CHAPTER 5

"Good Slut" Containment Strategies

You want to be known as a "good slut" so that you can be socially relevant, but you don't want to actually hook up or have sex. You want to be sexual and asexual simultaneously. Or maybe you do want to hook up or have sex. Regardless of what you actually want, you're terrified that you will get a reputation as a "bad slut," the kind who gets slut-bashed. What do you do?

One strategy, as we've seen, is reciprocal slut-shaming. Calling another female a slut in a pseudofriendly way, with the expectation of being called a slut in return in an amicable manner, is a survival strategy. But it's a big risk. The outcome may be positive; it may be negative. Reciprocal slut-shaming backfires frequently, and a girl could end up labeled a "bad slut."

Therefore, to prove they're not prudes but also not "bad sluts," to be sexual but not "too sexual," girls and young women turn to additional strategies:

- Wearing sexy clothes—tight leggings, bras revealed intentionally, supershort skirts and shorts.
- Sending guys they barely know sexually suggestive texts, photos, and videos.
- Hooking up with a guy, but only after getting wasted and being unable to control their behavior, which shows everyone that they're not *really* hooking up—they're not *that* kind of slut.

These are containment strategies—attempts to be sexually assertive while also establishing a threshold of how far one is willing to go sexually. Essentially, they are methods of exerting limited agency. These strategies nearly always fail. As with reciprocal slut-shaming, they are far riskier and fragile than young women realize.

To many adults, these behaviors indicate something gone horribly wrong. Depending on one's point of view, an adolescent girl who uses her phone to take a photo of her breasts and then hits the Send button, or a young woman who gets drunk at a frat party and then goes back to some guy's dorm room, is the product of bad parenting, a "pornified" world, feminism gone amok, stupidity, or a diseased "raunch culture."

It's true that something *is* horribly wrong. But hand-wringing, clucking, and lecturing girls to behave "appropriately" or "modestly" is as ineffective as a "Do Not Track" app. Even suggesting, as the American Psychological Association

Task Force on the Sexualization of Girls did in 2007, that "we need to replace [the plethora of] sexualized images [in television, music videos, music lyrics, magazines, movies, video games, and the Internet] with ones showing girls in positive settings—ones that show the uniqueness and competence of girls," is laughably naive.[114] If only the solution were so simple. The problem isn't that girls and young women have never learned how to dress without showing off their bodies, and it's not that they are simply mimicking media images of hypersexual females. Rather, they are making deliberate, careful decisions in an attempt to shape how others perceive them. The real problem is that they don't realize that they can't control how others perceive them: what to them appears to be self-evidently slutty in a "good" way is read as slutty in a "bad" way by others. Moreover, many believe that if they pretend they don't really care about their sexuality, even while they clearly are exhibiting their sexual allure, they won't face any consequences.

To add another layer of complexity, many young females also believe that presenting themselves as overtly sexual is necessary for their feminist empowerment. But if they are showing off their sexual selves to prove a point about where they stand on the prude-slut scale, how much power do they really have? It's true that one of feminism's central goals is sexual empowerment, but this can be achieved only within a context of sexual equality. Within the culture of slut-shaming and the sexual double standard, sexual equality does not exist and young females' efforts to subvert the system are turned against them.

If we want to guide young females to avoid sexualizing

themselves in situations when sexualization may be inappropriate or even dangerous, we have to understand why these females make the choices they do. We need to recognize that to many young females, these behaviors *make sense*. These behaviors are *understandable*. When femininity is equated with sexuality, when women have come to believe that looking sexy is what females do best, when being sexually attractive holds the promise of validation, when females are tracked, monitored, and judged, then looking and acting "hot" while protesting that looking and acting "hot" wasn't really their intention is *rational behavior*.

For example, one way that young women trick themselves into believing that they have their peers' permission to act "slutty" is to attend slut-related theme parties. Many students at college campuses have long held "Pimps and Hos" parties in which guests are expected to dress up as either a pimp or a slut and to role-play at the event. Like Halloween, it's an opportunity to dress in costume and perform, in this case as a "bad slut" with the authorization of one's peers. Donna Freitas, the author of *The End of Sex*, has compiled an impressive list of spin-off theme parties with names such as "CEOs and Their Secretary Hos"; "Dirty Doctors and Naughty Nurses"; "Maids and Millionaires"; "Golf Pros and Tennis Hos"; and "Sex [short for Secretaries] and Execs."[115] College students who regularly attended theme parties told Freitas that "they provided the only 'legitimate' opportunity for women to dress in revealing or sexy attire. There was a clear desire among many women students to dress in a certain manner that, outside of the 'safety' of a themed event, would garner them a permanent reputation as a 'whore' or 'slut.'"[116] If you're a female attending a "Pimps and Hos" party, *of course* you're going to dress up and hook up with random guys—that's the whole point! So no one can blame you for being a "bad slut" when all you're doing is fulfilling the raison d'être of the party.

If you're always at risk of being labeled a "bad slut" no matter what you do sexually, even if you've never done anything sexual at all, why *not* sexualize yourself? You come to believe that you have nothing to lose. With this mind-set, many young females adopt several strategies to control their image as sexy but not slutty. As we will see, there are limits to their agency; the line between "sexy" and "slutty" is razor-thin; and their reputation often spins out of their control.

Strategy #1: Wear Sexy Clothes

If you walk by a club, bar, or trendy restaurant, you will likely see clusters of young women tottering in stilettos as they tug at shorts that could be mistaken for underwear. When those of us who came of age in the 1970s or 1980s wore something skimpy or outré in our youth, we imagined ourselves to be daring and scandalous, and we tended to reserve those outfits for special occasions. Young females today, however, wear revealing clothes far more often than we ever did, and many claim that their outfits are not sexualized in the least. We may respond to them, then, with disbelief. We wonder: Don't young females today recognize that if they sexualize themselves, particularly in nonsexual contexts such as school, others will regard them as sexual objects? Are they *intentionally* courting disaster? Are they really so clueless?

"It used to be that empowered sexuality was about your subjectivity—how you feel," Amanda Marcotte, the feminist blogger, tells me. "But now it's about being an object—how you appear to others. You have to present yourself as a sexy virgin." Marcotte observes that this shift from feeling sexy to presenting oneself as sexy occurred in the late 1990s and early 2000s with the rise of the teen star Britney Spears. "The record executives behind Britney Spears had the stroke of genius of having her grind around in a schoolgirl uniform that was half undone while advertising her virginity. This marketing ploy worked because of a preexisting fantasy of 'defiling' an innocent virgin."

It's no mean feat to present oneself as both sexually attractive yet sexually unavailable, and girls and young women who have followed Spears's model often miss the mark. "As the first generations of girls raised with feminism as a given have matured," adds Marcotte, "there's been a growing obsession with squelching and exploiting female sexuality. Both are sides of the same coin—an attempt to reduce women to their sexuality in order to deny their growing power in the world." To many young females, it's as if the feminist victory of sexual ownership never occurred: to them, sexual empowerment means being sexy to satisfy the desires of other people. And as was true before women's liberation exploded in the late 1960s and 1970s, other people get to judge if one is sexy in the right way or in the wrong way. Along the way, young women's sexual agency is contained. Spears sings in "Oops! . . . I Did It Again" that "I did it again to your heart / Got lost in this game, oh baby / Oops! . . . You think that I'm sent from above / I'm not that innocent." Is she a sexual provocateur, or is she an innocent naïf? She defends herself as clueless, but most who see her red catsuit in the video conclude otherwise.

Putting together a sexy-but-not-too-slutty outfit, you should realize, is not easy. It's hard work. It requires careful planning. Yet high school girls don't want their peers to know the extent of their calibrations and deliberations. They strive for nonchalance, for a seeming effortlessness and insouciance. When they're called to task for dressing in an overtly sexualized way, they claim that they didn't realize they were projecting a sexual message. "Oops, do I look like a lap dancer? I had no idea! I'm just wearing this see-through top and these short shorts because they're comfortable!"

It's easier than ever before to experiment with sexy clothes because clothes in the "fast fashion" market are inexpensive. According to Elizabeth Cline, the author of *Overdressed: The Shockingly High Cost of Cheap Fashion*, "Fast fashion is known not only for its constant offerings of the latest fads but for being shockingly cheap. Forever 21 can sell cute pumps for $15 and H&M can peddle a knit miniskirt for $5."[117] Girls and young women can use their allowance money or earnings from an after-school job to buy lots of cheap outfits made from synthetic materials by exploited laborers in China, Bangladesh, Honduras, or Pakistan. Since the prices are so low, the clothes become disposable, encouraging the taking of fashion risks. If it turns out that the cleavage-baring, backless leopard-print top doesn't score approval points, a girl can just toss it into the throwaway heap.

Meanwhile, 28 percent of the clothes marketed to tween girls at stores such as Justice, Aéropostale, and Abercrombie

Kids are sexualized, according to a study led by two Kenyon College psychology professors, Sarah Murnen and Linda Smolak.[118] In 2013, the clothing retailer Victoria's Secret targeted tweens and teens with a lace-trimmed thong saying "Call Me" on the front, underwear with lace and the word "Wild" on the back, and another pair that said "Feeling Lucky?"[119] Abercrombie described its tween jeans in 2011 as "fitted with a little stretch for a sexy look to give you the perfect butt."[120] Since the function of sexualized tween clothing, the researchers of the Kenyon study say, is "to socialize girls into a sexually objectified role," girls are forced to grapple with sexual objectification years before they are ready to do so.[121]

Feeling the pressure to look ever-so-slutty, and possessing a large number of cheaply made sexy clothes, middle school and high school girls get dressed in the morning and pull out of their closet body-hugging or skin-revealing attire. In general, these girls claim that they make clothing choices *for themselves*, not for male attention. This, my friends, is a smoke screen. We know that admitting the truth about desiring male attention is a fast track to "bad slut" hell, because one of the central definitions of a "bad slut" is a girl who "tries too hard." Pretending that they choose their outfits for reasons other than seeking male sexual attention, therefore, is essential. It is a way to cover over their true effort, much in the way a woman hobbling in four-inch stilettos absurdly claims, "These shoes are so comfortable!"

In June 2012, students at Stuyvesant High School in Manhattan, a prestigious, selective public school, protested the dress code, which read in part:

Students should wear the appropriate attire to school. Guidelines include the following:

- Sayings and illustrations on clothing should be in good taste.
- Shoulders, undergarments, midriffs and lower backs should not be exposed.
- The length of shorts, dresses and skirts should extend below the fingertips with the arms straight at your side.[122]

Many female students complained that administrators enforced the dress code subjectively, and that in doing so, they slut-shamed the girls. A senior wrote in the school's newspaper:

For the most part, I don't consider myself to be a particularly inappropriate dresser—even my mother would agree—but this year, I've been called out nearly every single time I've worn a skirt, dress, or pair of shorts (maxi skirts not included). Once I even lost my ID card over a belted dress that just reached my fingertips—and, once the belt was off (as I showed the administrator) actually went beyond. I'm not sure what it is about me that causes me to become the administration's target girl. Not all my friends have the same problem; few girls I know get called out as frequently as I do, and of course boys barely have to acknowledge the existence of a dress code at all. Perhaps this simply stems from some sort of miscommunication about the rules of the dress code. One day I came in wearing a jean skirt that actually extended beyond my fingertips (I had checked!) and, although wary of being called out, I was not totally surprised to be stopped anyway. What did surprise me was being informed that it wasn't enough for the skirt to simply reach past my fingertips (à la the rules as stated in the student planner), it had to "go well past." When I complained, indignant, that they just didn't make dresses or skirts long enough to pass—not for teenagers, anyway—I was advised to "think knees," or just wear pants. I was released with a warning, and left feeling like I'd been called out for wearing a bikini top to school, or a garter belt. It was an unpleasant, shaming experience.[123]

This student describes two outfits: one involving a belted dress, the other a jean skirt. As described, the belted dress did not comply with the dress code because it was too short, though the student implies that she alone was singled out when other girls wearing similarly too-short dresses were not. If true, enforcement of the dress code was unfair. With regard to the jean skirt, since the code states that skirts must extend below the fingertips, but not "well past" them, the skirt should have been deemed acceptable and she should not have been reprimanded.

But notice her defense. With regard to the dress, this student points out that when she removed her belt, her dress passed the length requirement. Yet she *was* wearing a belt, so what difference does it make what the length was when the belt was removed? And is it really true that no dresses or skirts exist that extend past her fingertips?

My point is not to embarrass this student, who found the

experience not only "unpleasant" but "shaming." I empathize with her, and I don't blame her for feeling upset. She seems to have been singled out when others were not, and she was reprimanded when she should not have been. At the same time, I want to point out that her defense is an exercise in denial of agency. A dress that just reaches the fingertips is, by almost anyone's standards, short. It is a minidress. Why wear a minidress unless you want to show off your legs? I am not blaming the student for wanting to show off her legs. But then why can't she admit that this was her intention? Why does she not concede that she wanted to appear sexy?

The answer is that this student, like so many young females, has been ensnared by the pressure to be sexy without being slutty. And one of the smartest ways to fit into this pinhole is to disavow your agency by pretending you're looking sexy by accident. If you admit that you're deliberately attempting to show off your body, you run the risk of being labeled a slut. Therefore, the only rational thing to do is deny your attempts at sexualization. You can then be sexy but in a "good" way. Moreover, if you're stopped by a school official who calls you out for being "too" sexy, you can protest that you're being slut-shamed. This preemptive measure adds another layer of protection against actually being slut-shamed by one's peers.

To protest the dress code itself, as well as the haphazard enforcement of the code, students called for a "Slutty Wednesday" in which they dressed as . . . you know. Boys and girls alike wore tank tops and short shorts, with some girls wearing spaghetti strap tops. Jessica Valenti, a feminist writer and a Stuyvesant alumna, supported the students. In an essay in

The Nation, she condemned not only the subjective enforcement but the code itself. Valenti argued that the code violated female students' rights, and that "the thinking behind the code sends a dangerous message to young women—that they are responsible for the way in which society objectifies and sexualizes them." She quoted the school's principal, Stanley Teitel, now retired, who had said, "Many young ladies wear denim skirts which are very tight and are short to begin with, and when they sit down, they only rise up, because there's nowhere else to go. . . . The bottom line is, some things are a distraction, and we don't need to distract students from what is supposed to be going on here, which is learning."

Valenti responded, "It's not the responsibility of female students to mitigate the male gaze. You find female bodies 'distracting'? That's your problem, not women's. Society teaches that women exist to be looked at, objectified and sexualized—it's up to others to make sure that they don't contribute to that injustice. . . . Whether or not [the students at Stuyvesant] wear tank tops or shorts [while learning] is so irrelevant."[124]

Singling out curvier students for wearing too-short skirts while turning the other way when less physically developed girls do the same thing *is* a form of slut-shaming, because it signifies that curvier girls are "bad sluts" while less curvy girls are "good sluts" or not even "sluts" at all. The Stuyvesant students were justified in their indignation. But I believe that as long as the dress code is enforced consistently, there is nothing slut-shaming about it. In fact, if it were up to me, I would eliminate the fingertip rule, because different people's arms have different lengths, so the fingertip rule does not establish a single standard for clothing length. In addition, in general a skirt that extends precisely below the fingertips of most girls is—yes, I'm going to say it—too short for school. The principal merely was noting a fact of physics when he pointed out that a short skirt rises up and can reveal a girl's underwear, however unintentionally, when the wearer sits. A better rule could be that skirts and shorts must be at least four or five inches above the middle of the kneecap.

The fact is that these girls, like many high school girls around the country, deliberately dress to resemble "good sluts." Yes, this is a distraction for everyone involved—the girls (because they're competing with each other and eyeing each other), the heterosexual boys (because in adolescence, chances are they find breasts spilling out of the low-cut top of the girl sitting next to them more attention-grabbing than problem sets), and the teachers (because they are all too aware of the various dynamics at play). Girls are sexualizing themselves with their attire. It's not a leap to point out that as a result, everyone who sees girls in sexualized attire will think of them in a sexualized manner.

When I taught at a New York City public high school that required a uniform T-shirt for all students, I observed two reactions among the girls. Some seemed to have accepted that they were stuck wearing an unfashionable, asexual shirt; they didn't put in any noticeable effort to sexualize their appearance within the school building during school hours. They wore jeans and sneakers and a minimal amount of makeup and jewelry. But the majority of girls did everything they could to subvert the school's imposed asexuality. (Although I have no reason to believe that the school's intent was to clamp down on girls' expression of sexuality in dress, that was the result. As far as I could tell, the school's goals were to instill a sense of school pride and to reduce competitiveness over clothing.) These girls routinely took off the uniform shirt in between classes, hoping they wouldn't be reprimanded. Beneath the uniform shirt they wore revealing and trendy tops. They also favored miniskirts, low-slung jeans, dramatic jewelry, and stylized hair and makeup. I didn't blame them, and I don't blame the Stuyvesant students either for trying to subvert their dress code. Nobody, especially teenagers, likes to be told how to dress—or what to do in general. Clothing is a way to express oneself and to define one's identity; both activities are central aspects of being a teenager. And many teenage girls, as we know, crave sexual attention. They believe that they must always look sexy, and that looking sexy is the best or only way to attract positive attention.

Yet there is a time and a place for looking sexy. School is not the right occasion for intentional hypersexual presentation. I found my students' attire distracting, just as former principal Teitel did with his students at Stuyvesant. It is difficult to focus on academics within a sexually charged environment.

"The girls dress this way because they're rewarded," notes Katie Cappiello of the Arts Effect. "It makes them popular and appealing and desirable and attractive to boys. They say they feel great in these clothes. They say they feel confident. They would rather get rewarded for looking hot than for getting an A on their midterm. They put more time and energy into what they'll wear the next day than studying or doing homework. Guys tell them they look hot; they're not telling them, 'Good job on that history paper.' For these girls, it's like they're on the pages of *Us Weekly* every day of their lives. Their lives are tabloid."

"But," I pointed out, "the girls don't admit that they're wearing these clothes to be desirable and attractive to boys. They say, 'Well, I'm wearing them to be comfortable.'"

"But they *do* feel comfortable," Cappiello told me. "It's true. They feel comfortable because they feel they look great. It's *that* sense of 'comfortable.'"

They feel "comfortable" because they look sexy. But looking sexy is not easy, which makes their choice to describe their clothes as "comfortable" ironic. To girls and young women, "comfort" is not necessarily about physical ease. It is a state of mind, and it is also an expression of an attitude of effortlessness. After all, "comfortable" clothes imply that no thought or labor was put into wearing them. The wearers are not *trying* to don something that makes them look like a "good slut." It just sort of *happens*. They choose clothes that they *like for themselves*, that make them feel at ease because they feel confident. In the narrative these girls tell themselves, they erase the labor they expend in putting together their slutty outfits. Therefore, when school administrators call them to task, they are quick to deny any agency—because they are denying it even to themselves. Through this strategy, they can be sexual and asexual, prude and "good slut," sexy and virgin, all at once.

The college students I spoke with behave similarly, although they don't have to contend with dress codes. Nevertheless, they have their own ways to assert their sexuality through clothing without crossing the line into full-scale sluttiness. They too choose sexualized clothes that give the impression that not much thought has been put into them. In my interviews, two words cropped up repeatedly: "yoga pants." Wearing yoga pants—with material thinner than denim but a touch thicker than tights—is widely regarded on college campuses as a safe way to appear sexually attractive. Such pants reveal the contours of the body without displaying any skin. Yoga pants are sexy but extraordinarily casual, and therefore make the wearer appear to have demonstrated little or no thought into her sexually charged appearance. "Yoga pants," by the way, have had different iterations over the years. Had I spoken with college students ten years earlier, no doubt they would have mentioned the body-hugging velour tracksuits that had been popular in the early 2000s. Whether the fabric is velour, spandex, Lycra, or Modal, the effect is the same: revealing the shape of the body. (Perhaps it is a coincidence, perhaps not, but the rise of sexy athletic clothes occurred when Britney Spears, the famous "sexy virgin," became an international sensation.)

"I find that the women here wear tight-fitting pants that look almost like tights," Jalisa, a black senior at an elite college on the East Coast, tells me. "The default is to be sexy, even if they're not thinking about it all the time. People say they're wearing yoga pants because they're comfortable, but they know their ass looks a certain way in them. They project a coolness that says, 'I don't care about anything.' They are putting in effort, but they want you to think that the effort is really easy."

Brittany, a nineteen-year-old white college student from the East Coast, agrees. "So many girls walk around in yoga pants every single day. You wear yoga pants to get attention. That's what you wear when you want to look hot. Chances are, you're not on the way to the gym. It's a way to look hot and attractive for guys. It's a way to wear tight clothes but there's less of a chance that someone will call you a slut because you're not wearing a miniskirt." Since yoga pants convey the pursuit of fitness or athletics, they convey a sense of purpose, even if the wearer never steps inside a yoga studio.

To hide their effort, these women say they are wearing clothes to please themselves—and it's just a *coincidence* that they are sexy. Repeatedly the college students I spoke with assured me, "I just like to wear these clothes"; "This is just my style"; "I like to look good for myself." Molly, the twenty-year-old white college student from Kentucky, explained her choice completely with regard to the fabrics involved. "Yoga pants are really comfortable," she told me. "They're not a tough material on your body, and I like that. Sometimes I just don't want a thick material on my body."

Some women are refreshingly honest about their clothing strategy. They admit that they choose clothes that make them look sexy but that don't scream "slutty." Maria, the twenty-one-year-old Latina student, told me, "I wear tight skinny jeans to show off my curves. If someone saw me on the street, they wouldn't think I'm dressed in a slutty way. I don't wear short skirts. The sluttiest way a woman will dress here on campus is heeled boots, not actual heels, and a sheer top with a bra showing." Vicki, a white twenty-two-year-old senior, sums up the students' thoughts succinctly: "Yoga pants are super comfortable, but also it feels good to get attention. Your ass looks nice in those pants."

My argument is not that young women need to cover their bodies, although I do believe that high school girls should follow their school's dress code if one exists. I reject the idea that sexual assault can be blamed on the victim's attire. Nevertheless, it's time we had an honest conversation about the sexual messages that high school girls and young women send out to the world when they wear clothes that call attention to their bodies as sexual objects.

Everyone gets dressed with the intent of making herself or himself look attractive. But if you're female, especially a young female, you interpret looking "attractive" as looking "sexy" more than "pretty" or "cute." The pressure to look sexy can pose a huge problem if you're trying to manage your sexual reputation, because as we know, one person's sexy is another person's slutty. The goal for most young females is to look like a "good slut"—sexy but not too much so. (Even fashion designers are aware of women's conundrum; Anni Kuan, who designs dresses worn by, among others, Chirlane McCray, the wife of New York City mayor Bill de Blasio, describes her clothes as "sexy but not slutty.")[125]

Young females worry that if they own up to their intentions and effort, they run the risk of being perceived as "too slutty." And they are right to worry. Yet the strategy of deliberately sexualizing their appearance with the intention of molding others' perception that they are "good sluts" and nothing more is doomed to backfire. The bottom line is that they are unable to control how their appearance is interpreted by others. I believe, therefore, that the female students at Stuyvesant truly were shocked to be stopped by administrators for wearing skirts that were deemed excessively short.

Although the girls intellectually knew that they were exposing much of their legs, they erroneously believed that they alone had the power to determine if and when they would be perceived as sexualized in appearance. They thought that if they pretended (perhaps even to themselves) that they didn't put in a lot of effort into their attire, no one could accuse them of appearing hypersexual.

High school girls in particular are not mature enough to recognize their inability to control how others will interpret their clothing choices. They don't know that even though wearing X-rated clothes never gives anyone permission to sexually assault the wearer, many people in the world at large assume that a half-naked female is "asking for it." We must guide high school girls to understand the limits of their ability to control others' perceptions of their sexual identities. A girl may wake up in the morning intending to present herself as casually attractive—a "good slut"—but if she misses the mark in even the most subtle way, there is a high likelihood that those she encounters will conclude that she looks like a "bad slut."

Strategy #2: Send Naked Pictures

Sexting is another strategy in which girls and young women mistakenly believe that they can control their sexual reputation as a "good slut" and nothing more. The first alarm sounded in 2004, when an eighth-grade girl at the prestigious Horace Mann School in New York City sent a digital video of herself masturbating to a male classmate she liked. Her face was clearly visible. He (or someone he forwarded it to) uploaded it to a file-sharing network that students used to trade music. Hundreds of students saw the video, which then became available to an audience of millions.[126] Soon stories of the circulation of similar videos, as well as photos of girls either completely naked or naked from the waist up, became impossible to ignore. Again and again, girls were humiliated when a boy they naively thought they could trust betrayed them. Again and again, girls became known as "bad sluts" by dozens, hundreds, even thousands of kids within their social orbit.

We don't know exactly how many teenagers are involved in sexting. According to an Associated Press/MTV survey conducted in September 2009 by Knowledge Networks, 24 percent of fourteen- to seventeen-year-olds, and 33 percent of eighteen- to twenty-four-year-olds, have been involved in "some type of naked sexting," either by cell phone or on the Internet. Yet according to a Pew Research Center survey conducted in December 2009, only 4 percent of twelve- to seventeen-year-olds have sent and 15 percent have received "sexually suggestive nude or nearly nude images via text messaging" on their cell phones. However, the Pew numbers most likely are so small because teens were questioned only about cell phone sexting.[127] Chances are that the AP/MTV numbers are more reliable. The numbers suggest that so far, the majority of teenagers are not sexting, although this may change as the practice becomes more routine and commonplace.

There's nothing new about taking a naked photo of yourself. "I myself am entirely guilty. In going through a box of Polaroids that I took in high school, I stumbled across a series of photos that I took after having acquired a copy of *Our Bodies, Ourselves*," says danah boyd. "Taking a picture seemed like a much more reasonable way of figuring out what was 'down there' than trying to get a mirror angled right. Thank goodness my mother had no idea that she was housing child pornography produced by her daughter. In talking with adults from various communities, I was surprised to learn how many had taken photographs of themselves as teenagers, trying to be sexy or sexual."[128] Ah, the predigital days of Polaroids, when you didn't have to bring your film to the photo shop for development, and your image could not be duplicated or circulated. Even with regular film, photographic images were contained. Unless you actively gave someone the negatives, you could keep your pictures private.

Today, girls often believe that as long as they send their photo to someone with whom they are in a relationship, they can rest assured that their photo is safe. And in fact, boyd says that most teenagers who do sext are doing so within the confines of a relationship, and that most images are not mass-fowarded. "I've done 'Skypesex' with a boyfriend," Vicki tells me matter-of-factly. "You masturbate while you're on the phone with Skype and show him the images. I've done photos also, but always in relationships, not with random hookups."

But projecting yourself in this way ushers in myriad problems for girls in particular. Girls want to look perfect, hot, and effortless. "In a relationship, there's now pressure to send videos and pictures," Nona Willis Aronowitz, a twenty-eight-year-old white feminist writer, tells me. "One guy asked me to send him video and photos, and it really stressed me out. I ended up taking lots of photos, over and over, rejecting them because they weren't good enough. Especially since we don't see each other very often, I wanted him to preserve an image of me as really attractive. But it was so much effort and pressure, and I decided I didn't want to do it. And then I think of these young girls in high school doing the same thing. It's hard to fulfill this expectation of representing yourself."

In addition, although boys also send photos of themselves —girls and young women refer to them as "dick pics"—only girls' photos are mass-forwarded. When a boy sends a picture of himself, girls tend to laugh. His "dick pic" is regarded as humorous but not shameful. Girls tend not to perceive the self-photographed naked penis as erotic. They also tend to regard the act of photographing one's penis as being within the bounds of acceptable male behavior, so they don't see it as scandalous.

When a girl sends a picture of herself, however, she's at risk for being slut-bashed. Her photo or video is seen as pathetic, shameful, and disgusting. Although she is eroticized, paradoxically the act of photographing herself is perceived to be unfeminine; it is evidence of one's sexual agency—even though many girls use sexting as a way to avoid actually engaging in real sexual activity. *His* photo may be forwarded to a few select girlfriends for a little laugh. *Her* photo may go viral to teach her a lesson. Molly, the twenty-year-old white college student, tells me that in her high school in Kentucky, "A girl sent her boyfriend a picture of her breasts—her face was in it too—and everybody saw it. She had dated him for a month. I felt bad for her. I would never want that to happen to me. The picture ended up getting forwarded to one of the teachers, and there was a big investigation. The guy was not punished. There were so many people who had the photo, so the school couldn't pinpoint who had been responsible for forwarding it."

Theoretically, a girl could control distribution of her image with Snapchat, an app that promises that photos disappear automatically after a few seconds of viewing. But there are no guarantees with Snapchat, because in fact it's possible to take a screenshot of a photo before it disappears. Snapchat is supposed to inform the sender if the recipient has taken a screenshot, but this mechanism can be disabled. Snapchat users in 2013 sent two hundred million photos a day.[129]

Georgiana, the white twenty-two-year-old graduate student, informs me that she knows "several people who send naked pictures to their boyfriend or girlfriend thinking that it can't be saved" with Snapchat. But not only can you take a screenshot and save a Snapchat photo, "you can also press down and save it directly to your library or post it to your Facebook. The app tells you if someone took a screen shot, and how many they took, but what can you do? Nothing. Once it's out there, it's out there."

Teenagers under eighteen can be charged with a felony under child pornography laws, leading to prison time and sex offender registration requirements—and girls are treated more punitively than boys are. In some states, prosecutors have investigated and prosecuted girls who took or posted pictures of themselves and, at worst, sent their photos to one individual. In several cases, they have even gone after girls involved in "self-sexting." When they were students at the Georgetown University Law Center, LiJia Gong and Alina Hoffman analyzed prosecutions of "teen self-sexting"—when photos are self-taken and intended only for personal, private use—and concluded that most investigations are unwarranted and sexist because the harm of "self-sexts" is minimal.[130] More than twenty states have enacted laws making sexting in some form illegal for minors.[131]

In a legal note that Gong and Hoffman wrote in the *Georgetown Journal of Gender and the Law*, they analyze several incidents in which girls were punished for sending naked images of themselves.[132] In *Miller v. Skumanick*, local District Attorney George Skumanick Jr. threatened to prosecute several thirteen-year-old Pennsylvania high school students for child pornography because they had taken a photograph of themselves from the waist up, each wearing a white, opaque bra. One student was speaking on the phone and another was using her hand to make a peace sign. Another girl was photographed in a white opaque towel wrapped around her body; another was wearing a bathing suit. Skumanick said that the girl in the bathing suit was posed "provocatively," and ordered the girls to enroll in a counseling program.[133]

In another case, two female high school students had photographed themselves posed with phallic-shaped, rainbow-colored lollipops. They also wore lingerie and pretended to kiss each other. They had posted the photos on MySpace and Facebook, with the photos accessible only to those granted "friend" status, and on Photobucket, which required a password for viewing them. As punishment, the school suspended the girls from school activities and forced them to apologize to their school for bringing "discredit and dishonor" upon themselves and their school. The students and their parents brought an action against the school district and the principal in which they claimed that the punishment violated their First Amendment rights. The court ruled in the students' favor, but also found that the school district and principal were immune from damages.[134]

Gong and Hoffman are infuriated by the sexual double standard that was applied in these prosecutions and by the fact that girls were slut-shamed as a result. "If someone chooses to share a photo, and everyone involved has given consent, he or she should not be regulated," Gong tells me. "Clearly there's a double standard for sexual activity, especially among young people. Women's bodies are eroticized in a way that men's bodies are not." For a heterosexual girl, "getting a 'dick pic' [from a heterosexual guy] is considered hilarious. I've never met a female who finds that erotic—whereas pictures of women's bodies are considered scandalous and salacious. Why are schools and prosecutors concerned about the purity of women's sexuality but not men's?"

Hoffman adds that teens' sexting makes adults uncomfortable. "It forces people to confront the reality of girls' sexuality. It forces people to recognize that teenage girls are sexual beings, and that this is what their sexuality looks like. The more social media are integrated into our lives, the more people will use them to explore their sexuality. They are using electronic media to figure out who they are." Sexting is becoming a routine, normal part of adolescent sexual exploration. But because it produces evidence, it causes adults to panic and moralize. If a couple's sixteen-year-old daughter says she's going over to a boy's home to study but doesn't return till midnight, they can pretend to themselves that she must be a committed student. If their daughter comes home crying that everyone at school has seen a video of her masturbating, they can't ignore or deny the truth of her sexuality.

Many adults don't realize that sexting among teens often is coerced. Girls often send a photo or video to a guy because they feel that they have to, not because they want to. Georgiana tells me that during her sophomore year of high school,

One particular guy that my girlfriends had introduced me to sent a picture of himself totally naked. Full-body, totally naked. He was not interested in me; he just wanted to sleep with me. And he then wrote, 'Now you have to send me one.' I texted him back: 'I never asked you for this picture, so no, I'm not sending you one back.' He continued to send me naked pictures, and he would text and leave voice mails. He did it repeatedly—numerous times. I ended up sending him a picture of myself clothed just to get him to stop. He wrote back, 'This is ridiculous; this isn't what I wanted.' This went on for at least six months. He finally stopped after I told my girlfriends about it, and I guess he became embarrassed when he knew they knew. But I admit that I liked that he paid attention to me. I was definitely attracted to him. I went to an all-girls' school, so it was exciting to meet a guy and have him be interested in me.

I asked Georgiana why, if she was attracted to the boy, she never caved and sent him a naked photo of herself. "I was paranoid about my picture getting circulated," she explains. "Around the same time, a girl at school had sent a naked picture of herself to her boyfriend, and after they broke up, he forwarded it to a bunch of people and she got expelled. So I was more scared than anything else."

"What did you do with the photos he sent you—did you ever forward them or show them to your friends?" I asked Georgiana.

"No, I deleted them," she told me. Her reaction was typical: although there are exceptions, females generally don't collect or brag about the sexts they receive. They tend to want to distance themselves from the images.

Although Georgiana never sent a naked photo of herself, the boy's demands were coercive. "Now it's your turn to send me one" is a refrain my interviewees have heard repeatedly. Guys pressure girls to send them naked pictures and then amass a collection of photos. And the guys always want the girl's face in the picture—otherwise the body could be anyone's. When girls think they're outsmarting the system by sending headless shots, they're told that headless isn't good enough. Did Anthony Weiner, who resigned from Congress after it was revealed that he had sent photos of his penis to at least six women who had followed him on Twitter, use his photos as leverage? None of the women involved who have come forward have said so, but it's likely that Weiner photographed himself not only to show off but to initiate a negotiation over the acquisition of photos of naked women.

Once a guy has amassed a collection, he may use it to authenticate his own masculine status. Jessica Ringrose reports that in her research of British youth she has found that boys use photos of naked girls as "a form of popularity currency or a commodity to be collected, traded, shown to others and distributed, but could also be used to punish the girls in question via 'exposure.'"[135]

Mara, a nineteen-year-old white student in California, remembers that when she was a freshman in high school, a senior guy she liked sent her a picture of his abs. He wrote, "OK, now send me one. I'll never show it to anyone." So she sent him a picture of herself wearing a bra. "Then there was another guy who didn't even send me anything but kept asking me to send him pictures, and I just ignored him. In my high school, the guys were always pressuring the girls to send them pictures. Guys would say, 'Oh, I have a picture of so-and-so on my phone; come and look!' They would show the pictures to everyone. It was boobs but also sometimes full-body naked. And they would forward them as a way to brag. It was a pride thing, like, 'Look who sent *me* a picture!' One guy had a hundred photos on his phone, a collection."

Jasmine, the twenty-year-old student who is black and Latina, shares her high school sexting saga. "Once in high school a guy sent me a picture of his penis and asked for one back. It made me really uncomfortable. I refused. I said, 'No, I don't do that.' I was asked a lot in high school and a couple times in college. 'Hey, can I have a picture of you?' I've always said no. I was even hooking up with a guy once and he said, 'Hey, can I take a picture of you?' I had to grab his phone and hide it from him because he wasn't listening to me."

"My friend in the tenth grade, who's considered one of the most popular girls, literally gets a handful of dick pics a day," reports fifteen-year-old Abby, a white girl from Arts Effect in Manhattan. "There's this one guy I see in church who sent his dick pic to two of my friends. And they're best friends and he sent the same pic to both of them at the same time. She gets at least two a day, usually Snapchats. I figure that if the guy is sending you a dick pic, it means he's looking for something in return."

Kaitlyn, sixteen, chimes in, saying, "It's sent only for leverage. It's not like any of us actually want to see their dicks"—and the six other girls dishing about sexting laugh hysterically.

Nicole, sixteen, offers that "I had someone on video chat spontaneously take off all his clothes. In middle school, lots of people say, 'Hey, want to video chat?' And then you strip for each other. So there was this girl in my school who did that, and she didn't know it but the guy took a snapshot of her. Plus technically you can't record the video chat unless the other person accepts, but he had software where you could record your screen, and she didn't know. And she was masturbating for him. And now that whole video of her masturbating got sent around to everybody."

Christina, the fourteen-year-old Latina high school student in California, tells me in a Skype interview, her big eyes looking serious and sad,

It started in the eighth grade. Two different guys sent me pictures of their penises, and then they wanted me to send a picture to them. I said no to them. Their pictures were not expected, and I didn't want them. But I did send a naked picture to a boy who had been my boyfriend, even though we were not together when I sent it. It was my whole body, but not my face. It was the summer after eighth grade. He then sent it to all his friends, and then he threatened to put it on Facebook if I didn't send him more. I was crying, and I told my older sister and my mom. It was pretty scary even though my face wasn't in it. I never replied to him, and he ended up not posting it. His friends go to my school and are in my math class. It makes me uncomfortable that I have to see them. I guess I just have to live with it.

I asked her why she sent the photo—fully recognizing that since she was thirteen at the time, she was just at the beginning stages of navigating the manipulations of sexting communication (not to mention the manipulations of dating and sexual attraction in general).

"At the time, I wanted him to like me," she explains. "I wanted to get back together. I thought this would get him to like me again." Now at fourteen, she's older and wiser. "I would never send a naked picture to anyone again," she says.

Twenty-six-year-old Diane, the white feminist marriage and family therapist in California, points out that it's not just high school guys who repeatedly ask girls for naked photos. We speak with each other via Skype, and although the image of her face and dark blond hair fills my computer screen, I get a glimpse of several large, bold tattoos on both her arms. She reports that she recently was active on the dating site OkCupid.

There was a lot of "Before we meet, can I see other photos of you?" And then you haven't even met the person yet, and already you start texting and sexting. Because of my tattoos, I cover up my arms when I send a picture. So the pictures I sent were just my boobs without my face or arms—and they really could have been anyone's boobs. How would he even know they were mine? But always immediately I would get a picture back—a picture of a dick. It was like, there was no foreplay. Immediately there would be this photo of a dick in the guy's hand. It was always about showing me how big it was. And it would just be his dick, not the rest of his body, not his face. I started accumulating these dick pictures. At one point I had five at the same time that I would show my girlfriends. We would sit around and show them to each other. After they would send me their dick picture, they would always expect something else from me—usually a crotch shot— even though I had never asked for the dick picture. It was a power play or a control thing. And at this point, what, I'm supposed to meet them in person? Are we going to have dinner? So I would usually lose interest. [*Laughs.*] Because at this point, the guy has seen my boobs. If he wants to see more of me, then we are having dinner next—I'm not sending a crotch shot.

As an adult in her mid-twenties with a feminist consciousness and a master's degree, Diane possesses the maturity to laugh about the way these men relentlessly demand more and greater sexual access without really knowing her. But high school girls usually do not have the same amount of confidence.

One of the most disturbing aspects of sexting is that many girls seem resigned to the situation. They have become so accustomed to hearing, "I sent you one; now it's your turn" that they don't question or fight it. Besides, as scary as the prospect is of having their photo forwarded and shared, they don't see any other way to get the male attention they desire. Mara explains, "Some girls are just naive. The boy always promises to never show the picture, and they think that he will like them if they send the picture, and they believe that he won't show it to anyone."

But even after they wise up and shed their naiveté, many girls send their photo anyway—because they so much want guys to consider them sexually attractive. "There are girls who realize that the guy will show the picture to everyone, and they are OK with it," says Mara. "They are so desperate for male attention they would do anything."

Sharon, the twenty-year-old differently abled white student whom we met in chapter 3, observes that in her high school, "a lot of girls had disabilities worse than mine. So they wanted sexual attention even if it wasn't positive sexual attention. There were girls who wouldn't mind if a picture of their boobs was forwarded to lots of guys. They figured they would never get a boyfriend, so this was a way to get sexual attention." In the messed-up logic of the prude-slut conflict, being a slut—even a "bad slut"—is better than being a prude or being alone. Even social humiliation is preferable to invisibility.

Sending a naked photo may seem like a smart way for a girl or young woman to prove that she's sexually sophisticated and in control—without actually engaging in sexual activity—but as we have seen, the moment she hits Send, she loses control over her image. As with wearing sexually provocative clothes, the sexual suggestiveness of the photographic image cannot be contained. Girls and young women who think they are capably manipulating their identity as a "good slut" invariably discover that in fact they have put themselves at risk for being labeled a "bad slut."

Strategy #3: Hook Up with a Random Guy—Drunk

Young women who want to have sex but are not in a committed relationship sometimes choose to "hook up"—to have what we used to call a one-night stand. But wait a minute—if they have sex with guys they're not committed to, won't they be slandered as "bad sluts"? Indeed they will. To mitigate this outcome, many female college students, and high school students as well, turn to a well-worn coping mechanism: alcohol. They drink excessively not only to deal with the fact that affectionless sex can be demoralizing, they also drink excessively with the hope that being drunk offers evidence that they never intended to hook up in the first place—and therefore cannot be held accountable as a "bad slut" for doing so. Hooking up while drunk is yet another strategy to hide one's effort in being sexual. If you're drunk, you appear not to have planned your hookup, and therefore you can pretend that you put no effort into it. You're exerting agency, but not really. Thus, slut-bashing and slut-shaming are intimately connected with drunken hookups. If slut-bashing and slut-shaming didn't exist, young females would be less likely to initiate sexual activity while drunk.

Let's get the numbers out of the way, since conventional wisdom is that hooking up is far more common than it actually is. At the high school level, we don't have data about hooking up, only about sexual intercourse, which often occurs within the context of committed relationships. According to the Guttmacher Institute, the average age of first intercourse is about 17 for American teenagers. At the age of 15, 20 percent have had first intercourse. At 16, a third of teens have done so, and at 17, nearly half (48 percent) of teens have had intercourse. When they arrive at college at 18, the numbers jump to 61 percent.[136]

Meanwhile, hooking up on campus is prevalent but not universal. Between two-thirds and three-quarters of college students hook up at least once during college, report Caroline Heldman, a professor of politics at Occidental College, and Lisa Wade, a professor of sociology at Occidental College. Heldman and Wade define "hooking up" as including any or all of the following: "onetime sexual encounters (a 'random'); multiple encounters, generally on the weekends, often without any contact during the week (a 'regular'); infrequent sexual encounters with an acquaintance or friend late at night (a 'booty call'); and repeat hookups with a friend that do not involve a dating relationship ('friends with benefits' or 'fuck buddies')."[137]

The ambiguity of the term "hook up" leads to a great deal of confusion—just as ambiguity over the meanings of "slut" puzzles so many of us. For this reason as well, hooking up and slut-shaming dovetail. When we hear that a young woman "hooked up" with someone, we don't quite know what occurred: Oral sex alone? Intercourse? Neither? Other? Likewise, when a girl is labeled a slut, we also don't quite know what led to her reputation. I believe it's not an accident that young females who hook up are called sluts: one ambiguity is substituted for another in a fruitless effort to make sense of what has occurred.

Of those students, male and female, who do hook up, over four years 40 percent do so three or fewer times, 40 percent do so between four to nine times, and 20 percent do so ten or more times during their college years.[138] So of the students who do hook up, the vast majority do so approximately two times a year, on average. To put things in clearer perspective: By their senior year of college, four in ten students are either virgins or have had intercourse with only one person, according to the Online College Social Life Survey of twenty-four thousand students at twenty-one universities.[139] Many college students, then, are monogamous or minimally sexually active.

Many young women claim that they aren't looking for a committed relationship, that hooking up is exactly what they want. Hanna Rosin argues in her book *The End of Men and the Rise of Women* that women in college increasingly eschew serious relationships and delay looking for a spouse to protect their future professional goals. Yet being career-oriented doesn't mean that they want emotionless sex. Anna Latimer, a literary agent, writes that when she was in college several years ago, she did not seek a romantic commitment, but she still wanted sex to "come from a loving place—a desire to enhance intimacy."[140] Erica, the twenty-one-year-old sophomore at a New England college, emailed me the link to Latimer's article. She included a note telling me that Latimer had nicely summarized her own desires, adding that "at this point in my life, I'm not looking for 'hookups' or 'relationships' but just sex with friends that I genuinely love and appreciate." But the situation Anna Latimer and Erica describe is not easy to find. Hooking up with guys they don't care much about, and who don't care about them in return, may be collateral damage on the journey to sex with intimacy.

For women who truly don't want a relationship, or at least wish to postpone being in one, "I think hooking up can definitely be looked at as an act of feminist empowerment and as a sign of gender progression," writes Julie Zeilinger in her book *A Little F'd Up*. "Stereotypically, women are supposed to be the ones trying to trap men into relationships. . . . But hook-up culture proves to the world that girls (especially teen girls) are just as horny as guys."[141] In other words, the fact that girls have sexual desires just as boys do is becoming more accepted because so many of them hook up.

However, many heterosexual young women *do* want a boyfriend, and they see hooking up as the only way to initiate a romantic relationship. One of the girls in the group of Manhattan teens I met with insists that hooking up is an essential first step toward building a relationship. She says, "You don't start a relationship unless you've hooked up. So you hope that if you keep hooking up with a guy, at a certain point he will feel connected to you and want you to be his girl. And sometimes that does happen." In her mind, if a girl never hooks up, she will never become romantically involved with anyone; therefore, hooking up is not optional.

Many girls also worry that if they're honest about their desire for a boyfriend, they may appear to be emotionally desperate. Hooking up, then, is the best they can hope for under the circumstances. They are making a rational compromise.

Meanwhile, most guys don't approach hooking up with the same attitude. They aren't making any compromises. Women's expectations, then, are one-sided, and they often lead to anxious, hurt, or confused feelings. Hooking up within the framework of the sexual double standard means that the positive aspects are overshadowed by the negative. The guys, who are more likely than the women to be reluctant to commit, call the shots.

"For many girls, hooking up is the means to an end. For most guys, hooking up is hooking up," writes Zeilinger. "Even when they are participating in hook-up culture, girls still brag when they 'get' boyfriends (because, obviously, it's an achievement, just like they 'got' a reward . . .), and they still call other girls sluts for hooking up, even if they're doing the same thing. Whereas guys brag when they hook up."[142] Zeilinger continues, noting that hooking up "is still a largely male-controlled practice. It's a guy's game, and even when we tell ourselves that we're doing it for us, for our own reasons, and that we feel good about it, guys are still in control. They are the ones who dictate that they will not be in relationships, but that they will hook up."[143]

Zeilinger's insight is echoed by the *New York Times*. Despite an optimistic headline—"Sex on Campus: She Can Play That Game, Too"—the *Times* found that sixty female University of Pennsylvania students surveyed by the paper repeatedly noted that guys at Penn controlled the foundational presumptions of hookup culture. In fact, women at college *can't* play the game that men at college do. One interviewee explained, "The girls adapt a little bit, because they stop expecting that they're going to get a boyfriend—because if that's all you're trying to do, you're going to be miserable. But at the same time, they want to, like, have contact with guys." So they hook up and "try not to get attached." The Penn students said that the many females on campus change their romantic goals from finding a boyfriend to finding a "hookup buddy"—"a guy that we don't actually really like his personality, but we think is really attractive and hot and good in bed."[144] Their expectations diminish as they realize that what they want is out of reach. They want the same sexual agency that guys have, but they discover that sexual equality does not actually exist.

Guys tend to control the direction of romantic heterosexual relationships because of the traditional belief that that's what guys are supposed to do. Rachael Robnett, a doctoral student at the University of California, Santa Cruz, together with Campbell Leaper, a psychology professor, refer to this dynamic as "benevolent sexism."[145] Although benevolent sexism (the principle that women should be protected and given special treatment) seems preferable to "hostile sexism" (the belief that women should conform to stereotypical femininity), in fact it is a mechanism for men to direct women to take a passive role within romantic relationships. Benevolent sexism reinforces the idea that women are weaker than men, even though this idea is usually wrapped up in the guise of chivalry or polite manners.[146] As a result of benevolent sexism, men overwhelmingly are the ones who initiate marriage proposals. Even students at University of California, Santa Cruz, who are known for liberal attitudes, are "driven by a desire to adhere to gender-role traditions," Robnett and Leaper write with surprise.[147] This desire enables "men's hidden power" in heterosexual relations.[148] With hookups, men likewise exercise hidden power: they determine if a sexual encounter is a one-off event or if it is the initiation of a relationship.

When I met up with Zeilinger in person, she repeated her skepticism about how wonderful hookup culture is for most young women—although she was respectful toward those who find it satisfying. "Some girls feel empowered by hooking up, and that's a great thing for them," she said. "But a lot of girls feel they *have* to hook up. The refrain is, 'You should hook up because that's how relationships develop.' It's seen as a necessary evil. We're supposed to be virginal, but at the same time no guy wants us to actually be a virgin."

Gloria, the twenty-two-year-old Latina on the West Coast, confirms that hooking up can blossom into a relationship, because it happened to her. She saw a guy she knew at a dance club in Los Angeles, and "I pursued him because I just wanted casual sex," she tells me. "We went back to his apartment, where we had oral sex and intercourse. When I woke up the next morning, I felt good about it. We continued to hook up, and we established a relationship after that, and decided that we would only hook up with each other. I don't think this was an ideal way to start a relationship, but it happens." After that relationship ended, Gloria assumed that the next man she hooked up with could also become her boyfriend, but she was mistaken. "I got really screwed over," she says.

think he took advantage of me because of our age difference. I was eighteen and he was twenty-four. He was never willing to try to have a real relationship with me. I wanted a committed relationship, and he told me that he wanted a real relationship too, but he never really acted like he did. I think he just wanted to use me for the sex, although he would tell me his feelings for me, so I couldn't understand it. For me, hooking up is with the hope for a future relationship. When you're hooking up, it's hard to hold the other person accountable because there's a sense that there's no responsibility, because it's just a hookup. There's no real commitment when it's just a hookup. When you have a relationship, you are explicitly deciding to be monogamous. But hooking up is unstable, and you never talk about your status.

Men have long misrepresented their romantic intentions, so what happened to Gloria was certainly nothing new. But never before having experienced the instability of hooking up, Gloria didn't realize that for many guys, even adults in their twenties, having casual, uncommitted sex without establishing a serious relationship is the ultimate goal.

Ella, a twenty-four-year-old student in Pennsylvania whose mother is black and whose father is white, also reports that guys pretend to consider elevating a hookup to a committed relationship just to get the woman to agree to have sex in the first place. She finds that white men are guilty of this practice for racial reasons.

A lot of white guys want to sleep with a black girl. They say it right out loud. They aren't trying to hide it. But they're nervous about going with a full-fledged black girl, so they look for someone who's half-black, like me. They sleep with a half-black girl a few times, and then they're gone. They act like they're going to commit to you, but in reality they just want the experience. For example, there was a really good-looking guy during my senior year of high school. He was a college student at [another university], and we knew each other for a few weeks. My mom worked the night shift, and he slept over one night and we slept together. Then he disappeared. He told his friend that he just wanted to sleep with a black girl, and his friend told me. This kind of thing happened to me two other times. They use me as a notch in their belt, so that they can say, "Oh, I've slept with a black girl." Thankfully that's not the majority of guys, but there are plenty who think that way.

There are also guys who don't care about my race, they just want to have sex with me because they just want to have sex. They have no intention of making it serious. They mislead me to make me think they are interested in an emotional connection. But I want the emotional part too, not just the sex.

Like Gloria, Ella is dismayed with her lack of control within the hookup scenario. The guys she hooked up with controlled the encounters. The white guys additionally held a racial advantage that, overlaid with the sexual double standard, denied Ella her agency.

Aaron, a white twenty-one-year-old male college student in California, explained to me why after hooking up he often does not feel motivated to elevate the encounter to an emotionally attached relationship. He told me that from his perspective, hookup culture breeds insecurity among females—which he finds unattractive and alienating. He says,

After hooking up, girls always ask me, "How do I compare with other girls?" They want me to compare their bodies, their posture, their voices, their personalities, the way they are in bed, everything, My roommates had a screen saver on the monitor in our living room that was a slide show of fake boobs. Usually the screensaver shows a picture of mountains or trees, but for a week my roommates had a slideshow of fake boobs. So I was with a girl, and she asked, "Do my boobs compare with the ones on the screen?" I said, "But those are fake! You're my lover, and I appreciate your body, so this shouldn't be an issue." So as soon as I said that, then she asked, "OK, so how do I compare with other girls you've hooked up with?" It was like as soon as I answered one question to make her feel secure, she had to ask another. Girls are always asking questions that basically say, "Hey, I know that you hook up with other girls, and I want to know how I compare." They always want to know, "Where am I on the scale?" They express so much insecurity! This makes me want to, I guess, detach myself from those girls. They're so needy, and also they are implying that I have been with so many girls and therefore I am in a position to judge them on a scale. It's so awkward. Why do all these girls think this way? Why can't I find a girl who *doesn't* compare herself to other girls and who doesn't want to talk about her insecurity with me?

I told Aaron that I empathized with him, because most people don't want to be intimate with someone excessively needy. But I also asked him to step back and assess the situation from the girls' point of view. I asked him to be compassionate for his sexual partners. Hooking up for them is unstable, usually one-sided, and risky in terms of managing their reputation. Their sexual reputation is in his hands. If he chooses to spread stories about their sluttiness, he can. If they want to pursue a more meaningful relationship with him but he does not, that decision is also in his hands. In many ways, then, he holds great power over the women he hooks up with. The question is not why so many of his lovers are insecure—but why would they *not* be?

It's no wonder that so many females drink to excess when they go to a party or a club where there's a chance they will find someone with whom to hook up. Drinking may be an activity that washes away insecurities. "Women drink to excess in public for many reasons, often the same reasons that men do. Sometimes people drink to excess in public as a coping mechanism," says Nicole Kubon, a social worker and an advocate for survivors of sexual assault. "If they've been victims of sexual assault previously in the same type of space, like at a party, they may drink to try to regain control of the situation. It may be an effort to convince themselves that they were not victimized or that their experience of victimization has not or will not change who they are or how they act." And what about women who have not been victimized in this way? "Beyond the standard reasons why many people drink to excess, they may also be triggered when they are in certain spaces to drink more than they should because they feel anxiety or discomfort in the situation," she explains. Drinking to excess at a party, then, may be a way for a woman to deal with the depressing, disturbing reality that hooking up—under the present conditions of benevolent sexism and the sexual double standard—is far from her romantic or sexual ideals.

"Alcohol is key to the perpetuation of hookup culture on campus. It plays a huge part in the poor decisions students often make—and later regret," writes Donna Freitas, who surveyed 2,500 college students about their sexual experiences.[149] Female Penn students told the *New York Times* that they would never hook up without drinking first "because they were for the most part too uncomfortable to pair off with men they did not know well without being drunk."[150] Nineteen-year-old Min, an Asian student, said in chapter 2 that many women on her Northeast campus equate sexualizing themselves with making a feminist statement. She adds, "Sometimes they are too wild or behave out of the confines of appropriate behavior. Sometimes they get very drunk as an excuse to be more touchy or flirtatious or to justify hooking up; they're only having sex with someone because they're not sober."

If you hook up drunk, you can always attribute your sluttiness to the influence of alcohol. You're a "good slut"—you would never just sleep with any old random guy. If not for the fact that you were wasted, you never in a million years would have given that guy over there that blow job. Hooking up drunk is a strategy to disavow agency and sexual desire—two ingredients in the definition of a "bad slut." It's easy to say, "I didn't mean to have sex; *it just happened* because I was wasted!" The drunk woman who hooks up surmises that she can't be held responsible for her allegedly slutty behavior because she was unable to police herself. Ergo, she's not really a slut. And if she is, she's the "good" kind.

When a girl or woman reports that "it just happened," writes Deborah Tolman, a developmental psychologist and the author of *Dilemmas of Desire: Teenage Girls Talk about Sexuality*, her words can be understood "as a cover story. It is a story about the necessity of girls to cover their desire. It is also a story that covers over active choice, agency, and responsibility."[151] "Oops, it just happened" erases sexual desire. Covering up desire is "unsafe and unhealthy," writes Tolman.[152] "Healthy sexuality means having sexual desire, but there is little if any safe space—physically, socially, psychologically—for these forbidden and dangerous feelings."[153]

"Girls want to get drunk because it gives them permission to have a wild side come out so that they can become slutty. They can use alcohol as an excuse," explains Jessica, the twenty-three-year-old Latina in California. But, she warns, women are not in control. "It becomes expected of you to drink because a guy will buy you drinks, and he will be persistent to get you to drink, because he thinks that if you get drunk you will do what he wants. So then it's like you *have* to drink." Mara, nineteen, agrees. "Girls want to be in a carefree situation," she says. "But also, there's a huge element of peer pressure because drinking is so prevalent" on her campus.

How does the strategy of getting drunk while hooking up backfire? The same way the other sexual containment strategies do. No matter how much effort a girl or young woman exerts to control her image as slutty in a "good way," invariably it will be translated as slutty in a "bad way." Min tells me about a popular girl in her high school who was well liked and regarded as "pretty" and "cute" until she hooked up drunk.

One night she got drunk at a party and made out with two boys, and I think maybe "threw herself" on two others. After that, she became known as the "messy slut" and was slut-shamed by both genders. Apparently there was a discussion in the boys' locker room where it was agreed that she was "no longer attractive" and a boy who was seen walking with her into a room was chided by his friends. The slut-bashing eventually blew over, but she still had a reputation as a "messy bitch" because she frequently got drunk. After the incident, I talked about it with a male friend of mine who defended people's calling her "sloppy" because of her drunkenness. He disagreed with me that the term "sloppy" was gendered or linked to the word "slut."

Min's classmate violated one of the most important rules of "good slut" femininity: she expressed desperation and neediness by "throwing herself" at boys. Even though she was drunk, her actions were held against her. Note that her peers used the adjectives "messy" and "sloppy" to refer to her. We know from its etymology that the word "slut" historically has been linked with notions of uncleanliness; for six hundred years, "slut" conveyed a woman who could not or did not keep herself tidy. Even in the twenty-first century, "slut" continues to refer to a female who lacks the necessary control to keep herself "clean."

Hooking up drunk also backfires at the level of physical pleasure. If a woman thinks that her sexual encounter will be worth it, despite its limitations, because at the very least she will have an orgasm, she may be in for a surprise. Research shows that women are much less likely to have an orgasm during casual hookups than in committed relationships. Men aren't focused on pleasing women in hookups, explains Paula England, a New York University sociologist who oversaw the Online College Social Life Survey, because of "the lingering sexual double standard, which sometimes causes men to disrespect women precisely for hooking up with them."[154] She found that only about 40 percent of women had an orgasm during their last hookup involving intercourse, while 80 percent of men did. Approximately three-quarters of women in a committed relationship, on the other hand, had an orgasm the last time they had sex. Because women are still stigmatized for having casual sex, says England, they "are not feeling very free in these casual contexts to say what they want and need."[155] England's statistics were confirmed by a similar study led by Justin R. Garcia at the Kinsey Institute at Indiana University.[156]

We have no data on how many hookups involve intercourse, how many involve only oral sex, and so on. But anecdotally, girls and women say that random hookups, especially when they're drunken, are fellatio affairs. When hooking up, females are much more likely to give males oral sex than to receive it. Aaron confirms that the guys in his peer group receive but do not give oral sex when they are hooking up. "The girls I know rarely receive oral from the other guys," he tells me, adding that for him, "it's part of foreplay. But most guys will say, 'OK, I'm trying to get my dick sucked tonight,' and they don't even want to learn the girl's name."

One Penn student told the *New York Times* that during her freshman and sophomore years, her sexual encounters often ended with fellatio because she always drank to excess. She said "that usually by the time she got back to a guy's room, she was starting to sober up and didn't want to be there anymore, and giving the guy oral sex was an easy way to wrap things up and leave."[157] Repeatedly in my interviews, the subject of one-sided oral sex came up within the context of drunken hookups. In my group conversation with the Manhattan teenage girls, we discussed the fact that even in high school, girls are drinking to excess at parties. When they hook up with boys, "the boys are really benefitting," says Kaitlyn, sixteen.

Sometimes I feel like hooking up with a guy is like going over to his house to do his homework for him. You feel like you're not benefitting from it. Even though I do want to hook up, it's not about getting off. When I'm hooking up with a guy, I feel like I have a boyfriend for two hours. It's an emotional thing. But for him, it's often not emotional. For him, it's beneficial because he knows that by the end of the night he will have come. If I feel like I'm going to his house to do homework for him, than what really am I getting out of it? If it's a onetime thing where I'm doing something because I just want to be with someone for the evening and it's obvious that that person only cares about getting off, that's not a good situation. If I can tell that the guy likes me as a person, then that feels really good.

But they don't really care about whether the girl gets off. Once they come, they're done. They don't want to keep hooking up after that point. There's maybe a 2 percent chance they will make any effort [to give the girl sexual pleasure]. They won't go down on a girl if it's a onetime thing. Also if they don't want to feel like you're doing their homework for them, then they will try. Or they want the power of making you get off because they think it's hot, or because it will help them get off. But in general, if they know you're going to give them a blow job anyway, they won't go down on you.

Nicole, sixteen, agrees with Kaitlyn, adding, "Girls go to parties all the time and get drunk and hook up with guys and give them blow jobs. But boys don't do that. Boys don't just go to a party and go down on a girl and then not see the girl again. If a boy goes down on a girl, it generally means that he's in love with her, or that they are in a relationship." The other girls in the room agree. "It's only equal when you're in a relationship," Nicole concludes. "It's not equal when you're just hooking up."

A young woman who hooks up drunk is *lucky* if the worst that happens to her is humiliation or an unsatisfying consensual sexual encounter. The worst way this strategy backfires is with sexual assault. Hooking up is an inherently ambiguous situation to begin with, since there are no clear parameters of what sexual activity or level of commitment may be involved. When alcohol is added to the equation, the boundaries of consent and coercion are blurred. Sexual refusal that may be obvious when both parties are sober becomes less clear in the fog of intoxication. Males who are predatory or severely compromised in their judgment can interpret a female unable to give consent as a female who would give consent if she could.

Sexual assault on campus is frighteningly common. According to the US Department of Justice's Campus Sexual Assault Study of 2007, 13.7 percent of women have been the victim of at least one completed sexual assault while at college. Over half of these women were unable to give consent because they were incapacitated, primarily by alcohol, and nearly all the assaults were carried out by someone the victim knew and not by a stranger.[158] Drinking increases the likelihood that a hookup will lead to sexual assault. The problem is most acute during a college student's freshman and sophomore years. Female college students in their first two years surveyed by William F. Flack Jr., a psychologist at Bucknell University, and his colleagues reported that 48 percent of all unwanted sexual activities took place during a hookup, and 81 percent of all incidents of unwanted sexual activities involved alcohol.[159]

One Penn student told the *Times* that during her freshman year, she went to a party with a boy who lived on her floor, drank too much, and told him she wanted to go back to the dorm. Instead, he brought her to his room "and had sex with her while she drifted in and out of consciousness. She woke up with her head spinning. The next day, not sure what to think about what had happened, she described the night to her friends as though it were a funny story: I was so drunk, I fell asleep while I was having sex!" Humor may have been the only way she could have attempted to seize control over this nonconsensual sexual act and also stave off development of a slutty reputation. She explained to the *Times* that when a girl has been drinking, "Guys assume that the default answer is always yes."[160]

What young women perceive as a protective measure ends up being the opposite: it renders them unsafe. Being drunk at a party to show she's nonchalantly sexy is confused by men with her being willing to have sex with anyone, even if she says no or can't say no because she is too drunk, or even blacked-out. Girls and women who drink excessively must recognize that they are putting themselves at risk whether or not they plan to hook up, although they never are at fault if they are assaulted. If they are unable to control their behavior, including the ability to affirmatively give consent, they may be dismissed as "bad sluts"—and many guys believe that it's fair game to coerce or assault a "bad slut."

We see that the three sexual containment strategies are doomed. Wearing sexy outfits, sexting but not actually having sex, and having sex but only when drunk may seem like shrewd ways to attract sexual attention without appearing slutty. But each strategy cascades into the next: when a young woman wears sexually provocative clothes, guys feel entitled to ask—even demand—that she send them sexual images. Once she's complied, guys want what they see as the next step: a hookup. Meg McInerney of the Arts Effect points out that when a girl sexts, she raises expectations of what she will do in person, in real life. She says, "After sending pornographic images and sexual texts, how do they tell a guy in person, 'I don't really want you to touch me' or 'No, I don't actually want to give you a blowjob'? When intimacy is at a high level electronically, it becomes much harder to say no when they're in person."

This isn't to suggest that young women lack sexual desire, and that they're just going through the motions with no agency at all. Many freely express their interest in sexual activity—but on their terms. Yet they can't have sexual activity on their terms, under their control, under the present conditions of the sexual double standard and benevolent sexism. Thus, their sexual agency is severely compromised.

CHAPTER 6

"Bad Slut" Coping Mechanisms

Few who have been slut-bashed—or who have witnessed slut-bashing—go unscathed. For girls in middle school or high school, the experience is traumatic and their actions in the immediate aftermath often are severe. My interviewees who were slut-bashed in adolescence tended to go in one of two divergent directions: either they became excessively sexually active—even if they hadn't been sexual before they acquired their reputation—or they shut down sexually. Both responses are dangerous for girls' physical and emotional health. Other girls developed eating disorders or turned to drugs. Tragically, a number of slut-bashed adolescent girls have taken their lives.

As noted in chapter 3, nearly half of girls in grades seven through twelve experience sexual harassment in some form, mostly verbal harassment, according to the American Association of University Women. This means that nearly half the female student population in middle schools and high schools across the country may to some extent turn to unhealthy behaviors in an attempt to cope with their harassment. The girls in the other half are hyperaware that they could be slut-bashed too, even if it hasn't happened yet, and therefore they may also turn to similar behaviors. After all, once a girl is labeled a slut, the thinking goes, she may as well act like one—she's got nothing to lose. And since *all* girls are potential "sluts," they *all* may come to believe they have nothing to lose.

College-age women, meanwhile, also may engage in very harmful behavior that can have devastating consequences. They learn to manipulate their sexual history as a protective mechanism. A few years older and wiser now that they're out of high school, they may believe that they're gaming the slut-shaming system. They proceed in what appears to be a normal and age-appropriate sexual development trajectory, but they become anxious about being perceived as slutty; as a result, they don't use contraceptives, or they lie about their sexual history, even to health care professionals, endangering their own health.

We must recognize girls' and young women's coping mechanisms not as evidence that young females today are hopelessly wild or misguided, or that their parents deserve an F in child-rearing. Rather, we must take a step back and recognize that their responses are symptoms of the sexual double standard and the culture of slut-shaming. We need to listen to what girls and young women are trying to tell us:

that being shamed as a slut—particularly in the digital age of wall-to-wall humiliation—makes their world a living hell and that they will do anything to make the pain go away. In many cases, they turn to coping behaviors to manage guilty feelings because they may believe they deserve to be publicly humiliated. Those of us who have girls or young women in our lives need to show them that no matter what they've done sexually, they do not deserve this label.

If You Can't Shed It, Own It

A common reaction to being slut-bashed is to become extremely sexually active with multiple partners. On the face of it, this response is counterintuitive. If your classmates are calling you a slut, wouldn't it be logical to protect your reputation by behaving in a manner that is antithetical to sluttiness? Yet this is not the way slut-bashed girls approach the problem. From their perspective, they can't control being called a slut. Their reputation is being shaped by others. But there is one thing they can control—their sexual behavior. By "owning" the reputation, they assert that they "own" their bodies—that no one, no matter what names they hurl, can take their bodies away from them. Girls who follow this line of reasoning misinterpret feminist notions of empowerment. They are not truly taking ownership over their sexuality because they are behaving defensively in a highly pressured environment of sexual inequality; they are not free agents with real choices. Once again, we see that the sexual double standard restricts girls' choices, and that the act of fighting back is itself constrained because it too is conducted within the sphere of the sexual double standard.

The satiric 2010 movie *Easy A* explored the phenomenon of "owning" the "slut" reputation—even when the so-called slut is not sexually active. Olive, played by Emma Stone, is under the radar and desperately wants the kids at school to notice her. In real life, any student who looks like Emma Stone would be impossible to ignore; despite this ludicrous premise, the film is actually quite astute. Olive lies about losing her virginity, and although her plan isn't for the lie to spread around school, she's not displeased when that occurs. "I gotta admit," Olive says, "I kinda liked being on the map."

To continue being the center of attention, Olive creates a slutty alter ego and embraces the identity. As her gay male friend Brandon says, "You're not even a real slut—but you're acting like one." Brandon concocts his own reputation-management scheme. He wants the kids in school to think he's straight so that they will stop tormenting him, so he asks Olive to pretend that the two of them have had sex, and she agrees. Brandon wins: he gains status as heterosexual and masculine. Olive loses: her "slut" reputation is sealed, and everyone thinks she is a "dirty skank." Olive decides, "So fine. I will be the dirtiest skank they will ever see." She goes to school dressed like Miley Cyrus in a bustier and tights with no skirt or pants. Soon every guy who needs a boost in status asks her for the right to tell the kids at school that he's had sex with her. Olive agrees, but each guy has to give her a gift card in exchange for their pseudosex. Her mocking narration makes it clear she thinks the sexual double standard is absurd and that the boys' sexual desperation is ridiculous.

Olive's fake identity goes too far when a boy who's been having an affair with the school guidance counselor lies and says that his sexually transmitted disease is from Olive. She chooses to allow the lie to stand, protecting the female guidance counselor, who risks losing her job and marriage. This being a Hollywood movie with A-list actors, all's well that ends well, with a romantic conclusion. A hunky classmate played by Penn Badgley doesn't believe the slut stories and saves Olive as the two ride off on a lawnmower.

Easy A portrays the very real coping mechanism of "owning" a "slut" label. As with many real girls:

1. Olive would rather be known as a slut than not be known at all.
2. Once she's known as a slut, she plays the role to the hilt.
3. Her identity as slut is necessary for her community; it supports masculine status. It also covers up an adulterous affair.
4. The slut is sacrificed to protect everyone else.
5. Her identity as a nonslut is restored only through a monogamous heterosexual relationship.

However, there are two crucial differences between Olive's fictional situation and those of actual girls. First, Olive has a lot of parental support. Her parents do not make her feel ashamed. They openly talk about sexuality, and they don't appear concerned about their daughter's reputation. If teenage girls had the same level of support at home, they would be less likely to resort to unhealthy coping mechanisms.

Second, in real life, girls who "own" the label don't fake having sex. They really do have sex. As a result, they don't get to ride off into the sunset. Olive, you see, remains a virgin despite her wild reputation—a false note in an otherwise remarkably perceptive script. Hollywood reinforces the sexual double standard because the audience knows that Olive isn't *really* having sex.

In the real world, girls who "own" the label end up having sex that is unhealthy. Please note that I am not arguing that sex is unhealthy, or even that sex among adolescents is unhealthy. Rather, I'm arguing that sex sought out for reasons disconnected from affection, intimacy, emotional pleasure, or physical pleasure is unhealthy.

Erica, the white twenty-one-year-old college sophomore, decided in the tenth grade that since everyone *thought* she was sexually active, despite the fact that she was not, she *should be* sexually active, but on her terms. She explained to me how her decision to embrace the label through her behavior spiraled out of control:

I started to think I should act a certain way. I started making out with people. I started hooking up with a number of guys. I wore leopard push-up bras. I decided to "own" the label. I think it was a normal reaction to the situation I was in. There was so much pressure on us [girls] to show our value through our sexuality, so then we think we need to defend the label. I thought I was deriving power from having lots of sex. Also, girls were labeled either "prudes" or "sluts." If you're a girl and you want to have sex, the only thing you know is to be slutty.

When I graduated from high school, I didn't even know you *could* be in control of your sex life. I thought that the girls my age just had a lot of casual sex that they might not have wanted. I thought that that's just what teenage girls did. I didn't know I could choose when, why, or how.

I was having sex with whomever, however. I removed my emotions from it. During one four-month period, I slept with twelve guys. I was successful in proving to myself that sex and emotions could be separated. It was exciting at first. Nobody was pulling at my emotions, which felt great. But after four months, I didn't feel in control anymore. It wasn't fun anymore. It became negative, and also I didn't have anyone I could talk to about it.

There was a turning point where I had sex with someone who was really drunk, and it was very scary because I had no control. He was over six feet tall, and he overpowered me. I consented to the initial act, but then I wanted to get out of it, but I couldn't. He was too big and strong and drunk. I tried to get him to stop, but he wouldn't.

Lacking models of healthy sexuality, Erica believed that having sex with multiple partners in a short period of time was what she was expected to do. Although she "owned" her label to assert control, in fact she had minimal control, because she was ignorant of other sexual options. When she was physically overpowered in an act of sexual assault, she literally lost control. She had framed her sexual activity within a slut-shaming narrative, the only narrative she knew, which closed off the possibility of choosing to say no or yes and meaning it.

Elizabeth, a white twenty-nine-year-old educator who grew

up in New York City and now lives in the Southeast, was a very early developer—she first menstruated at age ten—and became known as a slut beginning in the seventh grade, when her family moved upstate and she was the new girl in school. One girl in her grade was a ringleader who "started a campaign" against Elizabeth, who stood out because she wore a bra and wore fashionable clothes and eye makeup. "I wasn't trying to present myself as sexual," she says. "I was just interested in fashion. I loved Madonna's look." The girl yelled out "slut" to Elizabeth in the school hallways, egging on her friends to do the same.

Like Erica, Elizabeth became known as a slut even though she had zero sexual experience, but after being known as a slut she became sexually active. Unlike Erica, she had only one sexual partner. Nevertheless, she too had sex to prove a point, and as with Erica, she was pressured into sex she did not want.

Elizabeth became sexually active when she was in the eighth grade with Robert, a fellow eighth-grader and the son of a woman in the community with whom she had become very close. Elizabeth told me that Robert's mother became her "surrogate mother" because even though Elizabeth lived with her parents, she felt estranged from them emotionally. Her father had been emotionally abusive to Elizabeth and to her mother, and Elizabeth started to realize that her family was unbalanced. She became good friends with Robert's younger sister and started sleeping over at their house, which is when she started having sex with Robert.

"I was definitely sexually curious," she says, and "in some ways, maybe I felt that the label gave me the license to experiment, whereas if I hadn't been called a slut, I would have been too scared to be sexually active even if I had wanted to be. If you're scared of getting labeled then you don't do [sexual] things, but if you're already labeled then it doesn't matter." Elizabeth thought of herself as sexually empowered, but she had never been properly educated about what "sexual empowerment" really means.

I listened to a college radio station and heard Riot Grrrl music, and I had some feminist punk ideals. I tried to piece together an empowered sexuality, although I have to say that the sex I had was not very empowering. I was not in touch with what I wanted or needed, and we were drinking, and we were so young. I remember feeling like intercourse was a big step, and I expressed reservations about it, but then it happened very quickly. He and I had sex four or five times. I'm not sure about consent. I definitely consented to foreplay but not to intercourse. I was on the fence about intercourse. I would say things like, "I'm not really sure how I feel about this." He pressured me. I don't remember him overpowering me, but he definitely pressured me. I don't think he was even aware of it.

At school, Robert did not acknowledge Elizabeth, but the kids were aware that the two of them had had sex. "I didn't expect him to date me necessarily, but the fact that he didn't even acknowledge me at school made me think of myself as a slut." Elizabeth told an adult friend that she was having sex with Robert, and the friend used the word "rape." Elizabeth was confused. "I thought rape was something that happened by a stranger in an alleyway. I didn't want that label for my experience. I didn't know what language to use. Today I would say that the sex was nonconsensual but not rape." The story that she had been raped got around school, and her surrogate mother found out. She called Elizabeth, angry not only that she'd had sex with her son, but also that she was supposedly spreading a rumor that Robert was a rapist, although Elizabeth tried to explain that she didn't try to spread the rumor; the story was being spread around by other kids. "So then this woman who been so supportive of me was angry with me, and my support network totally crumbled out from under me."

Elizabeth had had sex with Robert because she'd been labeled already, so she figured she could do no wrong; how could things get worse than being called a slut? Yet indeed they did. She had nonconsensual sex, became the subject of yet another rumor, and lost the support of someone important to her who had offered stability. In addition, she believed that having sex would dovetail with her feminist vision of "empowered sexuality." The idea that having sex ipso facto is "empowering" led her, as it has led so many others, astray. As we have seen repeatedly, sexual activity within a framework of the sexual double standard and sexual inequality can undermine one's power.

Cynthia, a white twenty-one-year-old student in Pennsylvania, became known as a slut after she was molested by her brother for two years beginning when she was eleven. He is four years older than she. "It was physical abuse that usually was not sexual, but sometimes he also dry-humped me and masturbated in front of me. But mostly it was him physically beating me up," Cynthia tells me matter-of-factly. "I always fought back. I thought this was normal brother-sister fighting, so I never talked about it."

No one would have known except that when she was in the eighth grade, Cynthia confided in her school counselor, and the full extent of the abuse came out. Charges were brought against Cynthia's brother, including molestation charges. Cynthia and her parents tried to keep the charges private, but her brother was sent to juvenile detention for a year and a half. Once his friends knew why, everyone knew.

The gossip started in ninth grade, she tells me. "Lots of rumors went around that I was having sex with my brother, which was not true. Random people would come up to me in the hallway at school and say to me, 'Didn't your brother rape you?' and then just keep walking."

Although the kids at school were aware of the charges, they didn't know all the details. But in the eleventh grade, a girl who had previously been Cynthia's best friend "revealed everything to a lot of people." I asked Cynthia to speculate why her friend had punctured her privacy. "I think she was upset with me because we weren't friends anymore, and the reason was that she fell into a crowd that did drugs, and I didn't want to hang out with druggies. She might also have been upset with herself too for being with them, and she was also offended that I didn't want to be with her anymore." Cynthia added, "She did the worst form of bullying I ever encountered. Because of her, people called me 'slut,' 'whore,' and 'skank.' They did it right to my face. They said it right at me in the hallways. And as the stories went around, the information got changed. The story became that I had slept with my brother, and that I had wanted it and enjoyed it."

Cynthia reacted the way so many girls in her situation do: "I tried to embrace the label." She continues,

kind of tried to take the slutty personality and work with it and make it cool. In a way, I took on the role of being promiscuous. I tried to be what people expected of me. I started hanging out with girls that other girls considered skanky. I decided to be a slut and be what people were saying about me. I had sex with four random older guys who were acquaintances. I was fourteen and they were eighteen or nineteen. I just met them and hooked up with them purposely so that I could lose my virginity. The first guy I approached told me that he never slept with virgins, so I purposely went and slept with someone else first, although I never even hooked up with him. At the time, I felt cool. I tried to appear cool, so I talked about my sexual experiences with my friends, which made me seem experienced and slutty. My new friends looked up to me as someone who was experienced.

I slept around to try to take back the power and control that had been taken from me when I was abused and when people called me names. It was really just about me trying to be in control. But then I realized—what am I doing? I wasn't respecting my body. I never got any physical or emotional pleasure. I didn't have an orgasm once, although they all did. If it's a one-night stand, the guy doesn't care if the girl gets off. It's not in his interest to care. I did like the power and control, but nothing else.

When Cynthia embraced the label, she received no physical or emotional pleasure. Every girl and young woman I spoke with who embraced the "slut" label to cope with her reputation ended up having sex that, for lack of a better word, was "bad." Not every sexual encounter was bad, to be sure. But ultimately these sexual relationships were bad because the girls and women ended up assaulted, coerced, or used. Sex that is intended to prove a point rarely does.

The Disappearing Slut

Having a lot of sex is one way to exert control. Another method is bodily deprivation. After Elizabeth embraced her reputation by having sex with Robert, she developed an eating disorder. "I connect it with my confused sexual awakening," she explains.

I made a conscious decision to be skinny. All of a sudden I started to feel really uncomfortable in my body. I thought I needed to look perfect. There was also so much pressure at school to be perfect. I was a very good student, but I wanted to be perfect at everything. And at the same time, I felt rejected by Robert because he wouldn't even acknowledge me in the hallway at school after we had sex, even before the rumor went around that he had raped me. I never thought I looked right, and I had trouble looking at myself in the mirror. I never felt that my body was attractive or beautiful. So I got really controlling about it.

Elizabeth first exhibited anorexic behavior. Then she turned to bulimic behavior. Five feet tall, she was down to eighty-nine pounds at her lowest point, although she never had to be hospitalized. "I think I was looking to create boundaries. The behavior gave me a sense of control over my body that was difficult to come by not only because of my sexual experiences but also because of the controlling dynamics in my household, and I didn't really have anyone to help me," she tells me. "I didn't have that support—not from my own parents and not even from my surrogate mother."

Elizabeth made a second conscious decision: not to explore her lesbian sexual desire. "If I hadn't been called a slut, I would have been queer in high school. But being labeled a slut put me in a heterosexual box. I did not want to be called a slut and also a 'dyke'—that would have been just too much. I didn't date girls until I was twenty-one, and I know that I would have done it sooner if I hadn't been labeled."

Refusing to eat is not only a method of controlling one's body. It is also a way to signal "I'm not sexual." Although being slender is equated with being sexy, being skeletal (by the standards of most people) is not. Also, the refusal to eat is a refusal of bodily pleasure, and therefore it is a rejection of one's sexuality. In some respects, developing an eating disorder is the opposite of "owning" a "slut" label because it projects an asexual persona. And since Elizabeth also decided to ignore her lesbian sexual desire, she crushed her sexuality doubly.

Abigail, a white twenty-one-year-old student who grew up in upstate New York, developed an eating disorder after she was labeled a slut when she was a junior in high school.

The kids were fascinated by my spiraling down. I was well liked, but people were just fascinated. This was a small town with no distractions, so it was like I was their soap opera. I'm five foot two, and I got down to ninety-one pounds. My body shut down and I was hospitalized. But in my senior year, I snapped back and ended the disordered eating, although I was clearly troubled. I did not sexualize myself at all. I always wore large, baggy clothes. The truth is that because I suffered from having the eating disorder, the 'slut' reputation didn't bother me as much as it might have. I then had other things to worry about.

Some girls also take drugs. Mia, a white twenty-nine-year-old woman living in Nevada, was harassed "incessantly" as a slut during her middle school years, even though "I was not sexually active." The entire grade of girls turned against her, she speculates, because she was a cheerleader and was considered popular and pretty with a curvy but athletic body and blond hair. In the summer before seventh grade, there was a party and everyone was talking about sex. The conversation went like this:

"Oh, I'm not a virgin; are you a virgin?"

"Of course I'm not a virgin."

"Nobody was telling the truth," Mia points out dryly, "because we were all virgins. So then they get to me and ask, 'Are you a virgin?' and I say, 'Of course I'm not a virgin.' So then they say, 'Who with?' and I led them to think it was my guy friend who lived down the street with me." A week later, when seventh grade started, word got around that Mia was having sex. One girl wrote a petition saying that Mia was a slut and deserved to die. She went to all the girls in the grade during lunch to sign it—over two hundred signatures. Mia still can't understand why the girl was so extremely aggressive. "She just wanted to create drama," she says.

When the school administration found out about the petition, everyone who signed was punished with after-school detention, which led to a backlash, and Mia was physically beaten up. "I'd be walking home from school, and a group of four girls would punch me. They also would do it in the locker room during gym. I was their punching bag," she recalls.

Mia fell into a deep depression. She turned to drugs, starting in the seventh grade. "I was hanging out with kids in high school and high school dropouts. I knew them from the neighborhood. I used ecstasy, acid, pot, and a little cocaine. I'd been beaten up on the way home from school, and I was crying, and this older guy came up to me and said, 'Have you ever smoked pot before? Because you really look like you could use some.' So I went with him to his friend's, and that's how the whole thing started. I enjoyed doing drugs because they were a great escape, but also I wanted to be part of a group that accepted me, that wanted me, and that didn't beat me up." Mia hung out with them until the end of her junior year of high school, at which point she graduated early and moved away to college.

Mia's new friends were sexually active, but—ironically—she was not for many years. As a result of her experience, she explains, "I've had problems with touch. Even today I have a sort of bubble around me, almost a phobia, with any kind of touch—even a hug or someone touching my arm." While she does now have sex, she elaborates that her issue is "more with everyday touching or cuddling or hugging. Being beaten up at school conditioned me to not want physical contact."

Throughout high school, after she had been slut-bashed, Mia also wore baggy clothing and refused to wear makeup. "The word 'slut' completely transformed my life," she says. "I had been an early developer and I was very physically fit, so I had a very good body. But I wanted to look tomboyish. I did not want to draw attention to myself. I did not want to be seen as sexual at all. I wore big, baggy jeans so that no one could see the outline of my legs. I wore men's medium or large T-shirts. It was like I was saying, 'Please don't look at me!' I have naturally blond hair, but I started dying it black. I've been dying it ever since; I never went back to blond."

Today, Mia has to dress professionally for her corporate career, but she never wears skirts or dresses. "I dress in a guarded way" is how she describes her adult style. "I don't want to attract attention. I still have a good body, but I don't like to show it."

When a woman is so profoundly uncomfortable with her body that she refuses to eat, shuts down her natural and developmentally appropriate sexual urges, takes drugs to escape the harshness of her life, does not allow even people she's close with to embrace her, or deliberately hides her body, something is severely wrong. These are among the short-term and long-term consequences of being labeled a slut.

Lying About the Number

College-age women, whether or not they personally have been singled out as a slut, tell me the consequences of feeling ashamed of their sexuality. Many recognize that the easiest and best way to avoid being called a slut is to lie about their sexual history. They lie not because they are untrustworthy people, or because they have a pathological problem. They lie because under the circumstances, it is the smartest, shrewdest way to navigate the sexual double standard. Lying in their circumstance is rational and understandable.

In the 2011 movie *What's Your Number?*, Anna Faris plays Ally Darling, a woman in her thirties desperate to ensure that her number of sexual partners never exceeds twenty. She has read a magazine article stating that women whose number is over twenty have little chance of marrying, and she's terrified. The problem is that she's already had twenty different sexual partners. She decides to go through her list of ex-boyfriends, looking them up one by one, hoping that one could become her future husband. If she marries someone she's dated in the past, she figures, her lifetime number will never exceed twenty. By the end of the movie, she comes to her senses and realizes that none of her previous boyfriends is right for her, and she ends up with number twenty-one.

Women college-age and older express the same terror Ally Darling does over their number. One of the Penn students interviewed by the *New York Times* regarding college hookup culture refused to tell the reporter the number of people she had slept with because even though her real name was not used in the article she still didn't want the number to appear in print.[161] Her anxiety was so great that she would not even say her number aloud in a completely anonymous context. I found the same distress among my interviewees.

"I have a bad feeling about my number, but it's external, not internal. The number is getting higher," says Vanessa, a white twenty-one-year-old student. "The other day I asked a guy friend, someone who's really cool, if he thought I was a slut. He said, 'You're not a slut, but you have a slutty number.' He said it jokingly, but it made me feel bad. He said, 'You don't seem like a double-digit girl!' He wasn't trying to hurt my feelings."

She continues, "Almost everyone lies about their number. In my mind, there's no such thing as an ideal number. But in terms of what most people think, the ideal for either a guy or a girl is between four and six. If you're a guy, your number shouldn't be lower than four, and if you're a girl, seven seems like too much. Also, guys tell me that they don't want to be with a virgin, because they say that a virgin will get too emotionally attached. So the preferred number for a girl is one or two."

Since her awareness of her number is causing her so much unease, I asked Vanessa if perhaps she should stop keeping track. Maybe not knowing would make her feel better about herself. It turns out that my suggestion is completely untenable, because women (and men, as we will see) can't stop themselves from keeping count. Besides, she told me that it's *worse* not to keep track. The implication is "Like, wow, you've had sex with so many people that you don't even know your number anymore!" she explained. "I have a friend who keeps a list on her BlackBerry of everyone she's ever made out with, although in my circle, generally blow jobs [alone] are not counted in 'the number.' In high school, girls are more eager to please, so they give blow jobs, but in college, at least in my circle, that's not done as much."

So if oral sex alone does not get counted in "the number," what does? Unsurprisingly, women tend to be as restrictive as possible so that their number will remain as low as possible. Heterosexual vaginal intercourse gets counted. Oral sex and—yes, this is going to sound strange—anal sex are not counted. In one large-scale survey, approximately 71 percent of adolescents considered themselves virgins even after having oral sex, and 16 percent considered themselves virgins after anal sex.[162] Therefore, when a woman answers "What's your number?," chances are that she is excluding everything that's not traditional heterosexual intercourse. Even guys play this game. A University of Texas alum told his college paper, "I usually give the vaginal sex number first, but if asked, I'll give the oral number. Oral sex can't get you pregnant, so it's not that big a deal."[163] These discrepancies are not surprising since the definition of "sex" is far from uniform. Researchers at the Kinsey Institute asked nearly six hundred students, "Would you say you 'had sex' with someone if the most intimate behavior you engaged in was . . . ?" and found that there is no general agreement regarding which sexual acts aside from penile-vaginal intercourse constitute "having sex." Only 40 percent of respondents said that oral sex counts as "having sex," while 81 percent of respondents said anal intercourse means "having sex."[164]

Aaron, the white twenty-one-year-old college student in California, revealed that many guys also have insecurity regarding their number. "The number" was one of the first things he asked me about when I told him that I was interviewing young women about their sexuality. He wanted to know what kinds of numbers I was hearing. I told him the range I'd heard at that point—from several to the mid-twenties, with a few outliers. He audibly breathed with relief. "I feel so much better knowing that," he said. "My number is in the mid-twenties. Except for the guys at the fraternity, nobody talks about this, so I don't really know."

Aaron continued that at his fraternity, the guys rank each other by their number. He ranks number two, "right behind my cousin, who keeps track of the girls he's been with in a little leather notebook. He's very obsessive about his number. But I reject the number concept." Aaron is embarrassed to tell me that he "used to judge girls based on their number." He believed that a woman's number should never exceed four. "I don't know how I came up with the number four, which is kind of arbitrary, but that was the number I decided on." But then he realized two things. "Sometimes I'm with a girl for months, and another time I'm with a girl only one time," yet each counts as one notch on his total number. That didn't sit right with him.

Also, Aaron recognized that it's not possible for guys' numbers to be higher than women's numbers. "If I'm making out with lots of girls then obviously they're doing the same thing," he explained. "If my number keeps going up, then girls' numbers have to keep going up too. For the math to work, the numbers have to go up for guys *and* girls. It's not like one girl is hooking up with all the guys, and I'm assuming that there's the same number of lesbians as gay men, more or less. So once I started thinking about the numbers that way, I stopped judging girls." Although some individual women or men have sex with more partners than others, his overall point is sound: it's not fair or realistic to presume that women's numbers will always be lower than men's numbers.

Unfortunately, many college-age women tell me that the men in their lives make relationship decisions based on the number of the women they're interested in. Gloria, the twenty-two-year-old Latina student, tells me that before she started dating her current boyfriend, she hooked up with another guy while they attended a skiing trip during their school's winter break. Her current boyfriend was on the same trip and suspected what had occurred. Before they started dating, he asked Gloria if his suspicions were correct. "I lied and said no, because I knew that if I had said yes, he would have thought that I hook up all the time, and he wouldn't have wanted to date me," she explained. But a week later, her boyfriend asked her again, and this time she told him the truth and admitted her reasons for lying. Her boyfriend agreed with her. He would not have wanted to date her had he known the truth from the outset. Yet now that they were dating, he realized that Gloria's previous hookup didn't really matter, and he didn't want to break up with her because of it. What will she do in the future when she's asked about her number? I asked. "I understand that there could be potential consequences if I went above a certain number," Gloria told me, "although I don't know what that certain number is. I'm sure to some people two is too many, and to other people ten is too many."

Many boyfriends reject their girlfriends because they believe that their number is too high. Erica tells me about a "regular hookup guy, not a boyfriend," who knew that she had hooked up a great deal during her first semester at college. A few weeks after they started sleeping together, he told her, "This isn't working. I've slept with five people in my whole life, and you've slept with five people *I know.*" So he broke up with her.

Similarly, Ella, the twenty-four-year-old student in Pennsylvania whose mother is black and whose father is white, dated a Chinese American guy during her sophomore year who told her that he wasn't looking for a relationship, he just wanted to have regular sex with her. She agreed to see him with this condition. But after they had been together for two months, "he told me that I wasn't girlfriend material because I had been with ten guys. I couldn't believe he said that because his number was also ten!" Ella explains that her boyfriend apparently had looked up information on the Internet about "the number," and based on what he read, he concluded that her number was too high.

He compared me with Chinese women, and said that they didn't sleep around as much, that their number is lower than mine, or at least that is what he thought was true. I had never heard anyone talk like that before, so I didn't know what to say. First of all, why was it OK that his number was ten but not OK that I had the same number? Also, I told him that from my point of view, most of the guys I'd been with had used me, so it didn't seem fair to take them seriously as part of my number, and that he should have been bothered about the fact that they had used me, not about the fact that they added to my number. But he was going to use me too, so he didn't care.

Ella puts the number in a context of appropriate behavior. In her mind, the number is not important; it is the quality of the relationships that should count.

Jasmine, the black and Latina twenty-year-old student on the West Coast, observes that "the number" is not only a method of judging others. The reason people ask each other for their number, she tells me, is that "it's a justification system. If you know someone is more active and your number is lower, then you can think, 'Oh, I'm not that bad.' It's a way for the person asking the question to feel better about themselves." She is bisexual, so "the number" enables her to situate herself in relation to both male and female partners.

Jasmine previously had admitted to me that she herself had lied by giving partners a false low number. "So you're messing up their justification system," I told her.

"I've only lied two times to guys who asked me for my number and I worried they thought I was some sleazy whore," she responded. OK, fair enough. Who could blame her?

"What number is too high?" I asked.

Jasmine offered the highest number ranges of anyone I'd spoken with. "Unfortunately it does vary by gender," she prefaced. "For a male partner, I'd say that over forty is too high. For a female partner, I'd say that over twenty is too high," she said, adding that the numbers are "arbitrary." She continued, "I would have a problem with a woman with a high number. If I had a female partner with a number in the twenties, on the one hand I would be a little impressed but I would at the same time have judgment against her." Jasmine is embarrassed that she judges women more harshly than men using the logic of the sexual double standard, "which makes me very frustrated. No matter how open you are, at the same time you're always conditioned to these social norms," she says sheepishly. I can't help but wonder if, as she gets older, she will revise her threshold of the "too high" number for both male and female partners. Otherwise, her own "justification system" will be at risk, because surely her own number will continue to climb.

Women lie about their number not only to themselves (by manipulating which sexual acts count as legitimate) and to their partners. They also lie to their health care providers. Samantha, the white thirty-one-year-old waitress on the West Coast, told me that whenever she goes to her health clinic for her annual checkup, she's asked how many partners she's had sex with over the course of her lifetime. "The last time I went, I said sixty," Samantha told me. The nurse reacted with surprise. Samantha asked her what number women typically say. The nurse told her twenty. "I think either they're lying or I've been with way more people than normal." Either way, the nurse should not have expressed any judgment. Even putting aside the ethics of the exchange, if a patient is made to feel judged, she may not come back or may provide misleading information to her to "protect" herself, which could ultimately hinder her from receiving proper health care.

The nurse's expression of judgment was not an isolated incident. Jessica, the Latina college senior, went to the health services clinic on her campus last year when she was twenty-two "because I had a rash in my private area," she says. She was a virgin and this was her first visit to the campus clinic. The nurse questioned Jessica's honesty about her lack of sexual history, saying to her, "Well, there's no other reason for you to have this rash unless you're sexually active. Are you *sure* you haven't been sexually active?"

Jessica is convinced that the nurse did not believe that it was possible to be a twenty-two-year-old virgin, or even a twenty-two-year-old with only one sexual partner, with a vaginal rash. Jessica theorizes that the nurse believed that she had multiple partners. In fairness, the nurse may have been taking into account the fact that many women do indeed lie about their sexual history, and therefore Jessica's disavowal may have seemed implausible from her perspective.

It's like she wanted to believe that I was having sex with at least one person to explain why I had the rash, but because I said that I was a virgin, it was like she thought that I was lying and therefore must have been having sex with more than one person. Because if I were in a monogamous relationship, why would I lie? So it was like she was annoyed that I didn't say that I had one partner. She tested me with swabs, but I'm not sure what for, because she never even got back to me with the results, which I thought she was supposed to do, and I didn't follow up. She had more power than me, and I figured that she knew more about the rash than I did, so I felt that she had the control, and I was really uncomfortable. It turned out that I was allergic to my clothing detergent, which I discovered by myself.

In a bizarre loop and leap of logic, the nurse speculated that Jessica had multiple sexual partners but was lying because she was worried that she would be judged and slut-shamed. Even though none of this was true, she was judged and slut-shamed anyway. Such is the strange world of slut-shaming, in which even virgins with detergent-induced rashes can be made to feel that there is something sexually wrong with them.

Twenty-six-year-old Diane, the white feminist marriage and family therapist in California, has also experienced being judged at a health clinic. "At my clinic, they ask for your number from the past twelve months," she says. "I feel like the nurses slut-shame, because of the looks on their faces when I tell them my number. At my first appointment, when I was eighteen or nineteen and the nurse asked me, I said nine. And she said, 'In the last *year*? Not in your lifetime, but in the last *year*?' I was like, 'You're a nurse; you're not supposed to look at me like that!' She made me feel ashamed. I feel like they are setting us women up to lie, which puts our health at risk. I felt like I didn't want to go back."

It turned out that the day after I spoke with Diane, she was scheduled to return to the clinic for a regular checkup. I asked her to inquire why they ask women about their number, and to please let me know their rationale. The next evening, she emailed me her report:

When I went to the appointment, I had to update my information for my file, and one of the questions was how many people I had sex with in the last year. I asked the nurse why they ask the question. She said it was to assess if the patient was at a higher risk for sexually transmitted infections, and that they also take into account how often the patient uses condoms (always, sometimes, or never), and if so, they would advise the patient to take a free STD test. I told her that there have been times when nurses would ask me my number for the year and they would give me judgmental looks. She actually apologized and said that those nurses sounded very unprofessional. We talked about how that would lead other women to lie to health professionals about their sexual history and put themselves at risk. She talked to me about the clinic always being a very busy place, and that the people working here should be focused on health and being able to see as many patients as they can. But that is all that was said, and she gave me my birth control and sent me on my way.

Even well-intended health care providers are influenced by the mind-set of the sexual double standard and the culture of slut-shaming. The idea that a health care provider needs to know a patient's lifetime number of sexual partners is "outdated," according to Jacques Moritz, MD, the director of the division of gynecology at Mount Sinai St. Luke's Roosevelt Hospital in New York City and a practicing obstetrician and gynecologist for two decades. He argues that asking such a question "may cause one to pass judgment. It's more important to know if the patient is sexually active with the same or other sex, and if the sex is protected."

Gloria Feldt, an author and reproductive rights activist, and the former president of the Planned Parenthood Federation of America, tells me that "the person taking the medical history should not express an opinion one way or the other, because the purpose is to obtain accurate information to provide appropriate health care. Patients are more likely to lie if they feel judged. I imagine that some clinic staff may be guilty of being judgmental about a patient's number of sexual partners. Even though they know they shouldn't express their opinions, human beings have a hard time being totally unbiased." Dr. Moritz adds, "We physicians try to check our judgments at the door, but it is very difficult to be perfect."

The next time you are asked by a health care provider for your lifetime number, respond with a question of your own. I recommend that you ask, "Why do you need to know my lifetime number? Isn't it sufficient to know how many partners I've had recently, whether or not I practice safe sex, and whether or not I've been sexually assaulted?" Offer to give your number over the last six months if you don't feel comfortable providing your lifetime number. If you suspect that you are being judged, ask, "Do you give women with a lower number different health care?" You should never feel judged when taking care of your health. On the flip side, if the provider treats you respectfully but insists that she needs to know the number, and you believe that her intentions are positive—to provide you with the highest level of care—then do not lie.

Many of my interviewees wanted to know my personal opinion regarding their number. At first, I was taken aback, unsure how to respond. In the beginning of my research, I told them that there is no such a thing as an ideal number; but they found that response unsatisfactory, since, as we've seen, some men will break up with their girlfriends because of their number, and health care providers may openly judge them because of it. The more I spoke with women about their number, the more I realized that saying it's meaningless is like telling a woman who asks if she's beautiful that only internal beauty is important. I came to recognize that the ideal circumstance is a sexual history without coercion, regardless of the number—which is what I subsequently told them when asked for my opinion. This was a response the women understood and accepted. When placed in a larger context of what can transform sexual activity from pleasurable to dangerous, the issue of one's number truly becomes insignificant.

Are You a Slut If You're Single and on the Pill? What If You're Pregnant?

The outcomes of women's efforts to manage their sexual reputation go beyond self-doubt, relationship breakups, and raised eyebrows at the clinic—although all of those are disturbing. Worse, many women I spoke with reported that they do not consistently use contraceptives, because they worry that doing so makes them appear slutty. They have good reason to worry: Look at what happened to Sandra Fluke, the former Georgetown student who testified before Congress, arguing that her law school's health insurance plan should cover the cost of contraceptives—which, she noted, often are prescribed for medical purposes. The radio personality Rush Limbaugh swiftly called her a "slut" and a "prostitute," and even suggested that women who use contraceptives covered by insurance should be required to post sex tapes online "so we can all watch." An economist at the University of Rochester, Steven Landsburg, wrote in a blog post that Limbaugh's analogy of Fluke to a prostitute was "spot-on" and that it's reasonable for taxpayers to be able to watch her having sex if they are underwriting the cost of her contraceptives.[165] (To his credit, the president of the University of Rochester, Joel Seligman, denounced Landsburg in an open statement on the university's website.)[166] Similarly, in 2014 former Arkansas governor Mike Huckabee said it was wrong to give women birth control without a co-pay under the Affordable Care Act because doing so tells them "they cannot control their libido or their reproductive system without the help of government"—equating women who use birth control with oversexed "sluts."[167]

Jennifer Castro was the president of the California State University, Long Beach, branch of Project Choice, a federally funded program that provides education about HIV and other STDs, from 2012 to 2013. Castro traveled around campus, talking about sex education. She went into classrooms for her lectures. "But when I talked about sex with girls, I didn't get much attention," she reveals.

In addition to lecturing, I distributed free condoms to the students, which I put in black bags in advance. I went around the room and gave each person one at their desk. The girls always said, "Oh, I don't need one, because it's the guys who need these." They didn't even want to touch them. So the girls didn't take them. Many of them left the bags on their desks or put them on my table. They didn't take responsibility. They wouldn't make eye contact with me. Guys from the fraternities took them. They said, "Oh yeah, I need these."

I asked Castro if the female students were reluctant to be seen taking the condoms in front of their peers, especially since someone could have taken a picture of them on their phone and posted it to Facebook.

"Yes, that is definitely possible. But girls didn't come up to me privately afterward," she said, so the obstacle wasn't only being seen in public; it went deeper. She continued,

What happened is that the girls didn't want to be seen as slutty. They said, "Well, I'm on the pill." But even with the pill they tried to keep it quiet and tried not to call attention to it, and the pill won't help with STDs. Even if the girl was with one partner, her partner may have had other partners, so she really should have used a condom even if she was on the pill. But they didn't want to hear it. My hunch is that this attitude was a widespread thing; it was not just on this campus. But I wasn't promoting sex; I was just promoting education about sex. I wasn't saying that the students were having sex. I was just trying to get them to take care of themselves.

At least these women can privately purchase condoms when nobody's looking. What do you do when you live at home and you have reason to believe that your own mother is tracking your contraceptive use?

Fortune, a twenty-two-year-old Latina college senior, lives with her mother, who repeatedly calls her a slut in Spanish.

The word she uses is *cuero*. It is slang for someone who is too easy and loose. It means someone who is dirty because she sleeps around. It's similar to *puta*. She says it when she thinks I've done something wrong, like if I don't clean my room. When she says it, it means: "You're acting bad. You're not behaving the way a young lady should behave." I tell her all the time that she shouldn't call me that, but she says that when she's upset and frustrated the word comes out. My other relatives must think it's OK, because they know that my mom insults me in that way, and they never speak up.

To me, I feel like being called a slut is a bad insult because I am clean. It really hurts me because I'm nowhere near a slut. I don't wear makeup. I don't dress anything like a slut. I dress very conservatively when I'm around my family because they're pretty traditional. I would never wear a dress or a skirt in front of my family, although I do when I go to a party. When I want to wear a dress for a party, I have to hide it and get changed somewhere else. Normally I wear jeans and T-shirts, and sometimes a sweater.

Fortune tells me that because of her mother calling her a *cuero*, she has to be very careful to hide the fact that she's on the pill. She keeps the prescription and the pills themselves in her backpack, and she never keeps her backpack at home unattended. In fact, her mother doesn't even know that her twenty-two-year-old daughter has a boyfriend. "It's bad enough my mom calls me a slut just because I don't act the way she wants me to act," Fortune explains. "If she knew I had sex, then she would have a reason to call me a slut."

Slut-shaming, then, is one cause of unintended pregnancies. Most unintended pregnancies occur because birth control is not used properly or at all, according to the Guttmacher Institute. Currently, half (51 percent) of all pregnancies in the United States are unintended. Nearly all (95 percent) of unintended pregnancies are caused by inconsistent use (43 percent) or nonuse (52 percent) of birth control. Forty percent of all unintended pregnancies in the United States end in abortion.[168] Slut-shaming, we see, can lead to unintended pregnancy and even abortion.

Birth control is available for free with no co-pay under the Affordable Care Act for forty-seven million women, and thirty million are already taking advantage of the benefit. Those without insurance can also get low-cost birth control from over seven hundred Planned Parenthood health care centers across the fifty states. But a woman has to want to obtain birth control, and slut-shaming often stands in the way of her need for this basic preventive health care.

Gabriela, a thirty-three-year-old Latina woman in New York City, relates that her mother also called her a slut. She connects her upbringing in the shadow of slut-shaming in her own home with her belief that guys alone must provide and use contraception. "When I was growing up, my mom was abusive and said many mean things to me that were unfounded. I don't know if it's because I lost my virginity at an early age." Gabriela had sex at thirteen with the son of her building's superintendant. When her mother found out, she cursed Gabriela for being a "slut." Gabriela concedes that she was "too young to have sex," and that "I was just a little girl, and I shouldn't have been doing that at that age." But because her mother called her a slut, "I thought of myself as one because I didn't know any better."

Gabriela did not have sex for the next several years. When she became sexually active again, "I realized that I needed to hide my sexual activity from my mother. I also thought that the guy is the one who should always take responsibility for birth control because I was raised to believe that the guy should be the one in charge. I only knew about condoms and I didn't consider any other form of birth control." When she was eighteen, she moved out of her mother's apartment because her mother was physically abusing her. She lived in a group home for a year.

"I was out of my mom's home," Gabriela continues, "but I continued to not take responsibility for condoms. I still always thought that the guy should carry condoms. It never occurred to me that I should carry them or have them. So then when I was eighteen, I got pregnant. We didn't use a condom. As it was happening, I didn't worry about the fact that we weren't using a condom. I wasn't thinking about diseases and I wasn't thinking about pregnancy, although I should have been." Gabriela became pregnant. She continues,

I got an abortion, which was really scary because I didn't have my mom's support, and I was basically alone. I went with someone who was basically a stranger to me; she worked in the group home where I was living, and she had to take me. I was so naive, and I didn't really even understand what was going on. I remember lots of people crying [in the clinic], and I was in a lot of physical pain afterward, and I remember thinking that I wished I could have been with my mom instead of this woman from the group home that I didn't know. But mostly I remember thinking that I could have stopped this from happening by protecting myself. So after the abortion, I took it upon myself to get on the pill.

Gabriela believes that she became pregnant because of having been labeled a slut. She says, "I wasn't aware of it then, but now I know that these labels do matter. Young women need to be educated about the whole slut thing so that they won't think about themselves the way I did."

Gabriela was lucky that abortion was available. Although the US Supreme Court ruled in 1973 in *Roe v. Wade* that abortion is legal without restriction until the point of viability (approximately twenty-four weeks of pregnancy), many states (nine as of this writing) have passed laws banning abortion after twenty weeks with limited exceptions for cases of rape and incest, and for the health of the woman; many other states are attempting to pass similar legislation.[169] Other state laws that make abortion exceedingly inaccessible include those mandating waiting periods, the requirement that the procedure take place in a hospital or with parental notification, and the lack of public funding. Between 2011 and 2013, over two hundred state restrictions were enacted, making twenty-seven states "hostile to abortion rights," according to the Guttmacher Institute.[170] These measures have no practical purpose but to shame and stigmatize women, since nearly 89 percent of all abortions take place during the first trimester, with 99 percent occurring before the twenty-first week.[171] The tiny number of abortions that take place after the twenty-first week predominantly occur because of desperate medical circumstances involving the woman, the fetus, or both.

Even within the first trimester, a large number of girls and young women don't realize they're pregnant for many weeks: home pregnancy tests are not foolproof, and they sometimes provide a false negative result; some women continue to bleed even during pregnancy, and if they have a history of irregular periods, they don't question this bleeding, because it's their norm; not everyone experiences morning sickness; and if a woman is overweight, she may not notice the extra pounds in her midsection.[172] Once a woman realizes she's pregnant and decides she wants an abortion, she may need several weeks to collect the funds to pay for it, including costs for traveling to a health care site that may be in another state, and to take off work without pay, which in some states may stretch out to a week when state law calls for a waiting period. So even if abortion is legal, very often it is not accessible—particularly for low-income women who don't have the money or the ability to take off time from work without penalty.

What drives abortion bans and restrictions? The belief that women who have sex for pleasure rather than procreation are sluts. Low-income women more than anyone else are profoundly hurt by obstacles to abortion access.

Andrea Grimes, an investigative political reporter who now advocates for the right of women to have access to safe and legal abortion, had been an ardent pro-life supporter when she was growing up in Fort Worth, Texas. She reveals that punishing women for having sex rather than concern over fetuses was the engine driving her pro-life rhetoric:

Because while I said it was about the babies, it wasn't. It was about slut-shaming. I absolutely *loved* slut-shaming. Because I was saving myself for marriage—well, oral sex doesn't really count anyway, does it?—I knew that I would always be right and virtuous and I would never be a murderer like those *sluts*. The issue couldn't possibly be up for real debate, to my mind: either you were a baby-killer slut, or you behaved like a proper Christian woman and only let him get to third base. Babies were simultaneously women's punishment for having premarital sex and beautiful gifts from Jesus Himself. That didn't seem like a contradiction in my mind. It was just another one of God's perfect mysteries. . . . In private, my anti-choice friends and I would laugh and laugh . . . about how stupid women were for having premarital sex. How evil they were for not being able to control themselves. How great I was for not having sex with my boyfriend.[173]

If those who want to outlaw abortion were truly concerned about fetuses, then why are women alone singled out for punishment—why aren't the men who create unwanted pregnancies also taken to task for their sexual activity? Why don't those who want to outlaw abortion combat ignorance about pregnancy through comprehensive sex education? Why don't they work to make birth control more, not less, accessible? Why do legislators continue to propose antiabortion bills with no exceptions for the health of the woman? The answer is that the desire to outlaw abortion is mingled with the desire for women with unwanted pregnancies to suffer because they are "sluts" who should have known better. Once again, we see the mind-set that "sluts" must be punished.

Three out of ten women in the United States have an abortion by the time they are forty-five years old.[174] And women who need abortions get abortions, whether or not the procedure is legal or safe, according to the Guttmacher Institute.[175] Blaming women who need abortions through slut-shaming is not only morally reprehensible, it also is medically irresponsible.

Better Dead Than a Slut

The most egregious and extreme consequence of slut-bashing is suicide. Since 2008, we know of at least eleven slut-bashed girls ages twelve to eighteen who have killed themselves.

One of the most widely covered stories was that of Hope Witsell. In June 2009, whenever Witsell, a thirteen-year-old from rural Florida, walked into a classroom, someone invariably said, "Oh, here comes the slut." No matter where she tried to hide at Beth Shields Middle School, kids taunted her. Turns out that Witsell had sent a photo of herself topless to a boy she liked. Another girl borrowed the boy's phone, found the photo, and forwarded it to some friends. The photo went viral. Everyone at school—even kids who went to a neighboring school—had seen it.

Witsell was a good student and the kind of untroubled child teachers love. A student adviser for the local chapter of the National FFA (Future Farmers of America) Organization who went to church every Sunday with her parents and enjoyed fishing with her father, Witsell wrote in her diary that, "Tons of people talk about me behind my back and I hate it because they call me a whore! And I can't be a whore I'm too inexperienced. So secretly TONS of people hate me . . ." Two weeks into the summer vacation, the school's administration learned about the photo and suspended Witsell for one week in September. Her parents took away her cell phone and grounded her for the summer, but they permitted her to attend an FFA convention in Orlando.

Several older boys staying at the same hotel met her at the pool, and called her room repeatedly to ask her for a photo of her breasts. According to a friend who was in the room, Witsell was scared of the boys and took a picture to get them to stop bothering her. She left the phone for one boy, who didn't have a phone of his own, to pick up and view. But an adult intercepted the phone and found the photo. When her school found out that Witsell had done it again, its administrators decided not to allow her to run for student adviser the following year.

When school started up again, so did the bullying. Witsell met with a school social worker, who noticed cuts on her leg and had her sign a "no-harm" contract in which she agreed to talk to an adult if she felt the desire to hurt herself. But the school did not call her parents.

On September 12, 2009, Witsell's mother went to kiss her daughter good-night. She opened the door to find that Witsell had hanged herself to death with a pink scarf tied to the canopy of her bed. The "no-harm" contract lay in the trash can. Witsell had determined that because everyone thought of her as a slut, she had no future, and that ending her life made the most sense.

In an excellent exposé, Andrew Meacham of the *Tampa Bay Times* recounts how Beth Shields Middle School botched up big-time. The school did not take any action against any of the students who forwarded the photo of Witsell or brazenly humiliated her. Instead, the school was relentlessly punitive toward Witsell.[176] Perhaps administrators reasoned that if she took topless photos of herself and sent them to boys, she was not worthy of sympathy. The school's reaction reinforced the belief that she was deserving of punishment rather than understanding.

We all need to be understanding, not punitive. It's true that Witsell initiated the chain of events that led to her reputation. She made a foolish mistake—not once but twice. But she was thirteen, and she felt the weight of enormous pressure. How can you be thirteen and *not* make a foolish mistake under these circumstances, perhaps even twice?

At the time that Witsell ended her life, Phoebe Prince, fifteen, was the new girl at South Hadley High School in Massachusetts. Her family had just moved from Ireland. Prince briefly dated a popular football player, as well as another boy. But wouldn't you know it—each boy had a relationship with another girl, either a former girlfriend or someone with whom he was still physically involved. Those girls did not take kindly to Prince's moving into their town and moving in on their guys. The girls enlisted their friends to launch an intense bullying campaign. Several girls regularly called her "Irish slut," and cursed her in the hallways and cafeteria.[177] Through texts and Facebook messages, others at South Hadley High called her a slut and a whore and told her she deserved to die. Prince was aware that there were threats to "beat her up" and "punch her in the face." Hours before she hanged herself with a scarf in January 2010, one of her tormenters threw a can at Prince as she walked home from school.[178]

As with Witsell, her school's administrators knew about the harassment but did not take action against any of the students who bullied her. As with Witsell, she was not sexually naive. But in Prince's case, criminal charges were brought against six teenagers who were indicted as adults on various charges ranging from statutory rape to criminal harassment to stalking. In May 2011, five of the teens were placed on probation, with several also sentenced to community service.

In *Sticks and Stones*, Emily Bazelon analyzes the complexity of Prince's suicide, concluding that although she was indeed bullied and called a slut, Prince had a history of depression and had attempted suicide previously before she even had moved to the United States. It would be wrong, Bazelon cautions, to establish a causal relationship between the slut-bashing and the suicide.[179]

Suicide is never caused by only one thing, and it's true that the relationship between slut-bashing and suicide is enormously complex. Slut-bashing alone may not motivate a girl to take her own life. At the same time, we should not ignore the association between the two. After all, a correlation between gay-bashing and suicide attempts has been documented, so it would make sense for correlation between slut-bashing—harassment that similarly focuses on the victim's real or alleged sexuality—to also exist.[180]

Hope Witsell's and Phoebe Prince's stories received a great deal of publicity, leading to public conversations about slut-bashing. The experiences of other girls who committed suicide after being slut-bashed likewise have been uncovered:

IN JULY 2008 in Cincinnati, eighteen-year-old Jessica Logan hanged herself one month after graduating from high school. She had sent a photo of herself nude to a boyfriend. After they broke up, he mass-forwarded the photo. Everyone at school saw the picture. They called her "slut," "whore," and "skank."[181]

IN MARCH 2010 in Long Island, New York, seventeen-year-old Alexis Pilkington hanged herself after landing a soccer scholarship to college. She had been called a slut on Formspring, but her parents said publicly that their daughter had suffered from depression; slut-bashing, they believe, did not cause her to end her own life. After her death, anonymous people posted graphic images of nooses around her neck on her Facebook memorial site.[182]

IN APRIL 2012 in Mantorville, Minnesota, thirteen-year-old Rachel Ehmke hanged herself after repeatedly having been called a slut and a prostitute in person and online. Two days before her death, an anonymous text sent to students at her school said that she was a slut, she should leave the school, and that the text should be forwarded to everyone they knew. Ehmke was in the seventh grade.[183]

IN SEPTEMBER 2012 in Saratoga, California, fifteen-year-old Audrie Pott hanged herself. The week before, she had been sexually assaulted by three boys at a party at a friend's house at which she had passed out drunk. The boys, whom she had known for years, took off her clothes and sexually assaulted her, including writing and drawing on her body with a permanent marker. They also took photos of her marked-up body, which then circulated among her schoolmates. At least one teenage girl was present in the room when the assaults occurred and encouraged the boys. Pott had written to a friend on Facebook, "I have a reputation for a night I don't even remember and the whole school knows."[184]

IN OCTOBER 2012 in Staten Island, New York, fifteen-year-old Felicia Garcia jumped to her death onto the track of an oncoming train. Several football players had tormented her with boasts about having had sex with her at a party after a game; other classmates joined in the name-calling. The night before she killed herself, she tweeted, "I cant, im done, I give up." Garcia's parents had died when she was a little girl; she was raised primarily within the foster care system, and had bounced around from home to home.[185]

IN OCTOBER 2012 in British Columbia, fifteen-year-old Amanda Todd hanged herself. When she was twelve, a stranger she had met through video chat convinced Todd to bare her breasts on camera and then circulated the photo online. The individual later created a Facebook profile using the same photo and even contacted her classmates. Soon after, she had sex with a boy who had another girlfriend; the girlfriend and a group of others physically attacked Todd. She tried to commit suicide by drinking bleach, but she survived; messages about her failed suicide attempt were posted to Facebook, and she was relentlessly teased by her classmates. A month before she killed herself, she posted a nine-minute video on YouTube titled "My Story: Struggling, bullying, suicide and self harm," in which she used a series of flash cards to tell of her experiences being bullied. After her death, she continued to be labeled a whore and a slut on online messages.[186]

IN DECEMBER 2012 in Hudson, New York, sixteen-year-old Jessica Laney hanged herself. Her friends said that she was called a "slut" and a "fuckin ugly ass hoe" on Ask.fm, the website modeled after Formspring that allows bullies to remain anonymous.[187]

IN APRIL 2013 in Nova Scotia, seventeen-year-old Rehtaeh Parsons hanged herself, leading to a coma; her family decided to switch off her life support machine several days later. When she was fifteen, she had been gang-raped by four teenage boys at a party when she was drunk. During one of the rapes, a bystander photographed the assault, and the photo was widely circulated in her school and town. "It went to every kid's cellphone," a friend reported. "Everyone assumed she was being a slut, that she wanted it." When Parsons explained that she had been raped, her peers "decided not to believe her."[188]

IN MAY 2013 in Queens, New York, twelve-year-old Gabrielle Molina hanged herself. Students had called her a slut online. Molina left behind a note describing the bullying and apologizing to her parents for ending her life.[189]

For a girl already depressed or anxious, slut-bashing may be the thing that finally pushes her over the edge and motivates her to take her own life. Even if the majority of slut-bashing incidents don't end in such horrific outcomes, it's clear that to stand by while this kind of bullying is occurring and not intervene is unacceptable.

Slut-bashing and slut-shaming often are justified on the grounds that they teach girls a lesson: that they should not be sexually active at all, or that they should not be "too" sexually active. If girls heeded this lesson, the rationale goes, they would adopt healthy behaviors. Yet we see that slut-bashing and slut-shaming cause the opposite to occur. Girls and women consistently turn to dangerous, damaging, and degrading behaviors. Calling a female a slut is like telling her, "Do not take care of yourself, because you are worthless." Tragically, some girls and women believe this to be true.

CHAPTER 7

The Rape of a "Slut" Is Rape

"If you've hooked up with someone like, three times," says fifteen-year-old Jocelyn, "there gets a point where you can't just, like, take off your shirt. You have to do more."

Kaitlyn, sixteen, agrees. "There was a freshman in my school who hooked up with a junior and wouldn't let him touch her boobs," she adds. "So people talked about her in a negative way because it was like, 'Why would she hook up with a junior and not do anything? He could get another junior girl who's hotter and will do things with him.'"

These girls are describing a social system in which females are valued only for the sexual pleasure they provide males. They are not appreciated for anything but their ability to provide a sexual service. Their own desires are beside the point. They "have to do more" than what they want to do. If they don't, the guy they're attracted to will "get another girl" who "will do things with him."

I was jolted by how blasé Jocelyn and Kaitlyn were in relating this state of affairs. The five other girls sitting with us on the floor of a studio in downtown Manhattan were just as languid. No one contradicted Jocelyn or Kaitlyn, or even seemed particularly disturbed by their reports.

How did we get to this point? I tried to keep my face neutral, and in a measured voice, I asked the girls how they feel about this pressure to go further sexually than they would like. What do they think about the fact that what they want to do sexually is less important to many guys than what the guys want—and that the guys tend to prevail?

"We kind of don't think about it," Jocelyn replied. "We kind of ignore it. This is just normal." I looked around at the girls, seated in a semicircle on the scruffy floor. *Yep*, their expressions said, *this is just normal*.

These girls' perception that they are expected to provide a sexual service to guys whether or not they want to was echoed in research conducted by Heather Hlavka, a sociologist at Marquette University. Hlavka analyzed interviews with one hundred girls between the ages of three and seventeen who had been victims of sexual assault, and found that the girls overwhelmingly did not even recognize acts of sexual assault as crimes. One white thirteen-year-old girl told her interviewer, "They grab you, touch your butt and try to, like, touch you in the front, and run away, but it's okay, I mean . . . I never think it's a big thing because they do it to everyone."[190] The girls in Hlavka's research did not recognize sexual violence unless it conformed to their limited conception of rape; therefore, as an example, they did not perceive an act of violently forced oral sex as rape because they recognized only violently forced vaginal penetration as an act of rape.[191] Hlavka concluded that the girls in this study "often did not name what law, researchers, and educators commonly identify as sexual harassment and abuse."[192]

As the girls I met with shrugged, *This is just normal.*

Males who sexually pressure or overpower females they consider to be "slutty" believe that their behavior is acceptable. They think: It's normal. It's natural. It's inevitable. After all, a "slut's" value comes from her sexuality. Therefore, it's OK to be sexual with her even if she doesn't consent. Otherwise, why did she sluttify herself in the first place? Wasn't it her choice, her decision, to turn herself into a sexual object? Isn't she "asking for it"? Anyone who interprets the act as assault has misunderstood; the act was consensual.*

We've seen that a girl or woman may be labeled a slut for a variety of reasons. Sometimes she sexualizes herself—she wears clothing considered provocative, or she seeks out males' attention. But sometimes she does not sexualize herself—she's labeled a slut because she is drunk, or she's considered a threat by her female peers, or she differs from them in some arbitrary manner. Either way, she becomes regarded by others as a sexual object.

Given the conditions at play today, in which, as we've seen, every girl or young woman is at risk of being regarded a slut, it's reasonable to argue that every girl or woman is also at risk at some point of being sexually overpowered or coerced.

---

* An act of "sexual assualt" or "sexual abuse" is any type of unwanted sexual activity, including inappropriate touching. "Rape" is an act of bodily penetration—vaginal, anal, or oral—which does not necessarily involve force. Most rape occurs through pinning, coercion, and threat rather than actual violence.

Once assaulted, the victim and not the perpetrator is blamed—because she is, after all, a "slut." The accuser rather than the accused is presumed to be lying; the accused rather than the accuser is seen as sympathetic, as one who has experienced a trauma. This mind-set seems like a throwback to an earlier era, before feminists raised society's awareness of the prevalence and seriousness of sexual assault. And yet this mind-set is astonishingly common. Many people use a victim's preassault actions to justify her assault. Victims are conditioned to accept this logic and conclude that they are to blame. Maybe they weren't *really* assaulted. They are uncertain. And their uncertainty feeds more assaults, because their uncertainty prevents them from reporting what has occurred. Their uncertainty protects the perpetrator and preserves the logic of slut-shaming.

Sexual assault, of course, is not new. As long as there has been sex, there has been sexual assault. What is new is that today, female bodies have no privacy. They are visible, tagged, posted, circulated, tracked, rated, judged, "liked." They are always available—sexually available. Not only is this the reality, this is the expectation: female bodies *should* be visible; they *should* be available; *they should be sexually available*. In addition, young women are supposed to want—to choose—to make their bodies visible, available, sexually available. This is the new normal.

We girls and women no longer own our bodies, because our bodies are in the public sphere every second of every day. When we relinquished our privacy in the world of social media, we also, unwittingly, gave away our bodily autonomy. Ma'lik Richmond, one of a group of teenage boys found guilty in 2013 of sexually assaulting a female acquaintance from West Virginia at a party in Steubenville, Ohio, told *The New Yorker* that it was acceptable for him to hook up with her, even though his friend had been physically involved with her, because she was "community property."[193] Richmond's language suggests that the Steubenville High School football players felt ownership over the girl's body, and that they believed they had license to do whatever they wanted with it. By this logic, the girl herself could not claim ownership over her own body.

Girls and women internalize the message that their bodies do not truly belong to them. As a result, they are perhaps more persuadable than ever before to do sexual things to which they do not consent. Sometimes girls and women *do* want to do these sexual things; they *do* have sexual desire, and they *do* want to act on their desire. But under these conditions, when a girl's body is perceived as "community property," how do they—and we—recognize where desire stops and coercion begins? Pretending to consent to one's own sexual objectification is now part of "normal" female adolescence. As one of the teenage girls sitting on the floor with Jocelyn and Kaitlyn tells us, "You have to display a sexual personality—it's like, 'Are you down to fuck, or not?'" Girls and young women must express a sexual identity showing that they are eager for sexual activity they have chosen, whether or not they truly want to be sexually active. Yet behind their pretense of sexual bravado, most girls and young women do not actually want to be treated as sexual objects.

Guys must listen to what young females say, not infer consent based on their outfit or their consumption of alcohol.

Those who do not ask for, or listen to, an expression of consent come to believe that female bodies are theirs for the taking. They feel entitled to partake in "community property." "We've all been affected by sexual aggression," says one of the girls, "like when a guy at a party grabs your boobs, and you don't want to say anything. You laugh it off and make it like it's not a big deal, because you don't want to be seen as a bitch or a feminist who makes things like this a big deal." It's not just teenage boys who go around seizing female bodies unsolicited. Elizabeth, the white twenty-nine-year-old educator who grew up in New York City and now lives in the Southeast, tells me that at dance clubs, men feel perfectly comfortable grabbing the bodies of women they encounter. She sighs, saying, "Sometimes you just want to dance and not worry that some random guy will grab you. You don't want to have to worry about being harassed or assaulted."

Coercion Is the Absence of Consent

Nearly one in five women in the United States has been raped or has experienced other sexual violence at some point in her life, according to an exhaustive government study called the National Intimate Partner and Sexual Violence Survey.[194] This statistic may shock you. You may wonder: Is it truly possible that so many women have been sexually assaulted? Yes—the answer is yes. Sexual assault really is this prevalent. Linda Degutis, the director of the government center that conducted the survey, admits that the one-in-five-women number may be "surprising" to many people. "I don't think we've really known that it was this prevalent in the population," she said when the survey was released in 2011. Bear in mind that this number includes not only acts of forced penetration (rape) but also acts of sexual violence other than rape.[195]

Regarding rape specifically, the youth of the victims is striking. Forty-two percent of all female victims have been raped before they turned eighteen, and 80 percent have been raped before the age of twenty-five.[196] More than half of female rape victims have been raped by an intimate partner, according to the study, and 40 percent have been raped by an acquaintance.[197]

Nearly half of women surveyed at a small liberal arts university (44 percent) had experienced a coerced sexual encounter (including unwanted touching, attempted rape, or completed rape) during their first three semesters, according to psychologists at Bucknell University led by William F. Flack Jr. Of these "unwanted" activities, 81 percent involved alcohol. (The researchers use the term "unwanted" rather than "coerced.")[198] The reason for rape most frequently reported (62 percent) was impaired judgment due to alcohol. The reason for unwanted fondling most frequently reported (67 percent) was that it happened before the perpetrator could be stopped.[199] Despite the prevalence of coerced sexual encounters, only 3 percent of students reported these incidents to university authorities, and only 11 percent of the women who'd experienced unwanted or coerced sexual intercourse defined the incident as "rape."[200]

The high incidence of "unwanted" sex, Flack and his colleagues argue, "demonstrates that men often get what they want, whereas women often do not" because "the man disregards either the woman's wishes or her lack of capacity to give consent; that is, some instances of unwanted sex constitute rape or assault."[201] Not all acts of unwanted sex, however, constitute rape or assault from a legal point of view. Flack and his colleagues point out that in other encounters, women "may feel as though they have little power (physical or social), and thus, little choice but to acquiesce"—that is, women may decide that it's easier to go along with the sexual encounter and get it over with as quickly as possible than to protest. Thus, the researchers conclude, the sexual dynamics on campus "are largely controlled by men and dictated by blatant, if not explicit, sexist attitudes."[202]

Flack's conclusions are confirmed by Lisa Wade and Caroline Heldman at Occidental College. In their study of hookup culture during students' freshman year of college, they found that on college campuses, male and female students consider male sexual coercion to be utterly normal. Women constantly "need[ed] to rebuff the advances of men in whom they were not interested," Wade and Heldman report, and many women consented to "sexual activity they did not desire, seeming to feel it was their only option, despite the absence of physical coercion, threats, or incapacitation." Several women told Wade and Heldman that they performed fellatio to get rid of men who wouldn't leave them alone. The researchers found that for many students, sexual coercion "seemed normal or inevitable."[203] Many men on campus believe it's normal to sexually take, even without the woman's consent. Many women believe it's normal to be sexually taken from.

Coerced sex is an act in which a woman's ability to exert power is taken from her. Three scenarios are possible:

- She protests and the man disregards her wishes.
- She is unable to protest because she's incapacitated.
- She wants to protest but chooses not to, because she perceives that protesting will not successfully stop the perpetrator and may cause him to become violent; she just wants the unwanted encounter to conclude as quickly and painlessly as possible.

In each scenario, the woman either protests or would protest if she could. She is robbed of her agency. Yet ironically, if she contends that she's been victimized, she is denounced for being assertive; and if she's assertive, she must be the type of girl who *invited* the unwanted sexual encounter—because that's what assertive girls do. Even when she speaks up to report that she's been violated, then, she is told that the sexual encounter was her choice.

Nicole, sixteen, relates the story of a friend, Leah, who was sexually assaulted when she was thirteen.

She had really big boobs, and she would wear tank tops. There was, like, nowhere else to look. So immediately guys were like, "Hey, wanna hang out?" She was really sweet and went with them and she let the boys touch her. It was really sad because immediately she was the slut of the school. So then she tried to become known as a prude. She hasn't touched anyone for, like, two years. Then she was raped because an upperclassman knew she was a slut and held her head down for thirty minutes and wouldn't let go until she gave him a blow job. You could argue that it was her choice to do it, because she put herself in the situation even though he held down her head—although who would want to suffocate like that? But that's what people were saying—that it was her choice and that she didn't have to do it.

Nicole is ambivalent about Leah's agency. On the one hand, she says that Leah "was raped" and she asks, "Who would want to suffocate like that?" Yet Nicole doesn't seem entirely sure that Leah truly was raped, noting, "You could argue that it was her choice" to give the older boy oral sex despite the fact that the conditions were coercive. If Leah was raped, how could it have been her choice? Nicole's uncertainty over Leah's ability to control the incident dovetails with one of the definitions of a "bad slut"—a girl or woman who exerts agency. A "bad slut" has done something she should not have done. Although rape is an act of stripping away agency, Leah's status as a "slut" overshadows her coercion and renders this sexual encounter wanted rather than unwanted. In the end, the story that Nicole tells is one not of coercion but of consent, of choice. Nicole leaves open the possibility that Leah initially chose to give the boy oral sex; therefore, when he held her head forcibly against his penis and did not release his grasp on her until after she had completed the act, surely that circumstance must have been her choice too.

This narrative of the slut who invites an act of rape and therefore has no right to complain about it after the fact is the dominant way people interpret reports of sexual assault. "The underlying skepticism that sexual assault survivors face when they disclose may be the single most damaging factor in our societal response," writes Kimberly Lonsway, the director of research at the nonprofit organization End Violence Against Women International. "It may also be the most powerful tool in the arsenal of rapists because it allows them to commit their crimes with impunity."[204] Thus, when the former Missouri congressman Todd Akin said in 2012 that women who become pregnant under any circumstances should give birth, even if the pregnancy is not wanted, since it's not possible to become pregnant from a "legitimate rape," he suggested that "sluts" cannot truly be raped. A "legitimate rape"—according to Akin's logic—is one in which the victim exerts no agency at all, and therefore her body mysteriously shuts down its normal physiological processes. Any woman who "chooses" to put herself in a situation in which sexual violence is a risk is a "slut" who implicitly consented to be assaulted.

The thing about rape is that people who want to protect rapists and normalize the act will look for *any* pre-rape behavior by the victim to explain how she "chose" to become victimized. Even an eleven-year-old girl who was gang-raped by at least two nineteen-year-old men, and possibly up to sixteen other males, in an abandoned trailer in Cleveland, Texas, was accused of inviting her own assault. The girl was threatened with being physically beaten if she didn't comply with the rapists, who then recorded the attacks on their cell phones. James C. McKinley Jr. of the *New York Times* chose to include in his story about the gang-rape that residents claimed the victim "dressed older than her age, wearing makeup and fashions more appropriate to a woman in her 20s. She would hang out with teenage boys at a playground, some said." He also quoted a resident who said, "It's just destroyed our community. These boys have to live with this the rest of their lives."[205] The eleven-year-old girl, who wore makeup and so-phisticated clothes and liked to hang out with boys—which eleven-year-old girls tend to do—is to blame for wrecking the lives of the men who raped her. The implication is that she is a "slut" who was not really raped because rape of a "slut" does not count as real rape.

In Billings, Montana, a male high school teacher named Stacey Dean Rambold admitted to raping a fourteen-year-old student at her school in 2008, when he was forty-nine. District Judge G. Todd Baugh sentenced the teacher to thirty days in prison; he explained his leniency by saying that the victim, Cherice Moralez, "seemed older than her chronological age" and was "as much in control of the situation" as the teacher. The girl killed herself in 2010 as the case went through the legal system.[206] Perhaps taking her own life was the only thing she truly could do to be "in control of the situation."

The YouTube entertainer Jenna Mourey, twenty-six, known as Jenna Marbles—"the woman with a billion clicks," according to the *New York Times*—reiterated this narrative in her nine-minute video titled "Things I Don't Understand About Girls Part 2: Slut Edition," released in December 2012. According to Mourey, as noted in chapter 2, being a slut is a choice, and any "slut" who chooses to have risky sex with random guys deserves to be judged. She excoriates "sluts" for making "bad slutty decisions," linking the "slut" label with a woman's active choice to be "slutty." It's not difficult to watch her video and conclude that a "slut" who's been raped invited the rape.

In her video, which has been seen by over five million

people, Mourey looks right into the camera and delivers her monologue. She says,

A slut is someone that has a lot of casual sex, and unfortunately I can't completely define "a lot," because it's different in different people's minds. . . . I want you to understand that I think that being a slut is a choice, so maybe I'm not making fun of you personally, I'm just making fun of your slutty choices, because I still love you, no matter what. . . . The next thing I want to talk about are stupid sluts, and I'm not using this lightly, OK. . . . Many girls go to school because they're like, I'm going to be a slut. That's cool, that's great. These are facts. And I'm going to use one particular slut that I know as a reference, one girl in particular justified sleeping with so many dudes, because she only did it in the butt. So they didn't actually count. I'm just going to take a second here to like let that sink in. . . .

Dear girls, when you're out and you see another girl that's like blackout drunk, and some dude is trying to take her home. . . . Just be a fellow vagina partner in life, go up to her and be like, Are you all right? That's all you have to say, and then all of a sudden you start to see the drunk gears turning in there just like, Oh, yeah, I don't know, I just met him, I'm not going home with them. I'm going to get a cab. Help them, help the sluts of the world makes less bad slutty decisions. . . .

Mourey expresses empathy for "sluts" and instructs her viewers to help "sluts," especially when they're drunk. However, her definition of a slut is a woman who chooses to have "a lot of casual sex." Although she concedes that "a lot of casual sex" is a relative thing, implying that different people have different opinions about what number of sexual partners constitutes "a lot," she can just tell when a woman is really a slut: "It's the girl that you're like, Yeah, yeah she is a slut, yeah that girl." You know a slut when you see her.

Mourey goes on to parse a category of "sluts"—"stupid sluts"—who are particularly open about their desire to have sex with multiple partners. (Mourey's denunciation of "stupid sluts" is similar to Nicki Minaj's judgment of "stupid hoes." In 2012, Minaj released "Stupid Hoe," singing, "Stupid hoes is my enemy, stupid hoes is so wack . . . You a stupid hoe, you a stupid hoe, you a stupid hoe / And I ain't hit that note but fuck a stupid hoe / I said fuck a stupid hoe and fuck a stupid hoe.") "Stupid sluts" are defensive about their desire, so they "justify" their actions through faulty logic (anal sex doesn't count as "real" sex). These "sluts" have a tendency to have sex while drunk, Mourey continues. She encourages her viewers to intervene if they see a man taking home a drunk woman who appears to be unable to give sexual consent. Yet after this monologue, will her viewers really want to help a drunken woman who may be targeted for sexual violence? Or will they judge her the way Mourey has—as someone who, if she ends up being raped, brought the rape on herself because of her "slutty" and "stupid" decisions?

Framing the issue of sexual violence within a rhetoric of choice puts the blame on the victim and renders her unsympathetic and, worse, not credible. I think that Mourey would agree that no one chooses to become a victim of sexual violence. But she opens the door to questioning the validity of rape victims' claims.

The concept of "choice" under the conditions of a slut-shaming culture is questionable. When you're conditioned and pressured to present yourself as a "good slut," what does it even mean to suggest that you are *choosing* to be a "slut"? We know that through reciprocal slut-shaming on social media, girls and women present themselves as sexually empowered—as "good sluts." When they do choose to be a "good slut," they are socially rewarded at first, but invariably their identity becomes interpreted as that of a "bad slut"—the kind who gets blamed for being sexually assaulted. No female ever chooses to be known as a "bad slut." So is there a real choice here? As Kathryn Abrams, a Berkeley Law professor, points out, "Women's agency under oppression is necessarily partial or constrained."[207] Young females are not powerless—no one is threatening them if they don't adopt a "good slut" persona—but they are not capable of shaping their choices, either. When you listen to the stories of actual women labeled "sluts"—which Mourey does not—you hear narratives devoid of real active choice. Even when they consent, they experience no sexual desire.

Sexual Assault Is Not Ambiguous Sex

Many people confuse sexual assault with sex for which consent is murky. As a rule, women who are unsure if they gave consent do not consider themselves raped. They admit that they could have communicated protest but made a calculation not to. They report that they engaged in unwanted sex they regretted after the fact, but they do not classify the act as assault.

Mara, the nineteen-year-old white student in California, tells me about a sexual encounter she did not want but was punished over anyway. Two years ago, when she was a high school senior, she went to her prom with a male friend, Cal. The two had no romantic connection, and the decision to attend together was made at the last minute. They went to an after party, where Mara became drunk. Cal was driving, so he remained sober. "The next thing I know," she tells me, "we were having sex in his car. My best friend, not knowing what we were doing inside the car, came over to the car with a bunch of guys. One of the guys looked inside the window and saw everything. When Cal and I came out of the car, people were already talking. I felt ashamed because I didn't even want to have sex with him, and I was blaming myself for having done it. I felt it was my fault. At this point, it didn't occur to me that maybe it was his fault."

One of Mara's classmates posted a picture of her prom group on Facebook. One girl singled out Mara, commenting, "Nice picture except for the whore in red in the middle." The kids at school gave her "looks and comments. They would say, 'How's Cal?'" Mara explains that at her high school, the prevailing opinion was that it was OK to have sex with your boyfriend, if you had one, but if you had sex with anyone else, you were a slut.

Several months later, when she was a freshman in college, Mara questioned what had occurred. She thought about the fact that she was drunk while Cal had been sober. She may have never expressed any protest, but because she was drunk, she was pliable—and Cal, whose judgment was not impaired by alcohol, knew it. "I came to the conclusion that I had been taken advantage of. What he did was really not OK. It was not rape, and I wouldn't call it rape. But it was unethical and immoral and it was just really not cool."

Cynthia, the white twenty-one-year-old Pennsylvania student, relates a similar narrative of a choice that wasn't really a choice to have sex. She classifies the incident, which took place last year, as "not rape, but not consensual." She went to a party, got drunk, and met a guy whom she asked to walk her home. She had just broken up with her boyfriend, whom she'd been with for two and a half years, she told me, so she wasn't used to walking home alone. "I wanted company for the walk home, but that is all I wanted. I definitely did not want to have sex with him." Yet she did end up having sex with him. "It wasn't rape because I never said no," she explains. "I never actually told him to leave me alone, and then it got to the point where I realized, 'I guess this guy is coming into my home with me.' He did everything and I just kept quiet until he left. I felt violated. The situation was creepy and weird."

Could Cynthia have kicked him out of her home? Yes. Then why didn't she? Because the choice to do so did not occur to her. In part, her judgment was impaired because she was drunk. But she also realized that the quickest and possibly least painful way to get him to leave was to acquiesce and let him have sex with her. She did not actively choose to have sex, but she did not actively choose to not have sex. As twenty-two-year-old Vicki explains to me, "I think girls often play a part in putting themselves in a bad situation. They are afraid to say no, even if having sex with the person makes them want to dry-heave. Maybe they don't want the guy to feel bad, or maybe they don't want him to think of them as a prude." Mara and Cynthia faced conditions in which protest was difficult, since both had been drinking, but they interpret what occurred as a violation rather than as a rape. Their assaulters may have had no idea that they had committed a violation. They may have considered these sexual encounters completely uneventful and normal. Mara and Cynthia did not report these events to legal authorities, because they recognize ambiguity in these specific experiences; they do not believe that these experiences were completely coercive.

But many people believe that reported rapes are similarly lacking in clarity. Indeed, many people believe that reported rapes often are false allegations. "Within the domain of rape," writes David Lisak, a longtime researcher on campus rape, "the most highly charged area of debate concerns the issue of false allegations. For centuries, it has been asserted and assumed that women 'cry rape,' that a large proportion of rape allegations are maliciously concocted for purposes of revenge or other motives."[208]

From one angle, it makes sense to presume that within a culture of slut-shaming, when the consequence of being labeled a slut can be disastrous, a young woman might lie about or otherwise misrepresent an act of sexual assault to protect her reputation. Lying or exaggerating may be logical when the social consequences of being perceived as slutty are so harmful. After all, we have seen that any woman who is perceived as actively choosing a sexual identity is at risk for being labeled a bad slut. Thus, one could argue that falsely claiming to be a victim of sexual assault is a wise strategy because it enables the accuser to present herself as someone lacking in control, as someone who had no role in being victimized, as someone who was passive rather than active.

But the data do not bear out these suspicions. In fact, study after study shows that only a very small percentage of accusations of rape are false, which is consistent with the rate of false accusations of all crimes. Lisak and his colleagues systematically evaluated seven studies on false allegations. The percentage of false accusations ranged from 2.1 percent to 10.9 percent. They also designed a new study analyzing sexual assaults reported over a ten-year period, from 1998 to 2007, to a police department at Northeastern University in Boston. Of the 136 cases of sexual assault that were reported, eight (5.9 percent) were coded as "false reports," meaning that a thorough investigation had been pursued and evidence demonstrated that the reported sexual assault had not occurred. The authors conclude, "The stereotype that false rape allegations are a common occurrence, a widely held misconception in broad swaths of society, including among police officers, has very direct and concrete consequences. It contributes to the enormous problem of underreporting by victims of rape and sexual abuse. It is estimated that between 64% and 96% of victims do not report the crimes committed against them, and a major reason for this is victims' belief that his or her report will be met with suspicion or outright disbelief."[209]

Since, as Lisak and his colleagues point out, the overwhelming majority of rapes are not reported at all, the percentage of false accusations of rape is far lower than the 2 to 10 percent range they have found among reported rapes. If

10 percent of only *reported* rapes are false accusations, the percentage of all false rape claims actually hovers between less than 1 percent to 3 percent.

Joanne Belknap, a sociologist at the University of Colorado, Boulder, sums up this thorny issue succinctly: "Although false rape claims are reprehensible, it is important to acknowledge that they are also incredibly rare. Clearly, as a group, victims are very unlikely to report rapes to the police, and even less likely to make false claims."[210] According to the data, we should always be inclined to believe those who claim they have been assaulted. Sometimes women do lie; as we have seen, the culture of slut-shaming is so toxic that some women may conclude that lying about sexual assault is the only way they can salvage their reputation. But overall, lying about sexual assault is very rare. Therefore, our impulse must be to presume that accusers are reporting the truth.

Rape Culture on Campus

Many college campuses support a culture in which male sexual violence is normalized. As a result, females on many campuses conclude that being sexually assaulted is nothing out of the ordinary. After all, as the White House confirmed in its 2014 report on campus sexual assault, one in five students has been assaulted, though only 12 percent of those who have been assaulted report the violence.[211]

Male students at even the most elite colleges appear to believe that coercing women into having sex that they don't want is acceptable behavior. According to Brett Sokolow, the

CEO of the National Center for Higher Education Risk Management, a consulting and law firm, between seven hundred and eight hundred campuses now use the term "nonconsensual sex" as a synonym for "rape" in their policies on sexual assault.[212] "Nonconsensual sex" linguistically evades "rape" and sounds much less serious than "rape." "Nonconsensual sex" sounds more normal and less criminal than "rape." Since most people think of sex as consensual, even putting the word "nonconsensual" in front of it fails to convey that "nonconsensual sex" is in fact a crime.

When a campus community perceives rape as normal, rape not only goes unpunished but is even encouraged. Members of a fraternity at Yale—the same fraternity that claims President George W. Bush as a member—line up and yell, "No means yes! Yes means anal!" A "Preseason Scouting Report" email ranks freshmen by name, hometown, college residence, and "how many beers it would take to have sex with them."[213] Yale formally found sufficient evidence against six rapists in the first half of 2013. One was suspended for one year and may return to Yale. One was put on probation, and the other four received written reprimands. None of the rapists was expelled until 2004, after the university came under national scrutiny for mishandling sexual assault complaints.[214]

In 2011, a member of the Kappa Sigma fraternity at the University of Southern California sent a widely circulated email to members with advice on how to get women to have vaginal and oral sex with them. Throughout the letter, women are referred to as "targets" because they "aren't actual people like us men. Consequently, giving them a certain name or distinction is pointless." Fraternity members are advised to avoid women whose genitals, called "pies," "are extremely meaty and resemble a cold cut combo from Subway," and they are encouraged to remember that "sometimes targets that look like a Mack truck ran over their face have the greatest bodies and some outstanding [vaginal] grip." Fraternity members are reminded that they will be ranked according to how much sex they have with beautiful women. They are warned to avoid ugly women, even if they are skilled sexually: "Many fatties and uglies do have great gullets and are particularly good at sex. They have to be more dedicated to their craft because no one would talk to them otherwise. Likewise, a target does not receive a reduced ranking if you get down to the pie and it resembles a slaughterhouse. It's unfortunate, but poor qualities like that do not lower her physical beauty."[215]

In 2013, eighty student leaders at Saint Mary's University in Halifax were disciplined after it was discovered via Instagram that they had led a chant during orientation week about the pleasures of sexual assault to an audience of four hundred students. Male and female students chanted, "SMU boys, we like them young. Y is for your sister. O is for oh so tight. U is for underage. N is for no consent. G is for grab that ass." It turns out that this chant had been popular on campus for five years.[216]

Why is the normalization of sexual coercion prevalent on campuses? Alex Barnett, a professor of mathematics at Dartmouth, believes that men's anxiety over their social status among other men, rather than a desire for sex, plays a big role. In an open letter to Dartmouth's president, Phil Hanlon, written in September 2013, after the government began an investigation of sexual assault at Dartmouth, Barnett noted that "college is not a 'safe space' for women, the reason being in large part, rather shockingly, their fellow male students."[217]

Campuses with a strong male athletics program appear to breed an environment in which men feel entitled to assault women. In fact, athletes typically comprise between 10 and 15 percent of the student population but account for 25 percent of assaults on campus.[218] Jessica Luther, a journalist, argues that National College Athletic Association (NCAA) programs and gang rape on college campuses are connected. In a 2013 article in the *Atlantic*, she noted that at two Division I football programs—Vanderbilt University in Nashville, Tennessee, and the United States Naval Academy in Annapolis, Maryland—multiple football players have been charged with rape. These circumstances were not anomalies; they mirror a widespread attitude among many male college athletes that they are entitled to treat women as sexual objects, even to the point of assaulting them. An Oklahoma State University football player found guilty of gang-raping a woman in a dormitory told the *Los Angeles Times*, "Well, speaking for myself and a lot of other people, we felt like we were above the law, like OU would protect us from anything." Luther concludes that the culture of men's college athletics in Division I "can be harmful to women."[219]

An additional reason that women at college may be particularly vulnerable to sexual assault is that pro-rape messages are the background noise of campus culture. A number of male popular entertainers, many of whom tour the campus circuit, sing blithely about sexually assaulting women. When an entertainer performs on a campus, it's not unreasonable to conclude that the institution that invited him approves of his messages.

Increasingly, student activists are fighting back. In 2004, students at Spelman, a black women's college, protested the appearance of the rapper Nelly for a campus fund-raiser. His music video for "Tip Drill" portrays women in bikinis shaking their behinds and clothed men throwing cash at them; a man swipes a credit card between a woman's buttocks.[220] In 2013, Harvard students protested the performance of the hip-hop artist Tyga at the college's spring concert, although the performance went on as scheduled.[221] In his song "Bitches Ain't Shit," Tyga raps, "Need a bitch that can fuck, cook, clean, right. / Turn a bitch out, make her lick twice." In "Bitch Betta Have My Money," Tyga raps, "Shut the fuck up and jump on this dick. Nothing but a motherfucking skank. / Fuck what you talking 'bout and fuck what you thank."

The normalization of sexual violence in campus musical entertainment reflects the normalization of sexual violence in music at large. Beyond college campuses, many male musicians sing about women as sluts who deserve to be raped. Reebok ended its relationship with the rapper Rick Ross after the feminist group UltraViolet created a social media campaign against the entertainer, who brags about raping women. He sings, "Put molly [Ecstacy] all in her Champagne / She ain't even know it / I took her home and I enjoyed that / She ain't even know it."[222]

Although black hip-hop artists have been most scrutinized publicly for their women-hating lyrics, a broad spectrum of white musicians also sing about "sluts" who should be assaulted or murdered if they can't provide sexual pleasure to men. Eminem sings in "Kill You," "Slut, you think I won't choke no whore / 'Til the vocal cords don't work in her throat no more?! / Shut up slut, you're causin' too much chaos." The hip-hop group the Cataracs sing in "Sunrise," "Ain't fuckin, then what the fuck are you for?" and in "Top of the World," "I'm just saying anything to get me up inside your throat. Is it working?" Waking the Cadaver, a death metal band, sings in "Chased Through the Woods by a Rapist": "Tonight this cunt will pay. / My dick will beat her face. / Her life and her cunt are mine. / This slut shall now see. / All night on this bitch I release my piece. / Yes. Yes. I am the man. / And I will kill when I can. / You can try to run. / But you're done."

If you hear these songs, maybe even humming or singing along, you begin to absorb their messages. In these songs—as in much other cultural entertainment—women are represented as nothing more than objects who provide a sexual service to men. Their value, these pop culture entertainers tell us, resides in being a receptacle for men's sexuality. But when women then want to be sexual themselves, they are blamed for being "too" sexual. If they are raped, it was all their fault.

Raped While Drunk

But perhaps the most significant reason for the prevalence of campus sexual assault, which the White House report on rape and sexual assault highlighted, is the consumption of alcohol and drugs on college campuses. "The dynamics of college life appear to fuel the problem" of campus sexual assault, the report reads, "as many survivors are victims of what's called 'incapacitated assault': they are sexually abused while drunk, under the influence of drugs, passed out, or otherwise incapacitated." The report goes on to say that rapists deliberately prey on women who are drunk or drugged, and may deliberately provide their victim with alcohol or drugs. As a result, most sexual assaults take place at parties and involve two people who know each other. In addition, "campus perpetrators are often serial offenders," with 7 percent of college men having committed rape or attempted rape, and 63 percent of those men having admitted to committing an average of six rapes each.[223]

Put simply, men who commit sexual assault target drunk or drugged women for sexual assault, and each of those men tends to assault multiple women.

Although we know from the data that men who rape use alcohol as a vehicle for their crime, the rhetoric of "choosing" to be "slutty" informs many people's understanding of the role of alcohol. Thus, when it comes to credibility, the rape victim who had been drinking faces the toughest hurdle. A woman who drinks is automatically assumed to be "slutty"—a "sloppy slut"—because she is said to have put herself in a risky situation, and therefore she does not deserve sympathy for being victimized. In a 2013 Navy hearing of the gang rape of an intoxicated Naval Academy student in Annapolis, Maryland, by three football-player classmates, one of the defense lawyers asked the victim if she had worn a bra or other underwear the night of the rapes, and whether she "felt like a ho" afterward. Another defense lawyer asked her about her oral sex technique. When the prosecution objected, he claimed that if she had performed oral sex with her mouth opened wide, it would indicate the "active participation" of the woman and therefore her consent.[224] Yet the woman was intoxicated and had passed out while the rapes took place.

Although drinking to the point of becoming incapacitated is unwise and risky for anyone, the blame for rape must be put on the rapist who preys on a drunk woman, not a drunk woman who becomes prey. If my car is stolen after I've parked it with the door unlocked in a neighborhood known for car theft, a crime has been committed, and I have the right and expectation to report the crime to the police. No one would tell me that the thief is the one who deserves sympathy, and that apprehending him would ruin his life. No one would tell me I'm a terrible person for getting my car stolen, and that I deserve to have my car stolen. They would be right to question my judgment, but not the fact that a crime has been committed. But when it comes to rape, the victim's pre-rape actions are used to justify the crime.

Many people presume that if she's not conscious, an intoxicated or drugged woman automatically gives sexual consent. Yet the opposite is true. Both participants must be fully conscious for consent to be present. "College students usually laugh when they hear this guideline," writes Alan D. Berkowitz, PhD, who helps colleges design programs that address health issues. Many college students "cannot imagine two completely sober people having sex." Yet "the greater the extent to which alcohol or other drugs are consumed, the greater the impairment of consent. Less consumption of alcohol or other drugs means that there is a greater chance that consent is present." Berkowitz clarifies that consent may be possible even if alcohol has been consumed, but "the greater the alcohol consumption, the less likely that consent is possible."[225] Just because a partner doesn't say no does not mean that she would say yes if she could. If she doesn't say no because she's excessively drunk (or passed out, or otherwise incapacitated), one must assume that she would say no if she could. Consent is present only if the ability to refuse is also present. If the ability to refuse is absent, there is no consent.

Jamie, a twenty-one-year-old biracial (Latina and white) college senior on the East Coast, was raped in her dorm room during her sophomore year. We meet for lunch at a diner near the office where she's interning part-time. Tall, with long brown hair and olive skin, she exudes confidence and competence. Before we've even ordered our meal, she says to me with a directness I appreciate, "Yes, I've been called a slut. I identify as a lesbian, but I've had my times with men." She is "absolutely" positive that her rape occurred because of her reputation as a "slut."

Over a chicken salad, Jamie tells me her story. During her first year on campus, she came out to the other students in her dorm as a lesbian, but in her second year, she began to hook up with guys as well. Her dorm mates teasingly called her a "lesbian whore." Jamie at first didn't take offense. "I don't think their intention was necessarily to hurt me," she explains. "They would say, 'I saw you making out with that guy at the back of the bar. Just because he bought you one drink doesn't mean you have to go and have sex with him!' They were trying to be funny. Since I was hooking up with girls and guys, they couldn't help themselves. They said, 'You're always with a different person!' They started calling me the Muff Master."

Unable to help myself, I snicker when I hear the vulgar label. I feel terrible about my gaffe, and I apologize profusely. But Jamie understands. "No, it's OK, I know it's funny," she assures me. "The name can definitely be funny!" She laughs with me. "I laughed too when I first heard it! It was not hurtful at first. In a way, I glorified it. I was like: I can hook up with whoever I want. In the beginning, I really didn't mind, and it was my friends who were using the name. I was excited that I had started experimenting sexually, and that I was being acknowledged for who I was."

But, as always happens, she lost control of the situation. It was one thing when the nickname was used between her and her friends as a joking term of endearment, another when her friends started to introduce her that way to strangers, as if this was the thing that defined her and they had license to spread stories about her. "Once the name spread to people who didn't know me, I didn't like it anymore. I would go to parties and I'd say, 'Hi, my name is Jamie,' and then one of my friends would come up from behind me and say, 'This is the one we told you about. She's the Muff Master.' That was when I was like, I don't think I like this anymore."

The name-calling went beyond just friends of friends at a party; it began to haunt her in her dorm, making her unsafe. Jamie's resident adviser created signs for everyone's door. But for Jamie's door, the sign did not say JAMIE. It read MUFF MASTER. The RA's action was particularly inappropriate since she was supposed to oversee the students' well-being. Instead, her action made Jamie feel threatened. Jamie took it down immediately, but her RA put up a new one. "What shocked me was that everybody had heard about me. From sophomores to seniors, they would say, 'Oh, you're the Muff Master! I've heard so much about you.' I'd say, 'What have you heard about me?' 'That you get around.' At that point, I would just walk away. I started telling my friends, "Enough with the whole Muff Master thing. Let's just go back to Jamie. I go by Jamie now." Jamie pauses and sighs. "I probably waited too long. Too much time had gone by. So now I had this reputation of sleeping with anyone. Guys would show up and say to me"— she impersonates a deep, masculine voice—"'So, I hear you're the Muff Master. Would you like to go the other way?'"

One night, her dorm had a party on the floor. Guys were walking in and out of different rooms. Her door sign still said MUFF MASTER. Jamie, who had been drinking at the party, went to her room at 1:00 a.m. Her roommate was away for the weekend, so she wasn't expecting anyone to be inside. She pushed open the door, and sitting at her desk chair was a guy she didn't know, although she recognized him because he worked part-time as the desk attendant in the lobby. "He is a very big man—probably six foot seven." Jamie said, "Can I help you?" He was clearly drunk. He said, "I hear you're the Muff Master, and I hear you like guys too, so how about the two of us, what do you think?"

"I was extremely scared," Jamie tells me. "Now, I'm a big girl; I can defend myself. I'm five foot eight and strong. But I was scared, and I didn't know what to do. He pushed me on the bed. Because of the party, it was very noisy outside my room, with music blasting. I could see that he was not going to leave until he had sex with me. I could see that there was no way I could stop him. I was really scared. So I managed to tell him, 'Listen, let's get a condom.' He didn't listen to me. He raped me, and he did not use a condom."

Jamie ran out of her room hysterical, crying. She found some of her friends, who went with her to her room, where the rapist was still sitting. Her friends told him he had to leave. Jamie again lowers her voice to a deep masculine boom, imitating his voice: "Well, she said that she was fine with it. I don't understand what's the matter." And then he left.

The next day, he sent Jamie a Facebook message: "Hey listen, I don't know what happened last night, but if you want to go in for halvsies on Plan B, let me know." Jamie did not respond. Because he worked in her dorm lobby, she saw him every Tuesday and Thursday at 8:00 a.m. He acted as if everything were normal.

Jamie doubts that he recognizes that he raped her. Even she sounds a little hesitant when she says the word. "I would say it was rape." She pauses. "But I do look at it as sort of my fault." She pauses. "I should have been decisive. I'm an assertive person. I wish I had handled it differently. Did I say no at first? Yes. Of course I said no. But he was forceful, and then I stopped saying no because I was fearful of my personal safety. I just passively let him do what he wanted. I figured, let me just get through it; it will be done soon; and then he would just leave." Jamie's experience shows that rape does not necessarily entail physical force.

Jamie attributes the rape to her reputation as a sexualized woman. "He must have thought, 'Well, she sleeps around all the time, so she'll say yes to me.'"

The "slut" label–rape–alcohol connection can operate in two directions. In Jamie's case, she was first known as "slutty" and then raped as a result of her reputation. The rape took place during a party in which alcohol flowed freely, which as research on campus rape shows is extremely common. The fact that Jamie had been drinking meant her defenses were down, and the rapist no doubt took her condition into account when he targeted her. But sometimes a woman becomes known as a "slut" *because* she is raped while drunk. The "slut" label in this scenario is a mechanism for others to make sense of the sexual assault. Instead of understanding the assault as a crime committed by the rapist, they understand it as a fabrication concocted by the drunken victim.

Melinda, a white thirty-nine-year-old educator in the Pacific Northwest, was raped twice as a teenager; both times, she was blacked-out from being drunk. Melinda grew up in a small town, and her home was "chaotic and violent," she tells me. "My mom was violent to me, physically and verbally. She would beat me and pull my hair, and she was also always very critical of everything I did. She and my dad had come from violence and poverty, and my household was very disjointed." When Melinda was fifteen, in the ninth grade, she went to a party and drank vodka for the first time. Not knowing her limits, she passed out cold. "I had never had sex before, but while I was passed out, I was raped, although I didn't know it. The next day, I felt sore, but I didn't know why."

I asked her how she found out what had occurred. "A guy came to my door the next day and asked me if I knew what had happened." Melinda discovered who had done this to her—a guy at the party who was eighteen or nineteen. It turned out that he had a girlfriend who went to Melinda's high school. Several days later, the girlfriend confronted her. "She called me a slut and a skank and told me to stay away from her boyfriend. All of a sudden, my social status changed. Before the rape, I'd been nerdy. I'd gotten good grades. Now the entire high school saw me as a slut. I was a girl who couldn't be trusted." Even the teachers knew about her rep. One day her French teacher told the class, "Today let's discuss Melinda's sex life." Melinda says wryly, "Since everyone had to speak only in French, I guess he thought it was OK." No one recognized that Melinda had been a victim of violence because she never told anyone, so only his version of what had occurred—that the two of them had had sex— went around.

"Why didn't you tell the girls at school that you'd been raped?" I asked.

"Because I blamed myself. I shouldn't have been drinking. I shouldn't have been at the party. I shouldn't have been pretending that I was a normal girl with a normal family. I felt an immense weight of shame. I became really depressed, and I decided that I was going to own the label. I thought, 'I'll just become the slut you think I am.' I started sleeping around. During the rest of my time in high school, I slept with ten to twelve guys. I drank and smoked pot. I dated the high school drug dealer. I shoplifted. I tried to take control because the story about me was out of my control. Also, I really just wanted attention. I'd only had negative attention, and I did anything to try to get some positive attention."

One year later, she went to a bar with her cousin at her cousin's college campus. She drank and blacked out again. Melinda was raped again—by a college student living in her cousin's dorm, and she became pregnant. She managed to hide the pregnancy from her friends and family. At two months, she deliberately took a home-pregnancy test and left the stick in the bathroom where she knew her mother would find it, but her mother pretended that she never saw it. "But

I knew that she had," Melinda says. "When I was at three months, I told her, and then she told my dad. They were furious with me. I explained that I had been raped, but they said it wasn't really rape and that I deserved it. My mother called me a slut."

Melinda had an abortion at fourteen weeks. "My mom drove me to the clinic and dropped me off, so I had to walk through the protesters by myself. Everyone in my family then pretended that none of this ever happened. I started obsessively going to the gym to try to gain control of my body. I weighed myself all the time and always counted calories. I never got down below 105, but my behavior was neurotic."

I ask Melinda which was worse: having been raped, or having been called a slut. She doesn't hesitate with her reply. "Being called a slut was worse than both rapes," she says. "Being known as a slut was like being branded. No one knew about the second rape. But the labeling was public."

Melinda's reputation occurred before the age of social media. Were she twenty years younger, she likely would have experienced the horror of seeing humiliating, denigrating photographic evidence of her assault, coupled with slut-bashing commentary, bouncing around Twitter, Instagram, and Facebook. Every day, it seems, another girl goes to a party and drinks too much—because she lacks the judgment and experience to know her limit, because boys encourage her to exceed her limit, or possibly, as was in Melinda's case, because she needed to cope with violence at home. She passes out, is raped by multiple perpetrators, is photographed, and is shamed on social media as the photographic evidence of her "sluttiness" is mass-forwarded. As we've seen, in recent years,

Audrie Pott, fifteen, of California, and Rehtaeh Parsons, seventeen, of Nova Scotia, committed suicide after they were gang-raped while drunk. In both cases, boys photographed the assaults and then circulated the photos, adding public humiliation to the private shame and psychological trauma of having been sexually assaulted. Branded "sluts" via social media, each girl determined that she would rather die than live with her reputation.

In Torrington, Connecticut, in 2013, two eighteen-year-old high school football players were charged with raping two thirteen-year-old girls, one of whom drank vodka and smoked marijuana with the boys but who said they did not want to have intercourse. The girls were subsequently taunted as sluts who deserved what they got. A Twitter message posted one day after one of the boys was arrested said, "Even if it was all his fault, what was a 13-year-old girl doing hanging around with 18-year-old guys." The message was reposted several times.[226] One student wrote on Twitter, "Young girls acting like whores there's no punishment for that. Young men acting like boys is a sentence." A high school sophomore told the *Times*, "The chick, she should get in trouble, too. It's probably a regular thing she does."[227]

But the mother of all "drunk raped sluts deserve what they got" narratives is that of the Steubenville, Ohio, victim. On August 11, 2012, a sixteen-year-old girl from West Virginia drank vodka and then went to a party in Steubenville where many popular wrestlers and football players were present, including the team's quarterback, Trent Mays, sixteen, with whom the girl had been flirting via social media. At around midnight, Mays and his friend Ma'lik Richmond, the team's wide receiver, went to another party, and the girl insisted that they bring her with them. At the next party, she threw up. Mays and Richmond carried her outside. She threw up again in front of the house on the street. Then she blacked out and doesn't remember anything until she woke up the next morning in the basement of a senior. She woke up naked next to Mays. According to Ariel Levy of *The New Yorker*, when her friends came to pick her up, "she seemed fine with where she was."[228] The girl had no memory of being raped, and was unsure if a crime had been committed.

Photographic evidence of the girl's sexual assault soon surfaced. An ex-boyfriend uploaded a photograph of the girl being carried by Richmond and Mays on Instagram. Richmond holds her by her ankles while Mays has her by the wrists, and she is clearly incapacitated, dead weight. The ex-boyfriend tweeted, "Never seen anything this sloppy lol." Another boy tweeted, "Whores are hilarious." A third boy tweeted, "If they're getting 'raped' and don't resist then to me it's not rape. I feel bad for her but still." A fourth boy tweeted, "Some people deserve to be peed on." In addition to the photo and tweets, a twelve-minute video of several boys laughing about the girl was created. A Steubenville student says, laughing mirthfully, "You don't need any foreplay with a dead girl" and "She is so raped right now."[229]

At the trial in March 2013, Mays and Richmond were accused of penetrating the girl's vagina with their fingers while she was incapacitated. Mays had texted to one friend that he had had intercourse with her, although he told another friend that he didn't because "she could barely move." To a third friend, he wrote, "I'm pissed all I got was a handjob. I shoulda raped her since everyone thinks I did." One witness said that he saw Mays kneeling over her, trying to insert his penis in her mouth, despite the fact that she had passed out. The witness said that "it didn't seem that bad." Levy writes, "The testimony left little doubt that Mays had been physical with the girl."[230]

These facts are horrifying: A drunken teenage girl is sexually assaulted by boys she trusts. The boys boast about their actions. They mock the girl they assaulted. They humiliate her in the most public way possible. They appear to have no recognition that any of this behavior is wrong.

Other people too—adults in the larger world—also regarded the girl as a sexual object who deserved what she got. After Mays and Richmond were arrested, people unconnected with Steubenville felt compelled to share their opinions on Twitter. They wrote:

> "There is no controversy nor is this up for debate: the girl put herself in the situation and two innocent guys are paying the price."
>
> "IMHO, the girl should be the one held accountable."
>
> "Sorry ladies, skimpy clothing is pretty much implied consent. Don't dress like a whore if you don't want to be treated like one. Simple."
>
> "Shouldn't they charge that Lil Slut for underage drinking???"
>
> "Those poor boys . . . All because the pictures and texts made that lil whore decide to play victim after it was over #Steubenville."
>
> "OMG. . . . U CANNOT RAPE THE WILLING!!"

"Those kids didnt rape that girl. the stupid drunk slut got everything she deserved. Her reputation got fucked up so she took it to the courts"

"That is ridiculous, she knew the possibilities of being taken advantage of when she was under the influence. It is her fault."

"So you got drunk at a party and two people take advantage of you, that's not rape you're just a loose drunk slut."

"Steubenville rape? Lessens 'real' rape, maybe she didn't consent but only cause she was too drunk she drank voluntarily lucky she's not dead"[231]

These responses come from a mind-set in which a "slut" cannot be raped because she invited her assault. She had a choice in the matter. Mays, Richmond, their friends, and everyone who offered these comments on Twitter do not recognize that nonconsensual sex with anyone, regardless of whether they are considered a "slut," is a crime. Levy writes that "the teens seemed largely unaware that they'd been involved in a crime." Prosecutor Jane Hanlin told Levy, "They don't think that what they've seen is a rape in the classic sense"—meaning a stranger jumping out from behind bushes at 3:00 a.m. and threatening to kill the victim if she doesn't comply. And when Levy asked Richmond what he thought when he saw Mays masturbating as he stood over the passed-out victim, Richmond replied, "I wasn't really thinking about, Oh, this is rape. I was just thinking, He talked to her, so I don't really care what they do." Levy explains that "talked to her" means that Mays and the girl had a flirtatious relationship through texting.[232] To Richmond, it was OK for his friend to have sex with the girl despite her inability to consent because she had demonstrated, through texting, that she was interested in his friend. He interpreted textual flirtation as sexual consent, despite the fact that a blacked-out girl not only cannot consent, she also cannot flirt.

"Steubenville happens every week somewhere in this country," says Jennifer Baumgardner, the creator of the powerful documentary *It Was Rape*, which tells the stories of eight diverse women and their experiences with sexual assault. The most striking aspect of the film is witnessing the strategies women use to cope with being assaulted. Not one of the women profiled in the documentary screamed during her assault. Already naked and vulnerable, they were afraid to do anything that would signal they were being coerced. Two of the women ended up dating their rapists after having been raped. As one of the women explains in the film, dating her rapist was a coping mechanism that "normalized things."

CHAPTER 8

Can "Slut" Be Reclaimed?[233]

When I planned to attend New York City's SlutWalk in October 2011, I had high expectations. I assumed the event, an antirape march, would be the protest rally I'd long been waiting for.

The logo for the SlutWalk was a lipstick-wearing Statue of Liberty holding up a placard reading, "No Excuse for Rape!" The tagline: "No one has the right to touch you without your consent." As with Take Back the Night marches, an annual fixture on many campuses, the goal was to raise awareness about the prevalence of sexual violence and to protest the common tendency to blame the victim because of her clothes or behavior. But Take Back the Night marches emphasize the danger of stranger rape and the need to stay safe while walking alone in the dark. This march highlighted rape committed by someone the victim knows, when the issue of consent is complicated because the victim doesn't express consent, yet the assaulter presumes consent is given, or just doesn't care.

How did a movement of antirape marches get the word "slut" in its title? The first SlutWalk took place in Toronto in April 2011 after a representative of the Toronto Police told female students at a York University safety seminar that "I'm not supposed to say this" but "women should avoid dressing like sluts in order not to be victimized."[234] Outraged students rose up in protest, and Sonya Barnett and Heather Jarvis, two Toronto feminists, organized the first event.[235] SlutWalks then took place in dozens of cities and college campuses across Canada and the United States and in hundreds of cities around the world. Within several months, an enormous, exciting international grassroots movement swelled. Although it largely fizzled out after 2012, SlutWalk had been the biggest grassroots feminist movement in decades.

The movement's primary message was that sexual assault is never the victim's fault. Simultaneously, SlutWalk also demanded that women have the right to be sexual without being slut-shamed. The genius of the movement—the reason it caught fire immediately—was that it finessed the paradox of women's being sexual without being sexual objects while also connecting this paradox with sexual violence.

As my excitement escalated in the weeks before New York City's SlutWalk, I hoped that the point of invoking "slut" in the title was to prod people to think twice before using the term. I figured that the term "slut" was finally going to get the critique it deserved. Lots of people would now have the chance to ponder the meanings of "slut" and would refuse to use the word ever again.

Yet when I arrived, I discovered that in fact the word "slut" was celebrated. Approximately three thousand people—mostly young white women—milled around Union Square with placards reading "Sluts Say Yes" and "I'm Only a Slut for My Man" while the band Witches in Bikinis (yes, they wear bikinis—along with wigs in neon colors) sang over and over, "If I wanna be a slut, so what? So what?" Humorously dismissing anyone who argues that a woman dressed in sexually provocative clothes is issuing an invitation to be raped, many marchers arrived wearing little more than boots, tights, and bras. They walked around the neighborhood for an hour chanting, "However I'm dressed, wherever I go, yes means yes and no means no." Soon the bras were discarded; a number of women remained topless. On their chests, many had written in marker slogans such as CONSENT IS SEXY. One woman penned, I AM MORE THAN THESE with arrows pointing to her breasts.

Is Reclamation the Best Strategy?

Is the time ripe to reclaim "slut"? Forgive me, sisters; I don't think so.

Since the Riot Grrrl feminist punk rock movement of the early 1990s, when Kathleen Hanna of the band Bikini Kill wrote SLUT on her stomach in lipstick, there have been localized feminist efforts to wrest control of the label. Instead of being shamed for our sexuality, the thinking has been, let's take ownership of this label and subvert its meanings. It's a brave, saucy move with doses of irony and humor mixed in, and one that's been gestating for a while. Years before the movement sought to rehabilitate the term, I started amassing a closet full of SLUT T-shirts given to me by campus groups after my lectures on slut-bashing. But I've never worn them. Simply put, most people aren't in on the joke, which creates more issues than it solves.

Certainly at the SlutWalk, everyone was in on the joke. I asked a young woman named Sonya, dressed in a Super-woman costume with SUPERSLUT printed on her chest in marker, what the word "slut" means to her. "Female empow-erment," she told me. "Being proud to be a woman." Another woman held up a sign reading, "I Am a Rape Survivor—No One Deserves It." I asked her what she thought about the word "slut." She too advocated reclaiming the term. "It's naive to think we can ever eradicate it," she told me. "I was called a slut in high school and later on my boyfriend raped me. I never thought of myself as a slut, because I was not promis-cuous. Reclaiming the word is good. We can take it back by changing the tone and the attitude." Another woman, wear-ing a SLUTS EVERYWHERE T-shirt, told me that "the ideal is to get rid of the word but we can't, so let's embrace it."

SlutWalk NYC, like the movement as a whole, was a serious call to action. Organizers chose to hold the event at Union Square to raise awareness of a nearby rape of a woman by an NYPD officer. The victim had approached the officer in 2008, asking for help getting home because she was drunk. The officer as-saulted her in her apartment while his colleague stood watch. At one point during the trial, the officer's defense attorney likened the victim's genitals to a Venus flytrap, suggesting that the victim was a dangerous predator rather than prey, and that her menace emanated from her sexuality.[236] The officers were charged only with official misconduct. In one way, this particular assault was anomalous: the victim and the rapist did not know each other. Although most people don't realize it, rape rarely involves strangers. But in other ways, the NYPD rape was all too typical: the defense claimed that the victim couldn't have been raped because her body showed no signs of physical force. Again, although most people don't know it, rape rarely involves physical violence. In this particular case, the victim was drunk, and therefore could not give consent.

The SlutWalk movement was an attempt to educate people about the realities of rape and to dispel the myths. Marchers wanted everyone to know that women should be able to wear what they want, drink alcohol, and be sexually active without the threat of sexual violence and, if assaulted, without blame for being a "slut." The movement was as much about women's right to be sexually active as it was about sexual violence. "By demanding sex without rape and insisting that consent distinguishes the two, [SlutWalk participants] are in effect declaring their sexual agency," writes Deborah Tuerkheimer, a professor of law at DePaul University College of Law.[237] SlutWalkers were saying that the best strategy to educate people about the nature of sexual assault is for women to showcase their "sluttiness"—to take ownership of their sexual selves.

My friend Alix Kates Shulman, the author of the bestselling novel *Memoirs of an Ex-Prom Queen* and an early radical feminist who helped organize the 1968 Miss America protest, in which feminists crowned a live sheep, believes in the power of the extravagant gesture in political protest. "My gut feeling," she told me, "is that the more outrageous the protest, the more attention it gets and the more awareness rises. When done with humor, it's like pricking a balloon. In my experience, the reclamation of a negative term—such as 'bitch'—defuses it. It might help people laugh at someone so dumb as to use the 'S' word as an epithet."

Shulman is right: The reason SlutWalks were so successful is that they were called, well, "SlutWalks." And contrary to the stereotype of the humorless, strident woman's libber ("How many feminists does it take to screw in a lightbulb? One, and that's not funny!"), SlutWalk participants were playful, even zany.

Still, I pause and question the strategy of organizing around "slut" as a unifying identity.

After a member of Femen, a Ukrainian women's rights group known for baring their breasts, staged a topless protest in Berlin in front of Russian president Vladimir Putin, calling him a "dictator," he smiled in amusement and put up two thumbs of approval.[238] "If you're a feminist and a stripper, and the guys watching you don't know that, does it really matter?" asks Andi Zeisler, the cofounder and editor of *Bitch* magazine.[239] You may think that your feminist message, or your feminist identity, is obvious, but chances are it's not only not obvious, it's an object of ridicule.

Cultural context is everything. When Shulman's women's lib cohorts threw off their bras in 1968, going braless was effective as a form of protest because women were expected to wear girdles and hosiery. In the 1960s, dressing in an overtly revealing manner was taboo. The contrast between convention and protest was jolting; eschewing a bra or going topless definitely made a statement. But in a culture where females are hypersexualized, embracing the word "slut" does not seem like a radical protest. It seems like a capitulation. Today, girls are pressured to dress and behave in an overtly sexual way, despite the conventional understanding that a "slut" is a woman who does just that. In this milieu, calling oneself a "slut" doesn't allow you to wrest the term away from those who would use it to judge and control women. Rather, it just confirms negative stereotypes of what it means to be female. You're merely adding ammunition to the arsenal.

From Slut Pride workshops at Harvard to the anti-GOP Rock the Slut Vote political movement to the social media campaign Sluts Unite, reappropriation of "slut" in a "good" way is fashionable. Yet when Yale fraternity pledges hold a sign reading "We Love Yale Sluts" or when millions of us receive spam emails advertising the availability of "Hot Local Sluts," the term is used in the traditional "bad" sense, referring to females as nothing more than sexual objects. A twenty-year-old male student at Brown University told me that an acquaintance, a male athlete, posted on his Facebook wall a photo of a woman from a SlutWalk with this caption underneath: "I like to pretend I was raped, but I was asking for it."

To feminists, "slut" means "sexually liberated woman." But to most people, "slut" means "disgusting woman who deserves to be shamed or even assaulted." This contradiction exposes the tension between different meanings associated with the word "slut."

I fear that that the weight of this contradiction is too much for the word "slut" to bear.

Yes, language is inherently unstable. It is constantly shifting, as we know from the etymology of "slut"; Chaucer used "sluttish" to refer to a man who was untidy, and the word has picked up a motley of meanings on its journey over the last six hundred years. Different people associate different meanings with specific words, and nobody can pin the meaning of any word as if on a museum display. I hope that the injurious meanings of "slut" will erode over time, and I look forward to the day when the word is either not necessary or is translated with positive associations. Yet I am deeply concerned that right now may not be the most strategic time to wrestle over the meanings of "slut" because the space for misunderstanding is cavernous. When you reclaim "slut," it's not clear to most people what exactly you are reclaiming.

SlutWalk performed on a grand scale what teenage girls and college-age women do when they posture as "good sluts." And as we've seen, the strategy of positioning oneself as a "good slut" never ends well. When a young female asserts her sexual identity in public, eventually she loses control and the "good slut" morphs quickly into "bad." It's impossible to truly control how the term is used in connection with one's own character. Even when a girl attempts to circumscribe her sexual identity within an in-group of peers, the porousness of social media leads to leakage, and her actions (real or contrived) become known—and judged—by others not in her inner circle. And when others call her a "slut," they are the ones dictating the meanings of the term.

Why should we assume that the results would be different for women at large? I believe that they won't be. Within the SlutWalk movement, a woman could define herself as a "slut" in the positive sense of "a woman who's unapologetically sexual without shame," but that was only really effective within the safe cocoon of movement protests. Because of the existence of the sexual double standard, few people outside feminist communities will regard her as empowered. They will denigrate her—and, as we've also seen, quite possibly assault her. This danger makes the reappropriation of "slut" fundamentally different from efforts to gain control over other negative stereotypes. For this reason, while I found the SlutWalk movement invigorating, I strongly believe that taking up "slut" as a crystallizing call to action is doomed to hurt women rather than help them—at least at this historical moment.

Is there any hope for reappropriating negative language? The word "queer" often is held as a reclamation success story because it is no longer automatically assumed to be an epithet suggesting that same-sex desire is deviant. Its negative associations have largely been diffused. It is understood by most people today as a confrontational yet celebratory word—as the activist group Queer Nation memorably chanted in the 1990s, "We're here! We're queer! Get used to it!"—or as a neutral descriptor of lesbians, gay men, bisexuals, and transgendered people.

Yet "queer" has its detractors, too. Not all in-group members support the term's usage. Also, the word means different things to in-group and out-group members. "Queer" was reappropriated not to replace "LGBT" but to refer broadly and inclusively to anyone with nonnormative sexuality, including straight people who identify as nonmonogamous; sadomasochist, bondage, and discipline aficionados; and fetishists. People who identify as "queer" use the term to contest rigid sexual categories based on sexual orientation. Yet most nonqueer people have failed to recognize the nuance, and have come to equate "queer" with "LGBT." Thus, while "queer" is now worn as a defiant badge of pride, it's a badge that often is misread and misunderstood.[240]

The reclamation of "queer" demonstrates that linguistic development is uncertain and impossible to predict. Likewise, there's no way to know how "slut" would be taken up by out-group members should reclamation become a more popular goal. Perhaps "slut" would be understood as "sexually empowered." Perhaps it won't.

"Bitch" is also often turned on its head to convey a playful reappropriation. Twenty-one-year-old Maria, the Latina college senior on the East Coast, reports that women on her campus call themselves "bad bitches" in a positive way. "It means you're a woman with an attitude, in a good way, and that you're having sex and you're proud of it," she explains. Owning "bitch" is an assertion of autonomy and sexual independence. It means you're not a docile doormat. But "bitch" can be appropriated in a way that "slut" cannot because "bitch" is fundamentally different from "slut." When used pejoratively, "bitch" is a commentary on a woman's attitude or behavior, not about her essence or about specific transgressions believed to mirror who she is as a person. If a bitchy woman changed her attitude and behavior and decided to behave submissively, no one would call her a bitch again. But when a woman designated a slut avoids any hint of sexuality, people continue to call her a slut anyway. "Slut" sticks for life, regardless of behavior.

Racism and the Risks of Reclamation

I admit that for personal reasons, reclaiming "slut" for myself is just not feasible. Having experienced slut-bashing in high school, I see no positives in trying to take ownership of the word that wounded me and still has the power to do so. Because of my personal history with the word, were I to label myself a slut, I would worry about impairing my professional, parental, and social credibility. I support sexual equality, and I believe that women should be judged on the same sexual scale that males are. But a public identity as a slut could invite harassment.

I'm not the only woman who hesitates. "If a woman has reported being sexually assaulted, participating in a SlutWalk could be used against her," Wagatwe Wanjuki, a twenty-six-year-old black social justice activist who has written and spoken about her own assault at Tufts University in 2007, warns me. "People who don't believe her could say, 'She couldn't have been raped because look at how she's dressed,' or 'Clearly, she's not really traumatized.' I still worry that I can't get away with doing 'slutty' things because they would be used as justification to not believe that I was assaulted and to invalidate me." Reclaiming "slut" is a luxury that many women cannot afford.

Women of color, particularly black women, worry that the pejorative meanings are inseparable from the word itself. Historically, white women and men have likened black women to sexual savages. The default assumption for women of color among white people is that they are "sluts," "hos," and "Jezebels"—that they are inherently and thoroughly hyper-sexualized and therefore impossible to truly rape. Reclamation of "slut" makes no sense for someone already assumed to be a "slut." In fact, it may be an act of self-harm; why denigrate yourself even more than you're denigrated already? Why deepen your own oppression?

A week before the 2011 SlutWalk in New York City, an organization called Black Women's Blueprint posted an open letter to the event's organizers, signed by hundreds of black female scholars, activists, and leaders; the letter was published on the *Huffington Post*. An excerpt of the letter reads:

We are perplexed by the use of the term "slut" and by any implication that this word, much like the word "Ho" or the "N" word, should be re-appropriated. The way in which we are perceived and what happens to us before, during and after sexual assault crosses the boundaries of our mode of dress. Much of this is tied to our particular history. In the United States, where slavery constructed Black female sexualities, Jim Crow kidnappings, rape and lynchings . . . "slut" has different associations for Black women. We do not recognize ourselves nor do we see our lived experiences reflected within SlutWalk and especially not in its brand and its label.

As Black women, we do not have the privilege or the space to call ourselves "slut" without validating the already historically entrenched ideology and recurring messages about what and who the Black woman is. We don't have the privilege to play on destructive representations burned in our collective minds, on our bodies and souls for generations. . . .

Although we vehemently support a woman's right to wear whatever she wants any time, anywhere, within the context of a "SlutWalk" we don't have the privilege to walk through the streets of New York City, Detroit, D.C., Atlanta, Chicago, Miami, L.A., etc., either half-naked or fully clothed self-identifying as "sluts" and think that this will make women safer in our communities an hour later, a month later, or a year later. Moreover, we are careful not to set a precedent for our young girls by giving them the message that we can self-identify as "sluts" when we're still working to annihilate the word "ho," which deriving from the word "hooker" or "whore," as in "Jezebel whore" was meant to dehumanize. Lastly, we do not want to encourage our young men, our Black fathers, sons and brothers to reinforce Black women's identities as "sluts" by normalizing the term on t-shirts, buttons, flyers and pamphlets.[241]

The argument put forth by Black Women's Blueprint is that only a woman with white racial privilege can reclaim "slut." The SlutWalk movement flaunted the privilege white women possess to play around with a "good slut" identity, erasing the history of Black women's sexual slander. "Slut" can't be reclaimed because out-group members use the word with its pejorative racist and sexist meanings.

Many white feminists similarly worry that "slut" is too dangerous for them personally, or for the women in their communities. "I was in *The Vagina Monologues* last year, and people paid a lot of attention to the 'Reclaiming Cunt' scene," reports twenty-one-year-old Cynthia, the white Pennsylvania student. "I noticed that now people use the word 'cunt' a lot—but in an abusive way. People on campus who don't believe in women's equality like to be able to use the word because they think it's acceptable and cool, and they don't even realize that in the play, it's supposed to be about women's sexual empowerment. And I think it's the same thing with 'slut.' The majority are going to use it in a negative way." If we normalize "slut," providing opportunities for people to use the word conversationally, they may wield it as a weapon under the cover of social acceptance. Georgiana, the twenty-two-year-old white doctoral student in comparative literature, succinctly sums up these concerns. "Try telling someone on my campus, where 'feminism' is a dirty word, that 'slut' is a positive word. It would not work at all."

Before and after SlutWalk NYC, the organizers of the event met to discuss the issues raised by Black Women's Blueprint, which were about the movement in general, not about the New York event specifically. Nicole Kubon, one of the white organizers, as well as other organizers involved, did not want to exclude any feminists "just because they didn't support this particular movement," she tells me. "There was a number of us that wanted to address the issues that were raised during the rally itself. We had long discussions and arguments about how to respond to the critique." But Kubon, who is a social worker and the vice president of the National Organization for Women's Young Feminists and Allies chapter, admits that not all the white organizers wanted to address the Black Women's Blueprint critique. "Some of the organizers worried that the critique took away from all the hard work we'd done to organize the event itself and to give voice to marginalized folks. We all recognized the role of racial privilege, but some of the organizers became defensive instead of examining the ways this privilege affected their point of view. Internally, we could not get on the same page. Not everyone 'got it.'"

Of the thousands who participated in the event, many were people of color, and three of the MCs were women of color, but the majority were white. There's nothing wrong with a white-dominated political event, just as there's nothing wrong with a black- or Asian- or Latina-dominated political event. What *is* a problem is when white feminists universalize the experiences of white women, suggesting that their concerns are shared by all women and excluding the problems of other women—a racial blind spot that many white feminists have long held. If reclaiming the word "slut" is a good idea for some white women, the thinking goes, then it must be a good idea for *all* women.

And then there was the notorious sign. A white participant at the 2011 NYC SlutWalk created a placard quoting John Lennon and Yoko Ono: "Woman Is the Nigger of the World." A friend, also white, was photographed holding the sign above her head, with white women standing around smiling, seemingly unperturbed. I didn't see the sign myself at the event, but in the days that followed, the photo made its way around the feminist social media blogosphere, with women of color and white women heatedly discussing the arrogance of the sign's messages—that the oppression of blacks (presumably black men) is a metaphor for the oppression of women (presumably non-black women); that black women don't exist; and that it's acceptable for white women to blithely use the 'N' word. "If SlutWalk has proven anything," wrote Aura Bogado, the author of the blog *To the Curb*, "it is that liberal white women are perfectly comfortable parading their privilege, absorbing every speck of airtime celebrating their audacity and ignoring women of color."[242]

"The fact that we are always Black and female at exactly the same time is a fact that continues to elude white women," wrote Brittney Cooper, an assistant professor of women's and gender studies and Africana studies at Rutgers University, on the website *Crunk Feminist Collective*. She continued,

The organizers of SlutWalk are genuinely baffled that this happened in the first place. To organize a movement around the reclamation of a term is in and of itself an act of white privilege. To not make explicit and clear the privilege and power inherent in such an act is to invite less-informed folks with privilege (in other words, folks who know just enough to be dangerous) to assume that reclamation can be applied universally. . . . "Woman" is not a universal experience . . . "Nigger" is not a catchall term for oppression . . . And "slut" is not the anchor point of a universal movement around female sexuality, no matter how much global resonance it has.[243]

The concept of reclaiming "sluttiness" presumes that a woman has other options for her sexual identity. She could "own" sluttiness, or she could "own" being a prude. A woman who is always assumed to be a "slut" and can never take on the "prude" persona no matter how asexual she may be or pretend to be can never have fun with the "slut" identity. Cooper explains that "sluttiness" and "slut-shaming" are "central to white women's experiences of sexuality. So to start a movement around that word is inherently to place white women and their experiences at the center." Black women "are always already sexually free, insatiable, ready to go, freaky, dirty, and by consequence, unrapeable. When it comes to reclamations of sexuality, in some senses, Black women are always already fucked."[244]

Yet some women of color openly embrace the "slut" label. Favianna Rodriguez, a Latina queer artist known for her politically charged work focusing on immigration and globalization, has created a series of "Slut Power" posters featuring brown women, bold colors, and eye-opening text reading POLITICIANS OFF MY POONTANG! MY UTERUS IS MINE and I'M A SLUT. I VOTE. SO DOES EVERYONE I SLEEP WITH. AND YOU'RE ABOUT TO BE MORE FUCKED THAN I AM. KEEP UR GOVERNMENT OFF MY PUSSY. Explaining the message of these posters, she writes, "Politicians and conservatives are waging an all-out war on women, our bodies, our access to health, our right to birth control, and our right to free, accessible and safe abortion. Everywhere you turn, the right wing is attempting to further limit and hinder our access to our reproductive rights through anti-contraceptive measures. I am fed up . . . I decided it was time for some slut positivity."[245]

The first time I spoke with Rodriguez was in 1997, when she was nineteen and a student at the University of California, Berkeley. She reached out to me to share her story of slut-bashing when I was conducting research for my 1999 book *Slut!*. She had been beaten up by her peers, who called her "slut," "whore," and "ho." In *Slut!*, I protected her identity by changing her name to "Rosalina Lopez," and I quoted her as saying, "I really think that being called a slut empowered me. The more people are marginalized, the more they see things in a critical way. You start to have almost a double consciousness: You see the role you're supposed to be in, but you also see that you're not in it."[246]

The Favianna Rodriguez I spoke with sixteen years later is a respected and popular artist who travels around the world talking about her art and her politics, yet in many respects she hasn't changed at all. She cuts a bold appearance with thick, curly hair, bright lipstick, and doorknocker earrings; her face is tempered by an inviting smile and soulful eyes. I asked her if, as a woman of color, she is concerned about describing herself as a slut. No, Rodriguez emphatically told me. Reappropriation of "slut" is central to her work, she explained:

Precisely because I'm Latina, there's an expectation that I'm sexually conservative, and a lot of Latinas have an unhealthy view of our sexuality. There's a lot of slut-shaming. But I am very sexually open. I am nonmonogamous; I have open relationships. I embrace the slut identity. This is my liberation. I challenge how women of color should be perceived, and it really messes with people's heads. They're like, Whoa! Which is why I keep doing it. People shouldn't assume that women of color all think about sexuality in a certain way.

I believe in the power of framing. I have lived on both sides of this issue, from slut-shaming to slut empowerment. Labels are used to disempower people, but I got to the point where I could turn this word around and make it something I could embrace. There is a power in satire and flipping things. There is a space for us to turn away from the "bad girl" narrative into a narrative of humor and satire. You know, a lot of moms buy my Slut Power posters for their daughters, and SlutWalks are very powerful. In the long term, the word will change because of these things.

Rodriguez's argument, that we need to wrest control of labels to void them of their power to hurt us, is important and seductive. She's right that we can't sit back quietly and passively while others define and name us.

What concerned me about the SlutWalk movement was not that "slut" was flipped around but that the act of flipping was presented as something feminists had to embrace to show support for women's sexual equality. Jaclyn Friedman, the author of the essay "My Sluthood, Myself" and an editor of the book *Yes Means Yes: Visions of Female Sexual Power and a World Without Rape*, told me that she felt uncomfortable with the prescriptive undertone at some of the marches. "I have claimed the term for myself some of the time," she said. "I find it useful in a way that takes the sting out of it. OK, what if I am a slut? What does that even mean? I'm not ashamed. But this is not the right strategy for everyone. Many women of color have said that this is not a safe strategy for them. There are different consequences for me than there are for other people." Embracing the "slut" label, then, works for some people, but those who support women's sexual equality should not be made to feel that calling oneself a slut or reclaiming the term is a required feminist entrance ticket.

Hurtful Words

Another eloquent rumination on the subject of reappropriating hurtful words is Judith Butler's book *Excitable Speech: A Politics of the Performative*. Butler, the acclaimed poststructuralist philosopher at the University of California, Berkley, who is white, Jewish, and queer, questions whether censorship of hate speech eliminates the wounds of hate speech. She observes that as painful as it is to be referred to by a slur, the slur opens opportunities to disrupt and subvert dominant assumptions. She writes,

One is not simply fixed by the name that one is called. In being called an injurious name, one is derogated and demeaned. But the name holds out another possibility as well: by being called a name, one is also, paradoxically, given a certain possibility for social existence, initiated into a temporal life of language that exceeds the prior purposes that animate that call. Thus the injurious address may appear to fix or paralyze the one it hails, but it may also produce an unexpected and enabling response.[247]

Using a hurtful slur is a method of telling someone that she is not as good as you. But using the slur does not cause her to become less good than you. To Butler, injurious speech is not conduct. She rejects the idea that hate speech is a form of doing, such as a judge stating, "I sentence you." Rather, Butler argues, hate speech merely initiates a set of consequences, such as when someone yells "Fire!" and others hurriedly exit a building. Most people understand "Fire!" in the context of an enclosed space as a persuasive statement meaning, "You guys really ought to hurry out of here if you want to be safe!" But yelling "Fire!" does not cause a fire. Likewise, Butler argues, a negative slur does not cause the slurred individual to become the thing she is called.[248] Therefore, we can tinker with the word's meanings and contexts. Hurtful words hold an "ironic hopefulness," Butler says, and "the conventional relation between word and wound might become tenuous and even broken over time."[249]

Randall Kennedy, a Harvard Law professor and the author of *Nigger: The Strange Career of a Troublesome Word*, affirms that the "N" word can be reappropriated successfully—though usually only by members of the in-group. When used by blacks among themselves, the word can convey warmth, affection, and a shared historical sensibility, he says. It was considered off-limits until the comedian and social critic Richard Pryor created performances that liberally used the "N" word to examine racism. Many entertainers—Chris Rock, Jay-Z, Ice-T, N.W.A—have deliberately imbued the word with positive meanings.[250] "To proclaim oneself a nigger is to identify oneself as real, authentic, uncut, unassimilated, and unassimilable—the opposite, in short, of a Negro, someone whose rejection of *nigger* is seen as an effort to blend into the white mainstream," writes Kennedy. The "N" word is a way to "keep it real."[251]

Kennedy believes that the "N" word today is not inherently racist; context is everything. In a nonracist context, even a white person, he believes, can use the word. However, he warns, it can be very difficult to make sense of the way the word is used and what precisely the context is. "This complexity has its costs. Miscues are bound to proliferate as speakers and audiences misjudge each other," he concludes.[252]

Jabari Asim, a writer and editor, also cautions that the spelling "nigga" in gangsta rap has opened a door that white people have entered, even though they're often not invited into the room. Because the new spelling seems playful and therefore acceptable, Asim writes in *The N Word: Who Can Say It, Who Shouldn't, and Why*, racist white people use it interchangeably with the traditional spelling.[253] Using the "N" word with either spelling is a risky endeavor for non-blacks because if the speaker and audience misjudge each other, negative stereotypes about African Americans are preserved rather than smashed. Kennedy and Asim point to the fact that in-group members often don't trust out-group members' linguistic savvy. Because of their history of oppression, people of color presume that those outside of their communities will wield the reappropriated slur as a new model of an old weapon.

To Butler, censoring or eradicating injurious words is a lost cause: "Keeping such terms unsaid and unsayable can also work to lock them in place, preserving their power to injure," she warns. Instead, those who are injured by hate speech should take on their "performative power" by appropriating the terms and turning the degrading meanings on their head.[254]

But censorship of the "N" word is sometimes necessary, particularly in mixed-race groups. Raediah Lyles, a graduate of Shippensburg University in Pennsylvania, served for two years as a resident adviser of a residence hall that was predominantly composed of white students, although there were African American and Latino students as well. The only woman of color in the hall, she immediately created a new rule: Absolutely no racial or gender slurs would be tolerated. "I grew up in inner-city Pittsburgh," she tells me.

My family used the "N" word all the time. But I noticed that students, including whites, were using the "N" word. In one instance, I could tell they were using it in a blatantly racist way. In the other instances, I honestly didn't know their intentions, but I would say that the racism was subtle. Perhaps they did not believe they were racist, but they were inconsiderate in not even thinking about how their words can affect others around them. They used the word to be "cool," and their justification was that their African American friends were using it. I wasn't alarmed when a student of color said it, but I spoke to them and explained, "I get that *you* use it as a term of endearment, but now whites think it's OK." When I spoke to the white students, they would defend and explain their reasons. I was friendly about it, but stern. I explained that there was a zero-tolerance policy for any derogatory slurs used by anyone, including racial slurs used against whites, which sometimes was done as a joke. Usually my scolding the student was enough, and the student would stop, although I did have to ask one white student to leave the hall. I had the same policy with "slut." If you hear your friends use it among themselves, you start to think it's OK to use it, and you just don't know any better. "Slut" was not tolerated in my hall.

Lyles distinguishes between in-group and out-group usage of slurs. She understands that when used exclusively among members of an in-group, a slur can be reappropriated and used safely. But when in-group and out-group members mingle, and out-group members conclude that they too can reappropriate, harmful stereotypes are resurrected.

I want to be hopeful about the transformative possibilities of recontextualizing injurious words. Alas, I am not—at least not right now. We have reached a historical point at which most people recognize that the "N" word creates and reopens deep trauma. (The white women at the SlutWalk who held the sign with the "N" word did not intend to send a racist message, although the meanings of their sign had racist effects. They erased black women out of ignorance, which is no small problem, but had they been educated about white privilege, they most likely would not repeat the gesture.) But others use the "N" word strategically to express racial prejudice or hatred. As Kennedy and Butler both point out, the context is central when reappropriating racialized hate speech.

Unlike the "N" word, however, "slut" in its negative, judgmental sense is regarded by the majority of Americans as a useful and necessary punitive term. It has never been seen as exceedingly inflammatory, despite its often disastrous and damaging impact—a disconnect that perhaps buoys its continued power. Because of the force of the sexual double standard, many people have internalized the belief that female sexual shaming is a good thing, that women (but not men) who enjoy sex with more than one partner, or who drink at parties, or who wear sexually provocative clothes, or who otherwise fulfill the stereotype of the "slut," deserve to be shamed. While racism is almost universally denounced—even by some people who may themselves be racially prejudiced—the sexual double standard is largely upheld, which is why feminism remains essential. In this climate, reappropriating "slut" may be riskier than reclaiming the "N" word because the pejorative meanings can't be pulled away. It's simply too likely that the effort will backfire, that bias against women believed to deviate from accepted conduct will result, and that violence against these women will escalate rather than diminish.

It's true that among members of a feminist in-group, the

"slut" label can serve as a poignant marker of solidarity. At the 2011 Boston SlutWalk, Jaclyn Friedman delivered an electrifying presentation in which she drew from the power of the word to unite women. She called on everyone present to identify as "sluts":

> If you've ever been called a slut, stand up now and say together—I am a slut. If you love someone who's been called a slut—stand up now and say, I am a slut. If you've ever been afraid of being called a slut, stand up now and say, I am a slut. If you've been blamed for violence that someone else did to you, stand up now and say, I am a slut. If you're here to demand a world in which what we do with our bodies is nobody's business, and we can all live our lives and pursue our pleasures free of shame, blame, and free, stand up and say it with me: I am a slut. I am a slut. I am a slut.[255]

Friedman used "slut" as an identity marker to create solidarity, she explained to me, because "If you're going to call one of us a slut, then we are all sluts. I was suggesting that if you come after one of us, you'll have to come after all of us. None of us deserves to be singled out and maligned."

Friedman's rhetorical strategy was successful in that moment because she was addressing people who had chosen to attend an event called "SlutWalk." She was speaking to the in-group. But outside the context of a SlutWalk, the in-group is not stable and identifiable. Women slut-shame each other, after all. Even feminists sometimes slut-shame other women. (Alexandria Goddard, the blogger who exposed the Steubenville rape case, turning it into a feminist cause célèbre, has referred to the female prosecutor as "Gravy Legs" because, as she told Ariel Levy of *The New Yorker*, "gravy spreads easily."[256]) With "slut," there simply may be no in-group outside the SlutWalk movement, which has lost momentum.

In addition, we have a mountain of evidence that reclamation of "slut" does not work. We have heard the voices of multiple girls and young women who attempted to embrace sluttiness to reclaim the term and the identity, and repeatedly we have seen the failure of this strategy. Girls and women nearly always lose control over their "good slut" image as it transmogrifies into a "bad slut" identity.

Still, many women feel empowered by taking back this hurtful, horrible term. Reclaiming the word may be a coping mechanism for some who have survived sexual violence or slut-bashing. No one can control the fluidity of linguistic development, and the meanings of "slut" will shift over time organically. And yes, activism *should* be fun, humorous, and joyous. Nevertheless, there is a real possibility that mass reclamation will trigger a terrible backlash against women.

I fervently hope for the day when we can all use "slut" as a feminist punch line that exposes the absurdity of the sexual double standard, but we are not there yet. First we must provide broader education about slut-shaming and sexual violence. Only when we have some degree of certainty that most people would agree that "slut" is a dangerous epithet can we begin taking back the word and making it ours.

CHAPTER 9

Creative Solutions to Eliminate "Slut"

If reclaiming the word "slut" isn't the answer, what is? The most strategic solution is to open up dialogue with girls and young women about the meanings of "slut." Through conversation and analysis, we can sharpen awareness that "slut" is a violent label; when females are called sluts, sexual assault and self-assault all too often lurk nearby.

But first there is an important distinction to make here: it's not female sexuality that is dangerous, but the sexual double standard. The way women are treated, not the fact of being a woman, is the problem. We must discard the sexual double standard, which cultivates "slut" as an acceptable label, without rejecting female sexuality. In a world without "slut," everyone would know that women and men both have sexual desire, that healthy sexuality requires active consent, that sex without consent is assault, and that victims of assault are never responsible for what has been done to them.

At this moment, it is not possible for a young woman to assert her sexuality outside of a monogamous relationship and not risk being called a slut. She should not have to change her sexual expression to avoid the label. Instead, all others must change their attitudes. Around the country, girls and women are taking matters into their own hands and chipping away at the mind-set that slut-shaming is acceptable and necessary.

Internet Activism

Social media and the Internet, which can help to oppress girls and women, can also serve as tools of liberation. The anti–street harassment group Hollaback! showed what was possible in 2005, back when a tweet was the sound a bird made, and "pinning" meant affixing a material item to a corkboard. One day a blond-haired man sat across from twenty-two-year-old Thao Nguyen on the R train in New York City, looked her in the eye, opened his pants, and began to mastrubate. Nguyen was alone and scared for her personal safety. She happened to have in her bag one of the early mobile phones with an attached camera. Nguyen snapped his photo, and left the train the first chance she got. She took the photo to the police to report the incident, but officers told her there was nothing they could do.

But Nguyen didn't want to dismiss what had occurred. This wasn't just a creepy interlude with a fellow commuter.

It was an act of sexual harassment. The masturbator wanted Nguyen to see him so that she would feel frightened and vulnerable. Chances are, he figured he would get away with his act, because in a culture with rampant slut-shaming, men have become accustomed to treating women as sexual objects and worthless "sluts." In fact, as a result of street sexual harassment, many women blame themselves after an incident of sexual harassment or assault for what they were wearing or for believing they could walk in certain public spaces. Street sexual harassment isn't a trifling matter; it undercuts girls' and women's sense of safety and makes them question what they can and can't do in public. It makes girls' and women's world smaller.

Nguyen decided that if the police weren't going to do anything about it, she would. She uploaded the photo online, and it went viral. It turned out that the masturbator, Dan Hoyt, was a well-known chef and a co-owner of a chain of restaurants specializing in raw food. Two other women recognized him and came forward to say that the same man had exposed and fondled himself in front of them, too. The story ended up on the front page of the New York *Daily News*, and Hoyt was sentenced to two years' probation after being convicted of public lewdness, a misdemeanor.[257] One thirty-one-year-old woman told the newspaper, "When it did happen to me I was in shock. It's a violation of my space and my sense of safety. It angered me that he thought he could get away with it."[258]

Another young New Yorker, Emily May, was fascinated with Nguyen's quick-thinking street activism. May talked about the incident with several of her female and male friends. When May revealed how commonly she encounters public acts of sexual harassment, one of her male friends said, "Emily, you live in a different city than we do." May and her friends set up a blog, which they named *Hollaback!*, and reached out to everyone they knew to submit stories and photos of street harassment and responses to it.

Within six months, *Hollaback!* was featured on *Good Morning America*. Activists in other cities got in touch, wanting assistance to set up similar websites across the country. Today, there are Hollaback! sites in over sixty-four cities and twenty-two countries, and you can download a Hollaback! app for your phone. Visit ihollaback.org, and you will find not only photos but testimonials, such as this one:

> I was walking from class home when these two guys yelled at me from the car, something about wanting to "break me." I just gave them a dirty look and kept walking. By the time they had circled back I was livid. When they yelled more obscenities at me I flipped them off. That's when they threw the bottle at me. I was so shocked at being hit and worried about the broken glass when it hit the concrete that I didn't get the license plate number. It pisses me off that they got away with it.

May is quick to explain that her motivation has never been simply about shaming harassers. Rather, it has been to encourage women to stand up to harassment that is never their fault. "We live in a world where, when women tell stories of sexual violence, it's assumed that they are lying, exaggerating, or being oversensitive," she says. "By sharing our stories, we are able to turn the lens away from ourselves and onto the people who are harassing us."[259]

Hollaback! shows the feminist potential of mobile technology. Because of smartphones, anyone victimized by street slut-shaming can document the act and share the details—visually or narratively—with others. All women feel safer because they recognize that women are part of a community that collectively is taking action. Although mobile technology and social media are often used against women by tracking and objectifying their bodies, these tools can be turned around to liberate women from being denigrated as "sluts."

Wagatwe Wanjuki also turned to the Internet to share her story and to rally others to share theirs. In 2007, Wanjuki filed a campus police report at Tufts University in Boston, alleging that she had been raped by another student with whom she had an abusive relationship. Tufts refused to investigate the charge, to move her into different housing, or even to provide counseling. Wanjuki believes that because she is a woman of color, she was looked at with suspicion; the administration did not take her claims seriously. They regarded her as not only a troublemaker but as a slut. She was expelled for not making academic progress, even though her GPA was above the minimum threshold; she told me that she believes the school expelled her because they considered her a troublemaker who, by speaking out, was tarnishing its reputation. (The irony is inescapable: a young, powerless woman whose reputation was ruined after being raped was considered a menace for holding the potential to ruin the reputation of a university with more than a billion-dollar endowment.)[260] Had she not been kicked out, she would have received her diploma in 2008.

"I was treated differently from white students," she told me. "I had asked if I could finish my schoolwork at home because being on campus and seeing my rapist was a trigger. They said no to me, but they said yes to a white girl with anorexia who made a similar request. I don't know why they made the exception for her. She was allowed to return home and finish her Tufts degree at another institution close to where she lives. But they wanted to get rid of me." Wanjuki created a website, RapedAtTufts.info, so that other survivors had a safe space to share their personal testimonies. One former student wrote,

I never really wanted to put this much of my own personal experience with Tufts into this website, but I think it is very important for it to be put out there. . . . The school refused to be understanding of my situation. Instead of asking what is wrong or instead of checking in to see how I was faring in such a harsh environment (being at a school that thought my rape is a joke created a hostile environment for me), the school remained silent until they saw it ideal to push me out of the door.[261]

Wanjuki created the site anonymously because she knew that if the administration could identify her as the webmaster, they would refuse to help her case go forward. As it happened, they refused anyway. Since Tufts did not bring justice to her case, she took her complaint to the federal government. Wanjuki filed a Title IX complaint, alleging that Tufts violated her equal right to an education, with the federal Office of Civil Rights. Title IX prohibits gender-based discrimination, including harassment and assault, in any educational program receiving federal funding. Colleges are mandated by the federal government to have a system for dealing with sexual assault complaints, and they can lose millions of dollars in federal funds if they are found to violate the law.[262]

Meanwhile, women at other universities—Amherst; Dartmouth; Swarthmore; University of California, Berkeley; University of Connecticut; University of North Carolina at Chapel Hill; University of Southern California; Yale; to name just a few—experienced the same thing.[263] They were raped on campus, but when they appealed to their university to investigate and to bring justice by exposing and punishing the rapist, they were accused of making a false accusation. They became aware that their universities cared more about protecting their endowments than ensuring the safety of female students. Students at dozens of schools filed complaints with the US Department of Education under Title IX, documenting that perpetrators were given a slap on the wrist, if that, while victims were blamed for being assaulted. They also filed complaints under the Clery Act, which requires schools to issue crime reports.

Joining with other activists, Wanjuki became a leader in the "Ed Act Now" movement for increased enforcement of Title IX and the Clery Act. In 2013, she and other activists met with Arne Duncan, the secretary of education, to demand that the Department of Education hold colleges accountable in preventing sexual violence on their campuses. In January 2014, the White House formed a task force to address rape on campuses, declaring that too many colleges were not in compliance with federal laws, and warning that they must curb campus sexual assaults and respond better to student complaints. In May 2014, the Obama administration released a list of fifty-five colleges and universities (now more than seventy) under federal investigation for mishandling sexual assault complaints, and the White House issued recommendations to colleges on how to eliminate sexual assault. A dozen members of Congress sent a letter to *U.S. News & World Report* asking the magazine to include sexual violence statistics in its college rankings. Meanwhile, the Department of Education concluded that Tufts had failed to comply with federal law by allowing a sexually hostile environment to persist on campus. Wanjuki's voice, along with those of other activists, was heard.

Wanjuki was able to mobilize a mass grassroots movement —she gathered over 176,000 signatures for her petition to the Department of Education—because of the Internet. "People listened to me because I was able to use the Internet to craft my story," she says. "And then we launched another petition to gain support for our recommendations for the White House task force.[264] We were told that our group was instrumental in the formation of the White House task force and the federal push to address campus sexual violence, which is a huge honor and extremely encouraging."

Wanjuki adds, though, that the progress to hold colleges accountable for sweeping rape under the rug is "bittersweet." On the one hand, "It was incredible to see the president of the United States talk about an issue about which I've been trying to bring awareness for years. I am so pleased to see survivors now have the community, support, knowledge, and resources that I did not have that allows them to more easily get retribution after being harmed by an abuser and a school." But on the other hand, she admits that "it's hard to also see these people get the justice that I never got while still struggling with the consequences of Tufts's apathy." In a sense, Wanjuki and the other activists who paved the way for the White House task force sacrificed themselves so that other students will now benefit.

Girls and young women who feel more comfortable speaking into a camera rather than typing on a keyboard also share their stories on the Internet. In August 2011, a thirteen-year-old eighth-grade girl from Vancouver, Sarah Sloan MacLeod, posted a four-minute video on YouTube under the name "astrorice" titled "Slut Shaming and Why It's Wrong." With her big, wide-set eyes, long light-brown hair, and braces, she looked like the child she was. But when she opened her mouth, her sophisticated analysis of gendered violence belied her age. She looked straight at the camera and, with tremendous expressiveness, said,

Slut-shaming is the unfortunate phenomenon in which people degrade or mock a woman because she dresses in tight or revealing clothing, enjoys sex, has sex a lot, or may just even be rumored to participate in sexual activity. The message that slut-shaming sends to women is that sex is bad, having sex with more than one person is horrible, and everyone will hate you for having sex at all. That message is complete and utter—excuse my French—bullshit. [*Rolls her eyes.*] Yes, I'm thirteen and I said the word "bullshit." Yes, I'm thirteen and I'm talking about slut-shaming. [*Pauses and puts on a pair of sunglasses.*] Deal with it.

MacLeod went on to inform her viewers that slut-shaming is connected with the widespread attitude that rape is not a serious crime because the woman who is raped is just a slut. She concluded,

'm noting a lot of other girls my age starting to say it, and it shocks me every time. How can they use such offensive language in such a casual manner? It's like they don't even know the meaning behind their words—and that's the thing. They don't know.[265]

Four months later, MacLeod's video had gone viral, with over six hundred thousand views. Anderson Cooper flew her out to New York to speak on his daytime television show for a program on teenage girls' pledging abstinence until marriage. On the program, MacLeod—who had yet to turn fourteen—told Cooper, "The abstinence movement promotes traditional gender norms, saying that women's worth and value come from their sexuality, which is completely untrue because my worth and value obviously don't come from anywhere like that. I have so many traits that I personally find better than that."

MacLeod's YouTube video, like Hollaback! and RapedAt-Tufts.info, is not only an example of a girl taking control over slut-shaming; it's also a call to others to spread the word. MacLeod recommended that her YouTube audience forward the link to anyone guilty of slut-shaming. "How awesome would it be to change the opinion of even just one person?"

MacLeod's video became an Internet sensation because of her mature presentation of adult ideas. No one expects a thirteen-year-old with braces to spout nuanced analysis of gendered violence. She was effective because she stood out as unusual. Yet I suspect that as she grows to adulthood, her videos will remain persuasive because she speaks accessibly, intelligently, and directly to ordinary people in plain language everyone can understand. Her message is clear: Slut-shaming is wrong and leads to violence.

Many other girls and young women also turn to simple, cheap, homemade videos to spread the message that slut-shaming is damaging to girls and women. After the YouTube personality Jenna Marbles uploaded her nine-minute video "Things I Don't Understand About Girls Part 2: Slut Edition," in December 2012, online reactions were swift and fierce. Franchesca Ramsey is a black comedian who riffs on racism and sexism and is best known for her hilarious send-up of offensive comments made by white women ignorant of their racial privilege in her YouTube video "Shit White Girls Say . . . to Black Girls," which has been viewed by over ten million people. Because of her edgy humor, her serious tone in the video "How Slut Shaming Becomes Victim Blaming" is all the more potent. She addressed the portion of the Jenna Marbles video in which Marbles suggests that "sluts" who have a "one-night stand" are taking a big risk because the guy they go home with may have "like, ten roommates in the other room that are all just waiting to close in and gang-bang you for the night." Standing in front of a stark white screen, Ramsey looks at the camera and says matter-of-factly,

This is not an attack on Jenna Marbles. This is really about a larger problem, and she's just kind of opened the door to the conversation. I've decided to chime in here because I actually have personal experience with this. Awesome! Of all the things I never thought I'd be sharing on the Internet, this is definitely one of them.

When I was eighteen, just past my eighteenth birthday, I was date-raped. That is how I lost my virginity. . . . For my eighteenth birthday, one of the girls that I worked with took me to a concert. She bought me concert tickets, and we went with her boyfriend and his roommate. Somewhere through the course of drinking all day and not really eating very much and kind of feeling pressured to drink because I was not really a drinker, when it was time to leave the concert, I was, like, beyond inebriated. Like, stumbling and slurring my words and having a hard time—and so clearly, I could not drive home. And in retrospect, I don't know if there was something in my drink because I've never, ever gotten like that post the situation. I blacked out—like, done-zo. Like, no recollection, was not conscious.

It wasn't until the morning that I even realized that I had sex and I was like, "Wait a second—what, what happened? This doesn't feel right." And I asked my girlfriend and she was like, "Yeah, you totally had sex with him, you were like, so bad."

I remember feeling mortified, just thinking, "Oh my god, why did this happen to me?" I mean, just all of those horrible thoughts going through my head, blaming myself. I told her, I begged her, "Please don't say anything about this at work." She told my coworkers. She told my manager, and they said horrible things to me. [*Chokes up and tears come to her eyes.*] They called me a slut, and I was the running joke. I was the running joke at work. . . .

I'm making this video because there are women that speak out about experiences that have happened to them, about their rape experiences. And time and again, everyone tells them, "Well, it was your fault. You shouldn't have done this, you shouldn't have done that." No. Can we stop telling girls that they "shouldn't get raped" and instead tell men to stop fucking raping women and to stop taking advantage of women? [*Chokes up again, and tears slide down her cheeks.*] . . .

There are people of all spectrums and walks of life that are affected by sexual assault and abuse, and the best way to prevent it and to make sure that those who are responsible are held accountable is to stop blaming our victims and to continue being smart and finding ways to protect ourselves and protect each other. I'll see you guys later.[266]

After posting this video, Ramsey decided that she would not participate in online comments. "I will not be answering any further comments on this video," she posted on YouTube. "Thank you for understanding." No further comments are necessary because her video speaks for itself. Girls' and women's individual stories offer evidence that no one deserves to be called a slut and that no one deserves to be sexually assaulted. Personal, intimate stories help make the case that slut-shaming must end.

Ramsey wasn't the only young woman who responded to Marbles. There are over fifty direct video responses on YouTube. Laci Green's video critiques the idea that sluts don't deserve respect because, she says, that leads to "women not deserving of respect."[267] In her own video response, Hayley

G. Hoover speaks directly to Marbles. She says, "You portray 'sluts' as different from normal or regular girls. Good things happen to regular girls and bad things happen to sluts." But, Hoover says, "when we make the separation, we start to justify that if a regular girl is attacked in an alley, that's rape, but if a 'slut' goes home with someone, making a dumb decision, that's her being stupid," and if she had made a better decision, she would not have been raped.[268] Some of the responses were created by men. Titles include "A Male Perspective: Jenna Marbles' Slut-Shaming"; "Response to Jenna Marbles and Slut Shaming Part 1: Rape is Not OK!!!"; "Things I Don't Understand About Jenna Marbles: Stupid Idiot Edition"; and "The Dangers of Slut-Shaming: Black Guy Edition."

A photo can be just as effective as a video. Sixteen-year-old Jada, a black girl from the Houston area, was raped in June 2014 after her drink was spiked at a party. Photos of her, half-naked and unconscious, were taken and circulated, going viral. Twitter users mocked her by mimicking her passed-out pose. But Jada (who has chosen to reveal her first name) seized control of the story. She posted a photo of her face and her fist, uplifted defiantly, with the hashtag #IAmJada. In this way, she reframed the narrative about her—that she was a slut—into an image of courage.[269]

Although the Internet enables slut-shaming messages to spread far and wide, it also provides a mechanism for resistance. But can resistant, lone voices alter public opinion? In the cacophony of videos and testimonials, will these voices stand out? If enough people shout, it will be impossible to ignore them.

The StopSlut Movement

These individual stories are inspiring. Yet it's unrealistic to expect that every young woman has the courage, savvy, or energy to fight back individually—nor should we expect a feisty response, on the Internet or in any other venue, to be her personal responsibility. Real change can only occur when masses of people come together to use their power and influence collectively.

An emerging social movement called StopSlut is leading the way. Katie Cappiello and Meg McInerney are at the forefront of this effort to educate young people. The kick-off for StopSlut took place in October 2013 at a conference held in New York City at the New School in Greenwich Village. Over two hundred people attended, most of them boys and girls ages thirteen to eighteen. Panels were held on meanings of the word "slut" (in which I participated) and what bystanders and young women can do to fight back against slut-labeling. In between each panel, a racially diverse group of teenage girls and boys bravely climbed up to the stage, faced the audience, and shared their own raw experiences with the word.

A girl told us that the doorman of her apartment building last year grabbed her breasts; when her parents pressed to get him fired, other residents paid for his lawyer. Another girl told everyone that she used to dance to Jay-Z's music, even when he made fun of "hos," until she realized that she and her friends were the ones being called "hos," and she decided that she didn't want to dance to her own degradation. A boy wanted everyone to know that his friend was called a slut just because she broke up with her boyfriend after he had pressured her sexually. Everyone believed the ex-boyfriend, a member of the wrestling team, while the girl stopped eating and became anorexic.

Throughout the day, the stories tumbled out nonstop. A queer girl got up on the stage to point out that any girl who expresses an interest in sexuality—with a boy or a girl—gets called a slut. A boy from an elite private school in the city shared that he knew the term "slut" was immoral when his guy friend, who "hooked up with random girls," called a girl who had hooked up with a random guy "a fucking slut." He said, "That made me a feminist." His guy friends ask him, "Why do you even care?" He tells them, "Every guy has a mother. A mother is a woman. You can't treat a woman as less than a guy. That's just stupid." A boy who introduced himself with the stage name Prince Akeem recited a poem he'd penned about the time he called his best friend a "slut" and a "freak" when she was thirteen, but then realized he had done something profoundly wrong. He concluded,

> She's not a bitch, hoe, or slut,
> She's a queen, angel, and a goddess.
> My final message to you, the people,
> Please! Do not for any reason make your best friend or
>   anyone else a target.
> Repeat after me,
> NO SLUT!
> NO SLUT!
> NO SLUT!

It could be my mother, my sister, or my niece.
Ban the word slut,
Keep the peace!

The culmination of the conference was a performance of a theatrical work, *Slut*, which was inspired by the experiences of a multiracial group of New York girls, who were also the performers. Cappiello and McInerney developed the theme with the girls, and Cappiello wrote the script, directing it with McInerney. The play explores the intersection of slut-shaming and sexual violence, and questions the wisdom of girls embracing the "slut" label for themselves, however well-intentioned and playful they may be. It was performed over a dozen times in New York City in 2013, including at the prestigious New York International Fringe Festival, as well as the festival's Encore Series. A galvanizing piece of theater, it could become the next *Vagina Monologues*; it has the potential to be staged by different communities and performed in varied venues. The *New York Post* called the show "hard-hitting," while the *Daily Beast*'s reviewer said the play makes "an important and underutilized gesture in creating a space for girls, their families, and the audience to communally work through a complicated and painful issue."[270]

The show opens with five high school girls, members of their school's dance team informally called the Slut Squad, joking around with each other in a friendly way about how sexy they are and calling each other sluts. "Is my outfit OK?" one girl asks. "Is it too slutty?"

It's Friday, and one member of the Slut Squad, Joey, has plans that night to meet up at her friend Conner's apartment for a party. Two of her girlfriends are supposed to come with her, but at the last minute, they have to cancel. Joey decides to go ahead without them, but first she attends another party, drinking vodka and hanging out with her male buddies. Three friends—Luke, Tim, and George—share a taxi with her to go to Conner's. Joey's had more vodka than she can handle, but she's not incapacitated. "I felt safe with them," she explains later. "They're my friends; we hang out every weekend. I mean, I made out with them a couple of times, but I never hooked up with any of them; we're just friends."

During the cab ride, George and Luke pin down Joey. They rape her by shoving their fingers inside her vagina. Tim, the brother of Joey's best friend, does not intervene. He pretends he doesn't know what's going on, looking steadfastly out the window during the rape. The driver has cranked up the music, so he can't hear what's going on in the back seat.

When they arrive at the party, Joey stumbles in and throws up. Someone snaps photos of her and posts them online.

Most of the play consists of Joey, who has brought criminal charges against the boys, speaking to the district attorney. We learn that everyone at school blames her for ruining the boys' lives. Her best friend's mother calls her "a little slut," even though her friend protests, saying, "But that could have been me! She is not a slut, mom. I know her. She is not a slut."

Every sexually provocative thing Joey has previously done becomes evidence that she is lying, that she's crying rape because she regrets what she's done and she's embarrassed, that she threw herself at the boys, that she asked for it. Even members of the Slut Squad don't believe her. "She's bringing down the whole school," one of them complains.

It turns out that as a joke, Joey had bought flavored condoms to the first party, and even had posed for pictures tasting them. She explains to the DA that this is all a misunderstanding; the condoms were part of a private joke shared with her classmates. In health class that week, a student had submitted an anonymous question to the nurse about flavored condoms, and everyone had thought it was hilarious. "I bought condoms, but that doesn't mean I wanted to have sex," she insists. But the pictures have been posted online. And then there are the other pictures of her drunk. And there's also the fact that as a member of the Slut Squad, Joey had been calling herself a slut for several years. So why should anyone believe her when she says she was raped?

"We use the term 'slut' in a positive, confident way," Joey attempts to explain to the DA. "We put a positive spin on it. It means we are confident and sexy. This is the only time I've been called a slut in a negative way, as a dirty whore . . . Do you think the fact that my dance team is called the Slut Squad makes people think I'm an actual slut?"

Joey comes to recognize that if she moves forward with her charge of rape, her credibility would be pitted against that of the boys—three popular, well-liked athletes bound for Ivy League colleges. "No one will believe me," she realizes. "*I* wouldn't even believe me."

The play is riveting because it lays out the reality faced by teen girls that no one wants to talk about even though it affects them to the core: "slut" may seem like a carefree term of endearment, and it is—until the moment a girl is assaulted physically or verbally. Girls don't know that "slut" is toxic, because no one discusses the situation with them. They are left on their own to figure things out for themselves—but by the time they understand the dynamics of "slut," it's usually too late.

Working on the play has deeply affected the young performers. None of them uses the word "slut" any longer. All of them worry about the connection between slut-shaming and sexual violence. After one of the early performances, one of the actors said during an open discussion with the audience, "There's pressure to dress in a sexual way so that boys look at you. You feel good because looking sexy makes you feel powerful, almost important."

I raised my hand and asked the girls if it's possible to be slutty in a good way—as the members of the Slut Squad attempt when they proudly call each other "slut" as a compliment —without eventually being considered slutty in a bad way. They shook their heads no.

And that is why the StopSlut movement is crucial. Teenage girls and young women need guidance. Adult women and men must help them.

Cappiello and McInerney have established the Girl Coalition to raise awareness and ignite the StopSlut movement in schools and communities. Their theater company, the Arts Effect, is working together with Equality Now, an international organization that works for the protection of human rights of women and girls around the world, as well as with several other institutions such as the Feminist Press, to support this initiative.

As of this writing, a hundred racially and economically diverse girls from all over New York City and New Jersey are participating in the Girl Coalition. They meet in small groups six times over a year with an adult mentor, becoming delegates within their schools. Each Girl Coalition participant creates a plan of action from the ground up that addresses the needs of her particular school's dynamics to confront and address slut-shaming, sexual violence, and sexual aggression, to spread healthier attitudes about female sexuality.

Slut-bashing and slut-shaming are isolating experiences, but members of the Girl Coalition are part of a larger community that supports teenage girls. By working together, they create a sense of sisterhood. Because so much slut-bashing and slut-shaming is committed by other girls, it's crucial that girls work together collectively. "We believe that one of the most important tenets of feminism is educating girls to make sure they understand how much we value their voices and experiences," Cappiello tells me. "We don't give them the solutions or impose solutions on them. We allow them to ask the questions themselves and to discover the solutions for themselves. The girls are the experts. They understand these issues better than we do, even better than any expert out there."

Cappiello and McInerney firmly believe that girls must explore issues for themselves rather than listen to what adults tell them. "With every question that comes up," adds McInerney, "we always ask them why. We turn around the question to have them answer it."

"If you're allowing the girls to ask the questions and frame the answers," I ask, "then what happens if they decide they want to reclaim the word 'slut'? Wouldn't that go against the whole idea of the Girl Coalition and the StopSlut movement?"

"If a girl said she wanted to reclaim the word, we would ask her why and then discuss," answers McInerney. "We've had so many conversations about reclamation," adds Cappiello. "We've talked about this for hours. When a girl wants to reclaim, we never say, 'You're wrong.' There shouldn't be an adult voice telling them what to think."

Although the girls are guided to recognize that reclamation has been attempted and has failed, they are the ones doing the thinking and the talking. This is their conversation. They need to figure out themselves what "slut" means rather than going along with current norms of behaving in a "slutty" way (however they define it) for the sake of fitting in. This movement gives them an opportunity to pause, step back, analyze, and decide what is the best route forward.

We need a huge cultural shift away from slut-shaming and toward girls' healthy sexual development. This conversation — facilitated by the StopSlut movement and the Girl Coalition — is indispensible for altering attitudes. Girls should not be fearful of their sexuality because they are afraid of being slut-shamed. We must listen to them as they speak out—in whatever medium or format—to make them feel part of a community that values them.

There is no good reason that a girl is shamed for sexting while a boy is not, that a woman's number must be lower than a man's, that a survivor of sexual assault has her credibility stolen from her along with her bodily integrity. For women to be truly safe, we must eradicate the use of the term "slut." Only then will female sexuality become transformed from a site of pitfalls to one of positivity and possibility.

Dos and Don'ts for Parents of Teenagers and College-Age Children

We've seen that girls and young women are bombarded by contradictory sexual messages within an oppressive environment of bodily surveillance, judgment, and shaming. Because they are perpetually at risk of being labeled a slut, they may perceive they have no choice but to act in ways considered to be slutty. The following behaviors stereotypically regarded as slutty by many people are often unhealthy from a developmental point of view; they also may reinforce and perpetuate the cycle of slut-shaming:

- Capitulating to coercive requests for naked photos, which can then be circulated against their will.
- Wearing sexually provocative clothes, or posting re-

vealing photos on social media, even when they are not interested in flaunting their physique, to avoid being harassed as a prude.

- Drinking to excess to cope with sexually uncomfortable surroundings or to evade sexual responsibility.
- Having sex with multiple partners to assert control over their body.
- Giving guys oral sex to feel desired or to get them to stop badgering for sex.
- Lying about their sexual history to friends, lovers, and health care providers to avoid being made to feel ashamed.

Girls may also develop self-destructive coping mechanisms as a reaction to having been labeled a slut or to the threat of being labeled a slut:

- Eating only a few hundred calories a day, melting away their breasts and hips with the hope of appearing undesirable and therefore not sexually objectified.
- Using drugs such as ecstasy, acid, marijuana, or cocaine to numb the painful experience of being publicly shamed.
- Attempting to commit suicide to end the experience of relentless public humiliation.
- Bullying other girls, or whipping up drama about them on social media, to call attention to their supposed sluttiness.
- Remaining silent, or participating in slut-shaming generated by someone else, without intervening when another girl or woman is targeted.

- Eschewing birth control under the false belief that "good" girls don't take charge of their sexuality.

What can we do to stop these behaviors and encourage healthy sexual development? Our ultimate goal is to wipe away slut-shaming, but until we succeed, we must focus on helping individual girls and women by teaching them to be aware of situations and behaviors that may lead to slut-shaming.

Those who harass, bully, or assault are the only ones who bear responsibility for their actions. It is never a girl's fault if she is called a slut. It is never a girl's fault if someone circulates a photo of her breasts. It is never a girl's fault if she becomes pregnant unintentionally. It is never a girl's fault if she is raped.

But as long as slut-shaming continues to exist, we must do whatever is in our individual power to help girls and women minimize their personal risks. They may end up harassed, bullied, or assaulted anyway; it's not possible to eliminate risk completely. Nevertheless, we must give them tools to help them avoid potentially dangerous scenarios and to handle perpetrators wherever they may be. And we must create a supportive and nonjudgmental environment where they feel comfortable being completely open about their experiences.

Do talk with your child, even well before adolescence, about the sexual double standard and slut-shaming.

Express openness about these topics so that your child will

feel comfortable confiding in you if she or he is harassed or witnesses harassment.

Don't express judgment against your daughter if she turns to unhealthy sexualized behaviors or coping mechanisms.

Likewise, don't express judgment against her friends or your son's friends. Remember, many girls today are reacting against a virulent culture of slut-shaming. Their behaviors are a symptom of a disease that we must attack and eliminate.

If you find out that your child sexts, do be understanding and not punitive.

If your daughter has sent naked photos of herself, she may have felt coerced. If she sent naked photos freely with no coercion, remember that you were a teenager once too. The same applies for your son. Engage in dialogue about the risks of sending sexually provocative photos, videos, and texts. Tell your child that if she or he receives a forwarded sext originally sent by a third person, it must be deleted immediately and never forwarded to anyone else.

Do teach your children to drink responsibly.

If your child is never permitted to drink even a sip of alcohol, you are setting her or him up to go wild and drink uncontrollably—and experience severely impaired judgment, not to mention physical illness—when she or he is not under your watch. Whether you like it or not, drinking is a major element of socializing on college campuses and even among many high school students. Chances are strong that your child will drink even when underage—to have a good time, to fit in with friends, or perhaps to cope with depression or anxiety. Coach your child to sip slowly and not to exceed the limit she or he can handle (for girls, this may be two drinks). That way, your child will appear to be sociable and agreeable without becoming drunk.

If you have a son, teach him that being wasted is never an excuse for behaving immorally or criminally. If he drinks and then bullies, harasses, or assaults another individual because his judgment is impaired, he and not the alcohol is to blame. Having sex with someone who is inebriated and incapable of consenting is criminal and immoral.

Don't insult your daughter over her clothing choices.

Don't tell her that her clothes make her look like a "slut," "ho," "skank," "*puta*," or anything similar. She probably puts a great deal of thought into her outfits. She may feel good about her appearance (and you want her to feel good about her appearance). If you strongly believe that her clothing is inappropriate for her age or for the occasion, calmly explain that your feelings are about her clothing and not a judgment against her personally. Say something supportive such as, "You look fantastic in that outfit! But unfortunately, many people are not as enlightened as you are about girls revealing their bodies, and they may treat you like a sexual object if you wear that outfit. They're wrong, but we need to watch out for people like that to stay safe. As your parent, it's my job to make sure you don't get hurt by people like that."

Don't threaten to throw away her clothes.

If you do, you take the risk that she will change her outfit after she leaves your presence, and you will lose all control.

Do be willing to compromise over clothing.

Even if your daughter is wearing clothes that are overtly sexually provocative, her intent might not be sexual. Work together with her to plan outfits that will get her the social approval she desires while minimizing unwanted sexual attention and objectification. Remember, she is still learning what is and what is not appropriate in different contexts, but her idea of "appropriate" and even "sexual" is vastly different from yours. For example, if she's wearing tight leggings and a tight top, you could talk with her about changing only the top and exchanging it for something looser, or vice versa. Let her feel in control of her style, but make sure you set firm limits as to how much of her body she exposes.

Don't tell your children (verbally or nonverbally) that teenage sex is bad and that if they are having sex, you don't want to know about it.

If your daughter or son becomes sexually active and perceives that you are unsupportive, she or he will not come to you when she or he needs advice or help. In fact, telling your daughter or son not to be sexually active could motivate her or him to become sexually active purely as an act of rebellion.

Do tell your children often that no matter what, they can always come to you with questions about sexuality.

Even if you strongly believe that kids in high school should never be sexually active, you need to be prepared that your children's reality may not match your ideals.

Don't avoid discussion of sexual assault.

Don't assume that sexual assault is something you don't need to talk about because it is rare. Sexual assault is much more common than you might think—nearly one in five women in the United States has been raped or has experienced attempted rape; almost half of these women have been raped before the age of eighteen, with 80 percent raped before the age of twenty-five—and it nearly always involves people who know each other and may even consider themselves friends.

Do talk about consent early and often.

It is never too early to discuss the idea of consent with your child. Your children need to understand that regardless of the circumstances, no one should ever touch another's body without explicit consent. If someone is unable to explicitly give consent because she or he is drunk or passed out, then consent is absent and touching that person's body is both immoral and criminal. It is never OK to take advantage of someone who is drunk, even if you don't respect her or him for getting so drunk in the first place.

Do talk to your children about the responsibilities of bystanders.

Your daughter and son should know that if they see someone being victimized or vulnerable to being victimized, it is their responsibility to intervene—even if they dislike the victim. As Franchesca Ramsey advises in her video "How Slut Shaming Becomes Victim Blaming," "there's no reason that a guy can't step in at a bar and say, 'Hey, dude, this girl is wasted, I don't think she wants to go home with you. Let's put her in a cab.'" Likewise, your daughter can put her arm around a drunken female at a party, steering her away from guys who might think she's fair game for sexual activity despite the fact that she's unable to consent, and either watch over her or help get her home.

Do monitor your child's Internet and social media use.

Tell them in what ways and how often you are monitoring them. If your child is engaging in slut-shaming behavior online, initiate a dialogue on why this is a problem and how it can backfire. If your daughter posts only sexualized photos of herself, talk with her about the fact that many people will unfairly make assumptions about her sexuality, which may or may not be true, based on the images they see of her online.

Don't spy on your child's Internet and social media use without her or his knowledge.

If your child then finds out, she will be less likely to confide in you when she needs your help.

If your daughter tells you she's been labeled a slut or otherwise victimized, don't ask her what she did to provoke the victimization.

Whether she's been slut-bashed online or in person, had a naked photo distributed against her will, or been sexually assaulted, she did nothing to deserve being treated this way. If you ask her what she did to cause the victimization, you are suggesting that she is at fault. Help her construct a timeline of events leading up to the victimization in case she decides in the future to file a formal complaint. Make sure that when you ask informational questions about the order of events, you do not express judgment against her actions.

Do tell your daughter that you believe her if she tells you she's been sexually assaulted.

Being supportive by believing her is the most important thing you can do. Many people will not believe her. If she chooses to speak out about her assault, many people will intentionally make her feel isolated, scared, and humiliated. Your belief in her will help her heal.

Don't ever call other females "sluts," even in a humorous or affectionate way, and certainly never in a judgmental way.

The best way to eliminate slut-shaming is to stop using the word.

Do be a role model to your children by treating all girls and women with respect.

Show them with words and actions that you respect girls and women who have been called sluts and who have been assaulted. Let your children know that even if you disagree with an individual woman's sexual choices, she still deserves to be treated with respect.

The Slut-Shaming Self-Defense Toolkit

Girls and young women: It's never your fault for being slut-shamed or assaulted. The ultimate goals described in this book are to eliminate slut-shaming and to redirect blame for sexual assault onto those responsible for it: the assaulters.

Until we are able to achieve these goals, you can take steps to minimize your personal risk. Please remember that whether or not you take these steps, you never deserve to be harassed or assaulted.

Don't binge-drink.

Yes, you want to drink with your friends. Fine—but keep your drinking under control. Even friends can do terrible things to each other when they're drunk, so don't assume that you're safe no matter how drunk you become just because you're with your friends. If your friends pressure you to drink more than you want, hold a cup of alcohol in your hand throughout the evening, taking small sips occasionally. No one needs to know that you're deliberately controlling your consumption. If you choose to drink excessively, discuss it in advance with a trusted friend who is not drinking excessively, and ask her or him to look out for you.

Don't dress in a sexually provocative manner unless you want to be looked at sexually and can handle being reduced to a sexual object, since unfortunately that may be the result of your attire. Everyone's clothing choices send a message. If you don't want your message to be "I like showing off my body in public," then don't show off your body in public. If that is precisely the message you do want to transmit, then be aware of how others perceive you.

Think twice before sending a seminaked or fully naked photo of yourself to someone.
You trust him now, but will he be trustworthy in six months? Is he the type of guy who likes to show off for his friends? And what about his friends—how trustworthy are they? He may send the photo to one friend, and that friend might forward it to hundreds. Make sure your eyes are wide open about the risks involved before doing something like this.

Intervene when another girl is called a slut or a ho, or if she's in a situation in which she may end up being called a slut or a ho.
Don't stand by quietly without speaking up. Girls and women have to watch out for each other—even if they don't like each other. If you have your peers' backs, they will have yours.

If you are called a slut or ho, confide in an adult and keep a written log of all actions made against you.

Take screenshots and print out hard copies of all messages, photos, and videos sent to you that constitute harassment. You might need these records in the future if you ever decide to file a formal complaint.

Don't call other girls or women sluts or hos.

You might think it's funny and flippant, but the more we spread these words, the more acceptable they become, putting all females at risk for being maligned as sexually abnormal.

Bond with other girls and women at your school.

Create a club to discuss slut-shaming. Build awareness within your community that slut-shaming will not be tolerated. Get together with other women—and, if you feel comfortable doing so, with guys—to talk about sexuality. Invite teachers and other adults to join the conversation.

Remember: No matter what you have done, you are not a slut.

And neither is anyone else.

Resources

Information on Sexuality, Birth Control, and Abortion

ADVOCATES FOR YOUTH

http://www.advocatesforyouth.org/for-professionals/sex-education-resource-center
2000 M Street, NW, Suite 750
Washington, DC 20036
202-419-3420

Advocates for Youth is a nonprofit organization dedicated to sexuality education, the prevention of sexually transmitted diseases and teenage pregnancy, youth access to birth control, and equality for LGBT youth.

COMMONSENSE MEDIA

www.commonsensemedia.org
650 Townsend Street, Suite 435
San Francisco, CA 94103
415-863-0600

Commonsense Media advocates for children and families and studies the effects that media and technology have on young users.

GUTTMACHER INSTITUTE

www.guttmacher.org
125 Maiden Lane, 7th Floor
New York, NY 10038
212-248-1111
Toll-free: 1-800-355-0244

The Guttmacher Institute is a nonprofit organization that works to advance reproductive health, including abortion rights, through research, policy analysis, and public education.

PLANNED PARENTHOOD FEDERATION OF AMERICA

www.plannedparenthood.org
434 West 33rd Street
New York, NY 10001
212-541-7800

Planned Parenthood, a leading national provider of reproductive health care, is also a leader in educating Americans about reproductive and sexual health. More than one million youths and adults participate in Planned Parenthood educational programs every year.

SEXUALITY INFORMATION AND EDUCATION COUNCIL OF THE UNITED STATES (SIECUS)

www.siecus.org
90 John Street, Suite 402
New York, NY 10038

212-819-9770

SIECUS is dedicated to affirming that sexuality is a natural and healthy part of life. A pioneer in the area of comprehensive sex education, SIECUS develops, collects, and distributes information about sexuality.

If You've Been Harassed, Bullied, or Assaulted

EDACTNOW

http://www.change.org/organizations/ed_act_now

EdActNow is a national student collective of survivor-activists working to stop campus gender-based and sexual violence of all forms.

EQUAL RIGHTS ADVOCATES (ERA)

www.equalrights.org
180 Howard Street, Suite 300
San Francisco, CA 94105
415-621-0672

ERA is a legal organization dedicated to protecting and expanding economic and educational access and opportunities for women and girls. The organization enforces Title IX, the federal law that prohibits sex discrimination in schools.

GAY, LESBIAN AND STRAIGHT EDUCATION NETWORK (GLSEN)

www.glsen.org
90 Broad Street, 2nd Floor
New York, NY 10004
212-727-0135

GLSEN is an organization that seeks to end discrimination, harassment, and bullying based on sexual orientation, gender identity, and gender expression in K-12 schools.

HOLLABACK!

www.ihollaback.org/
30 Third Avenue, #800B
Brooklyn, NY 11217
347-889-5510

Hollaback! is a movement to end street harassment powered by a network of local activists around the world. According to Hollaback!, the real motive of street harassment is to make its target scared or uncomfortable, and to make the harasser feel powerful. Hollaback! encourages targets to expose harassers with their smartphones by documenting, mapping, and sharing incidents of street harassment.

NATIONAL CENTER FOR TRANSGENDER EQUALITY

www.transequality.org
1325 Massachusetts Avenue, Suite 700
Washington, DC 20005
202-903-0112

The National Center for Transgender Equality is a social justice organization devoted to ending discrimination and violence against transgender people through education and advocacy.

NATIONAL WOMEN'S LAW CENTER

www.nwlc.org

11 Dupont Circle, NW, Suite 800
Washington, DC 20036
202-588-5180

The Center litigates, gets new laws passed, and educates the public about laws affecting women's lives in education, employment, family and economic security, and health and reproductive rights, with special attention given to the needs of low-income women and their families.

OFFICE FOR CIVIL RIGHTS (OCR)

US Department of Education
www2.ed.gov/about/offices/list/ocr/index.html
400 Maryland Avenue, SW
Washington, DC 20202
1-800-872-5327

The Office for Civil Rights works to ensure equal access to education through enforcement of students' civil rights. The OCR addresses gender discrimination, sexual harassment, and bullying.

RAPE, ABUSE & INCEST NATIONAL NETWORK (RAINN)

www.rainn.org
1220 L Street, NW, Suite 505
Washington, DC 20005
202-544-3064

RAINN is the largest anti–sexual assault organization in the United States. It operates the National Sexual Assault Hotline and carries out programs to prevent sexual assault, help victims, and ensure that rapists are brought to justice.

THE WOMEN'S LEGAL DEFENSE AND EDUCATION FUND

www.legalmomentum.org
5 Hanover Square, Suite 1502
New York, NY 10004
212-925-6635

The Women's Legal Defense and Education Fund expands the legal rights and services of girls and women who have been victimized by harassment and violence.

Material Written by People Who Believe That Slut-Shaming Must Be Eliminated

Bitch (bitchmagazine.org)
Bust (bust.com)
Colorlines (colorlines.com)
Crunk Feminist Collective (crunkfeministcollective.com)
Feministing (feministing.com)
Jezebel (jezebel.com)
RH Reality Check (rhrealitycheck.org)

Feminist Communities

AMERICAN ASSOCIATION OF UNIVERSITY WOMEN

www.aauw.org
1111 Sixteenth Street, NW
Washington, DC 20036
1-800-326-2289

The American Association of University Women (AAUW)

is the nation's leading voice promoting equity and education for women and girls.

EQUALITY NOW

www.equalitynow.org
PO Box 20646
Columbus Circle Station
New York, NY 10023
212-586-0906

Equality Now advocates for the human rights of women and girls around the world by raising international visibility of individual cases of abuse, mobilizing public support, and wielding political pressure to ensure that governments enact or enforce laws and policies that uphold the rights of women and girls.

GIRLS INC.

www.girlsinc.org/
120 Wall Street
New York, NY 10005
212-509-2000

Girls Inc. focuses on giving confidence to girls. The oldest Girls Incorporated affiliate was formed in 1864 in Connecticut to provide programs for young working women as well as young daughters of mill families. The organization's tagline today is that it "inspires all girls to be strong, smart, and bold."

HOW TO LOSE YOUR VIRGINITY PROJECT

www.virginitymovie.com/resources
The website for this excellent documentary by Therese

Schechter includes a comprehensive list of online resources, a blog, and other entry points to help make discussion about female sexuality sane and reasonable.

PLANNED PARENTHOOD ACTION FUND

www.plannedparenthoodaction.org
1110 Vermont Avenue, NW
Washington, DC 20005
202-973-4800

The advocacy and political arm of Planned Parenthood Federation of America, the Action Fund engages in electoral activity including legislative advocacy, voter education, and grassroots organizing to promote the Planned Parenthood mission. These efforts include advocating for changes in public policy with a sharp focus on ensuring access to comprehensive, affordable reproductive health care for all.

STOPSLUT

http://sluttheplay.com/stopslut-movement/
Visit this site to sign up to join the Girl Coalition or to apply to become a mentor.

THIRD WAVE FOUNDATION

www.thirdwavefoundation.org
220 East 23rd Street, Suite 509
New York, NY 10010
212-2288311

This foundation is a feminist activist philanthropic organization supporting young women and transgender youth ages fifteen through thirty. Third Wave has given nearly

$2 million to more than one thousand individuals through scholarships and more than one hundred young women–led and transgender youth–led organizations, often as the first national funder.

WOMEN, ACTION, & THE MEDIA (WAM!)
    http://www.womenactionmedia.org/
    7 Temple Street
    Cambridge, MA 02139
    617-876-5310
WAM! is dedicated to building a robust, effective, inclusive movement for gender justice in media. It is also a strong, growing community of people engaged with media who are learning and sharing skills needed to build a media ecosystem that represents the diversity of women's lives and stories.

ACKNOWLEDGMENTS

Thank you to Jennifer Lyons for twisting my arm to write this book. Jennifer, I had thought I'd said everything I wanted to say about slut-shaming, but I was wrong—and you were right. Clearly, you are a superb agent. More important, you are a precious confidante and ally.

I had told Jennifer that there was only one editor I wanted to work with—Denise Oswald—and that I wouldn't go forward with anyone else. I was thrilled when Denise said yes— even though that meant I had run out of excuses: I had to go write the book. Denise, I knew I'd made the right decision a year later when you gave me your extensive editorial comments. Rather than telling me what you thought was best, or making the changes yourself in the manuscript, you asked me sharp questions that forced me to think more deeply. On every darned page. When I wasn't cursing you, I was grateful. You challenged me not only to rewrite but to rethink.

I'm especially indebted to the stellar HarperCollins team: Cal Morgan, Amy Baker, Julie Hersh, Trish Daly, Mary Sasso, Kathryn Ratcliffe-Lee, Gregory Henry, Amanda Pelletier, William Ruoto, and Nina LoSchiavo. To Douglas Johnson, I am exceedingly thankful to you for whipping the copy into shape.

To Jaclyn Geller, thank you from the bottom of my heart for reading my proposal and my first draft—and for being gentle in your precise suggested revisions. Thank you to Patricia Dunn not only for your excellent critique of my proposal but also for twisting my other arm to join twenty-first-century digital culture. To Jennifer Baumgardner, I am grateful for your support and energized by your exceptional feminist commitment. Thank you to those who persuaded me that an updated analysis of the slut label was necessary: Jean Halley, Suzanne Rumph, and Justin Matthew Smith. Your encouragement helped to move this project forward. To Diana Cage, Harriet Luria, Amy Moorman Robbins, and Shira Tarrant, thank you for introducing me to your thoughtful students and igniting discussion about slut-shaming in your classroom.

I am galvanized by the brilliant work of Meg McInerney and Katie Cappiello. Thank you for offering me your critiques, welcoming me into your movement, and guiding the next generation of young women grappling with meanings of "slut."

I am fortunate to work for the Planned Parenthood Federation of America and Planned Parenthood Action Fund with smart, dedicated, fearless colleagues. They push every day to ensure that American women have access to affordable, safe, legal health care—no matter where they live or who they are—and that no one is shamed for using birth control or having an abortion. I am honored to work alongside you.

Finally, I am humbled by everyone who spoke with me about their personal experiences with slut-bashing and slut-shaming. For many, our conversations were emotional and difficult. Please know that your contribution helps raise awareness that the sexual double standard is sexist, unjust, and immoral. By speaking up, you are fighting the good fight, and for that I am forever grateful.

NOTES

1   Felicity Barringer, "School Hallways as Gantlets of Sexual Taunts,"
    New York Times, June 2, 1993, B7, www.nytimes.com/1993/06/02/
    education/school-hallways-as-gantlets-of-sexual-taunts.html. An
    accompanying bar graph appeared in the print edition of the news-
    paper; it is not included in the online version of the article. The
    study upon which this article was based was published as a booklet,
    *Hostile Hallways: The AAUW Survey on Sexual Harassment in Amer-
    ica's Schools* (Washington, DC: American Association of University
    Women Educational Foundation, 1993). The bar graph that ap-
    peared in the *New York Times* also appears on page 9 of this booklet.

2   Through my travels as a guest lecturer to college campuses, and
    with the assistance of several academic colleagues, I was fortunate to
    speak with clusters of college students from five universities—four
    in Northeast and Middle Atlantic states, and one on the West Coast.
    I was able to meet with a group of adolescent actors from New York
    City with the help of the leaders of a theater program called the
    Arts Effect. I placed an announcement on my website, as well as an
    advertisement in the feminist magazine *Bust*, both of which led to
    additional interviews. Several girls and women approached me after
    a sister or a friend had already spoken with me; they wanted in, too.
    Whenever possible, I met with these girls and women in person; in
    other cases, we spoke on the phone or via Skype. On average, each
    interview lasted an hour. In several instances, the interviewee and I
    spoke and met multiple times.

3   For an excellent historical overview, see the first two chapters of
    Joseph Allen Boone, *Tradition Counter Tradition: Love and the Form
    of Fiction* (Chicago: University of Chicago Press, 1987).

4   Jaclyn Geller, "Critical Reflections on the Push for Same Sex Mar-
    riage," *Connecticut Review* 33, no. 1 (Spring 2011): 47–55.

5   Nancy F. Cott, "Passionlessness: An Interpretation of Victorian Sexual Ideology, 1790–1850," *Signs* 4, no. 2 (Winter 1978): 220.

6   Harriet Jacobs, *Incidents in the Life of a Slave Girl* (New York: Oxford University Press, 1988), 45.

7   Shabiki Crane, "Pride from Behind," in *Feminism for Real: Deconstructing the Academic Industrial Complex of Feminism*, ed. Jessica Yee (Ottawa, Canada: Canadian Centre for Policy Alternatives, 2011), 78.

8   Jessica Ringrose, *Postfeminist Education? Girls and the Sexual Politics of Schooling* (New York: Routledge, 2013), 94.

9   *Oxford English Dictionary* Online, s.v. "slut, n.," accessed August 14, 2013, www.oed.com/view/Entry/182346?rskey=L0N1dO&result=1&isAdvanced=false.

10   Frances S. Foster, "Ultimate Victims: Black Women in Slave Narratives." *Journal of American Culture* 1, no. 4 (December 1978): 846.

11   Ibid., 852–3.

12   Ibid., 852.

13   Ibid., 853.

14   *Oxford English Dictionary* Online, s.v. "ho, n. 7.," accessed August 10, 2014, http://www.oed.com/view/Entry/248633?result=6&rskey=LxtlZ8&.

15   Simon Reynolds and Joy Press, *The Sex Revolts: Gender, Rebellion and Rock n' Roll* (Cambridge, MA: Harvard University Press, 1996), 325.

16   Dossie Easton and Catherine A. Liszt [Janet Hardy], *The Ethical Slut: A Guide to Infinite Possibilities* (Emeryville, CA: Greenery Press, 1997).

17   Pamela Ryckman, *Stiletto Network: Inside the Women's Power Circles That Are Changing the Face of Business* (New York: AMACOM, 2013), 28.

18   Erin Gloria Ryan, "Slut-Dropping and Other Ways College Teaches Kids to be Sexist Assholes," *Jezebel*, October 9, 2012, http://jezebel.com/5950287/slut+dropping-and-other-ways-college-teaches-kids-to-be-sexist-assholes.

19   "A Statement from Rush," March 3, 2012, www.rushlimbaugh.com/daily/2012/03/03/a_statement_from_rush.

20   Richard Pérez-Peña, "After Barnard Gets Obama for Speech, Tensions with Columbia Bubble Up," March 5, 2012, http://www.

nytimes.com/2012/03/06/nyregion/with-obama-to-speak-at-barnard-strong-emotions-at-columbia.html?_r=0.

21 Ravenna Koenig, "Lewd, Hateful Language Should Have No Place in Campus Debate," *Women's Media Center*, March 3, 2012, www.womensmediacenter.com/feature/entry/lewd-hateful-language-should-have-no-place-in-campus-debate.

22 These comments were cited in Katie J. M. Baker, "Barnard, Columbia at War Over Obama, Feminazis, and Cum Dumpsters," *Jezebel*, March 6, 2012, http://jezebel.com/5890888/barnard-columbia-at-war-over-obama-feminazis-and-cum-dumpsters.

23 Amy O'Leary, "The Woman with 1 Billion Clicks, Jenna Marbles" *New York Times*, www.nytimes.com/2013/04/14/fashion/jenna-marbles.html.

24 Laura Collins, "Teen girls 'who made death threats to Steubenville rape victim' are held in custody 'to protect victim from immediate harm,'" *Daily Mail*, March 19, 2013, www.dailymail.co.uk/news/article-2295853/Teen-girls-death-threats-Steubenville-rape-victim-held-custody-protect-victim-immediate-harm.html.

25 Stephen Rodrick, "Serena Williams: The Great One," *Rolling Stone*, July 4, 2013, www.rollingstone.com/culture/news/serena-williams-the-great-one-20130618.

26 *Urban Dictionary*, s.v. "Slut," accessed August 10, 2014, www.urbandictionary.com/define.php?term=slut.

27 Guttmacher Institute, *Fact Sheet: American Teens' Sexual and Reproductive Health*, May 2014, www.guttmacher.org/pubs/FB-ATSRH.html.

28 Jan Hoffman, "'Fat Talk' Compels but Carries a Cost," *New York Times*, May 28, 2103, http://well.blogs.nytimes.com/2013/05/27/fat-talk-compels-but-carries-a-cost/.

29 Sara Rimer, "For Girls, It's Be Yourself, and Be Perfect, Too," *New York Times*, April 1, 2007, http://www.nytimes.com/2007/04/01/us/01girls.html?pagewanted=all.

30 Donna Lisker, "The Duke University Women's Initiative," *On Campus with Women* 35, no. 1 (Spring 2006), available at www.aacu.org/ocww/volume35_1/feature.cfm?section=2.

31 Ringrose, *Postfeminist Education?*, 91.

32 This quotation is from a personal interview with Elizabeth Semmelhack conducted in July 2009 as part of the research for my book

Bad Shoes and the Women Who Love Them (New York: Seven Stories, 2010). This quotation appears in that book on page 94.

33 Rimer, ibid.

34 Quoted in Penelope Green, "The Rivals," *New York Times Book Review*, February 15, 2004, www.nytimes.com/2004/02/15/books/the-rivals.html.

35 Catherine Hill and Holly Kearl, *Crossing the Line: Sexual Harassment at School* (Washington, DC: American Association of University Women, 2011), www.aauw.org/research/crossing-the-line/. The report is based on a survey of a nationally representative sample of 1,965 students conducted in May and June 2011.

36 Dan Olweus, "Annotation: Bullying at School: Basic Facts and Effects of a School Based Intervention Program," *Journal of Child Psychology and Psychiatry* 35, no. 7 (October 1994): 1173; Dan Olweus, "Bullying or Peer Abuse at School: Facts and Intervention," *Current Directions in Psychological Science* 4, no. 6 (December 1995): 197.

37 Tara Parker-Pope, "Web of Popularity, Achieved by Bullying," *New York Times*, February 14, 2011, http://well.blogs.nytimes.com/2011/02/14/web-of-popularity-weaved-by-bullying/; Robert Faris and Diane Felmlee, "Status Struggles: Network Centrality and Gender Segregation in Same- and Cross-Gender Aggression," *American Sociological Review* 76, no. 1 (February 2011): 48–73, http://www.asanet.org/images/journals/docs/pdf/Faris_FelmleeASRFeb11.pdf.

38 danah boyd and Alice Marwick, "Bullying as True Drama," *New York Times*, September 23, 2011, www.nytimes.com/2011/09/23/opinion/why-cyberbullying-rhetoric-misses-the-mark.html/.

39 Alice Marwick and danah boyd, "The Drama! Teen Conflict, Gossip, and Bullying in Networked Publics" (paper presented at the Oxford Internet Institute's symposium "A Decade in Internet Time: Symposium on the Dynamics of the Internet and Society," University of Oxford, September 22, 2011), http://papers.ssrn.com/sol3/papers.cfm?abstract_id=1926349.

40 Ibid., 1.

41 Tamar Lewin, "Teenage Insults, Scrawled on Web, Not on Walls," *New York Times*, May 5, 2010, www.nytimes.com/2010/05/06/us/06formspring.html.

42 Emily Bazelon, *Sticks and Stones: Defeating the Culture of Bullying*

and Rediscovering the Power of Character and Empathy (New York: Random House, 2013), 223.

43 Oren Yaniv, "Long Island Teen's Suicide Linked to Cruel Cyberbullies, Formspring.me Site: Police," *Daily News*, March 25, 2010, www.nydailynews.com/news/crime/long-island-teen-suicide-linked-cruel-cyberbullies-formspring-site-police-article-1.173441; Bianca Bosker, "Alexis Pilkington Facebook Horror: Cyber Bullies Harass Teen Even After Suicide," Associated Press, posted on the *Huffington Post*, March 24, 2010, www.huffingtonpost.com/2010/03/24/alexis-pilkington-faceboo_n_512482.html.

44 Jessica Guynn and Janet Stobart, "Ask.fm: New Social Site, Same Bullying," *Los Angeles Times*, August 20, 2013, http://articles.latimes.com/2013/aug/20/business/la-fi-britain-cyber-bullying-20130820.

45 Ibid.

46 Lizette Alvarez, "Girl's Suicide Points to Rise in Apps Used by Cyberbullies," *New York Times*, September 13, 2013, www.nytimes.com/2013/09/14/us/suicide-of-girl-after-bullying-raises-worries-on-web-sites.html.

47 Tina Kelley, "A Rite of Hazing, Now Out in the Open," *New York Times*, September 18, 2013, www.nytimes.com/2009/09/19/nyregion/19hazing.html.

48 Andrea Newell, "Sexting and the Slut List: The Double Standard is Alive and Thriving," *Ecosalon*, April 6, 2011, www.ecosalon.com/sexting-and-the-slut-list-the-double-standard-is-alive-and-thriving/; Rebecca Dube, " 'Smut List' the Latest in Cyber-Bullying," Today.com, March 21, 2011, http://www.today.com/parents/smut-list-latest-cyber-bullying-1C7398537.

49 David Picker, "At Jets Game, a Halftime Ritual of Harassment," *New York Times*, November 20, 2007, www.nytimes.com/2007/11/20/sports/football/20fans.html.

50 Anahad O'Connor, " 'Monologues' Spur Dialogue on Taste and Speech," *New York Times*, March 8, 2007, www.nytimes.com/2007/03/08/nyregion/08vagina.html.

51 Eyder Peralta, "Michigan State Rep Barred From Speaking After 'Vagina' Comments," NPR.org, June 14, 2012, www.npr.org/blogs/thetwo-way/2012/06/14/155059849/michigan-state-rep-barred-from-speaking-after-vagina-comments.

52   William McGuinness, "Tim McDaniel, Idaho Teacher, Explained 'Vagina' in Sex Ed Class, So He's Being Investigated," *Huffington Post*, March 28, 2013, www.huffingtonpost.com/2013/03/28/tim-mcdaniel-vagina-sex-education_n_2971710.html.

53   WCNC staff, "Facebook Apologizes for Removing Breastfeeding Photo," wcnc.com, December 30, 2011, www.wcnc.com/home/Facebook-does-about-face-on-breast-feeding-photo-136442808.html.

54   Lizzie Crocker, "'Fantasy Slut League': Earning Points for Sexual Encounters in High School," *Daily Beast*, October 26, 2012, http://www.thedailybeast.com/articles/2012/10/26/fantasy-slut-league-earning-points-for-sexual-encounters-in-high-school.html.

55   Spencer Kornhaber, "Horny CSULB Paper Earns Rebuke for Telling Guys to Be 'Aggressive' During Sextime," *OC Weekly*, September 28, 2010, http://blogs.ocweekly.com/navelgazing/2010/09/csulb_paper.php.

56   Terri D. Conley, Ali Ziegler, and Amy C. Moors, "Backlash From the Bedroom: Stigma Mediates Gender Differences in Acceptance of Casual Sex Offers." *Psychology of Women Quarterly* 37, no. 3 (September 2013): 1–16.

57   Ibid., 5.

58   Ibid., 6.

59   Ibid., 9.

60   Ibid., 5.

61   Russell D. Clark III and Elaine Hatfield, "Gender Differences in Receptivity to Sexual Offers," *Journal of Psychology and Human Sexuality* 2, no. 1 (1989): 39–55.

62   Terri D. Conley, "Perceived Proposer Personality Characteristics and Gender Differences in Acceptance of Casual Sex Offers." *Journal of Personality and Social Psychology* 100, no. 2 (February 2011): 15.

63   Ibid.

64   Ibid., 16.

65   Ibid., 20.

66   Michael Bamberg, "Form and Functions of 'Slut Bashing' in Male Identity Constructions in 15-Year-Olds," *Human Development* 47, no. 6 (November–December 2004): 331–353.

67   Ibid., 339–340.

68   Ibid., 341.

69   Ibid., 348.

70   Ibid., 349.

71   Common Sense Media *Social Media, Social Life: How Teens View Their Digital Selves*, June 26, 2012, www.commonsensemedia.org/research/social-media-social-life-how-teens-view-their-digital-lives.

72   Louis Althusser, "Ideology and Ideological State Apparatuses" in *"Lenin and Philosophy" and Other Essays*, trans. Ben Brewster (London: New Left Books, 1971), 173–74.

73   Cited on http://metareddit.com/r/spacedicks+CreepShots, accessed on November 26, 2013.

74   Michel Foucault, *Discipline and Punish: The Birth of the Prison* (New York: Vintage, 1979), 200.

75   Michel Foucault, "The Eye of the Power," in *Power/Knowledge: Selected Interviews and Other Writings, 1972–1977*, ed. Colin Gordon (New York: Pantheon, 1980), 156.

76   George Orwell, *1984* (New York: Plume, 2003), 3.

77   Sandra Lee Bartky, "Foucault, Femininity, and the Modernization of Patriarchal Power," in *Feminism and Foucault: Reflections on Resistance*, ed. Irene Diamond and Lee Quinby (Boston: Northeastern University Press, 1988). Reprinted in *Writing on the Body: Female Embodiment and Feminist Theory*, ed. Katie Conboy, Nadia Medina, and Sarah Stanbury (New York: Columbia University Press, 1997), 93–111.

78   Ibid., 95.

79   Ibid., 103.

80   Ibid., 107.

81   Strawberry Saroyan, "The XXX Files," *Los Angeles Times*, September 11, 2004, http://articles.latimes.com/2004/sep/11/entertainment/et-saroyan11/2.

82   Alex Kuczynski, "The Sex-Worker Literati," *New York Times*, November 4, 2001, www.nytimes.com/2001/11/04/style/the-sex-worker-literati.html; cited in Ariel Levy, *Female Chauvinist Pigs: Women and the Rise of Raunch Culture* (New York: Free Press, 2005), 25.

83   Jennifer Keishin Armstrong and Heather Wood Rudúlph, *Sexy Fem-

inism: A Girl's Guide to Love, Success, and Style (New York: Houghton Mifflin Harcourt, 2013), 56.

84   Ibid., 20.

85   Ibid., 29.

86   American Society of Plastic Surgeons, *Plastic Surgery for Teenagers Briefing Paper*, undated, http://www.plasticsurgery.org/news/briefing-papers/plastic-surgery-for-teenagers.html.

87   "Transcript: Cosmetic Surgery and Teens," *Washington Post*, October 26, 2004, www.washingtonpost.com/wp-dyn/articles/A63931-2004Oct26.html.

88   Rosalind Gill, "From Sexual Objectification to Sexual Subjectification: The Resexualization of Women's Bodies in the Media," *Feminist Media Studies* 3, no. 1 (2003): 100–106, http://mrzine.monthlyreview.org/2009/gill230509.html.

89   Ibid.

90   The cartoon, by Peter Steiner, was published in *The New Yorker* on July 5, 1993. See Glenn Fleishman, "Cartoon Captures Spirit of the Internet," *New York Times*, December 14, 2000, www.nytimes.com/2000/12/14/technology/cartoon-captures-spirit-of-the-internet.html.

91   Sherry Turkle, *Life on the Screen: Identity in the Age of the Internet* (New York: Simon & Schuster, 1995), 11, 263.

92   Sherry Turkle, *Alone Together: Why We Expect More From Technology and Less From Each Other* (New York: Basic Books, 2011), 166.

93   Ibid., 251.

94   Ibid., 181.

95   Ibid., 251.

96   danah boyd, "Social Network Sites as Networked Publics: Affordances, Dynamics, and Implications," in *A Networked Self: Identity, Community, and Culture on Social Network Sites*, ed. Zizi Papacharissi (New York: Routledge, 2011), 45.

97   Katherine Losse, *The Boy Kings: A Journey into the Heart of the Social Network* (New York: Free Press, 2012), 174.

98   Katherine Losse, "Feminism's Tipping Point: Who Wins from Leaning In?," *Dissent*, March 26, 2013, www.dissentmagazine.org/online_articles/feminisms-tipping-point-who-wins-from-leaning-in.

99   Sean Silverthorne, "Understanding Users of Social Networks," *Har-*

vard Business School Working Knowledge (blog), September 14, 2009, http://hbswk.hbs.edu/item/6156.html.

100 Cited in James P. Steyer, *Talking Back to Facebook: The Common Sense Guide to Raising Kids in the Digital Age* (New York: Scribner, 2012), 27. Nass discussed the research, which has not yet been published, with Steyer in a personal interview on May 19, 2011, at Stanford University.

101 Kelly Schryver, "Keeping Up Appearances," (unpublished honors thesis, Brown University, 2011). Cited in Steyer, *Talking Back*, 27.

102 Julie Zeilinger, *A Little F'd Up: Why Feminism Is Not a Dirty Word* (Berkeley, CA: Seal, 2012), 155.

103 Ibid.

104 Ibid.

105 Michael Stefanone, Derek Lackaff, and Devan Rosen, "We're All Stars Now: Reality Television, Web 2.0, and Mediated Identities," in *Hypertext '08: Proceedings of the Nineteenth Association for Computing Machinery (ACM) Conference on Hypertext and Hypermedia*, June 19–21, 2008, Pittsburgh, PA, 107, 108.

106 Jenna Wortham, "Facebook Made Me Do It," *New York Times*, June 15, 2013, www.nytimes.com/2013/06/16/sunday-review/facebook-made-me-do-it.html.

107 Claire Hoffman, "The Battle for Facebook," *Rolling Stone*, September 15, 2010, www.rollingstone.com/culture/news/the-battle-for-facebook-20100915.

108 Losse, *Boy Kings*, 127–28.

109 Danielle Wiener-Bronner, "Justin Doody's 'Rate BU' Web Site Angers Students," *Huffington Post*, December 8, 2010, www.huffingtonpost.com/2010/12/08/justin-doodys-rate-bu-sit_n_793248.html.

110 Gregory Gomer, "Updated: The Social Network Prompts Student to Reincarnate Facemash, BU-Style," *BostInno* (blog), December 8, 2010, http://bostinno.streetwise.co/2010/12/08/the-social-network-prompts-student-to-reincarnate-facemash-bu-style/, accessed April 30, 2013. The student's comment has since been removed.

111 Britney Fitzgerald, "One in Four Women Deliberately Posts Unflattering Pictures of Facebook Friends, Survey Finds," *Huffington Post*,

July 3, 2012, www.huffingtonpost.com/2012/07/03/one-in-four-women-unflattering-photos-facebook_n_1646499.html.

112   Clifford Nass, "Is Facebook Stunting Your Child's Growth?," *Pacific Standard*, April 23, 2012, www.psmag.com/culture/is-facebook-stunting-your-childs-growth-40577/.

113   Zeilinger, 157–8.

114   American Psychological Association, "Sexualization of Girls is Linked to Common Mental Health Problems in Girls and Women—Eating Disorders, Low Self-Esteem, and Depression; An APA Task Force Reports," press release, February 19, 2007, www.apa.org/news/press/releases/2007/02/sexualization.aspx.

115   Donna Freitas, *The End of Sex: How Hookup Culture Is Leaving a Generation Unhappy, Sexually Unfulfilled, and Confused About Intimacy* (New York: Basic Books, 2013), 81.

116   Ibid., 85.

117   Elizabeth L. Cline, *Overdressed: The Shockingly High Cost of Cheap Fashion* (New York: Portfolio/Penguin, 2012), 101.

118   Samantha M. Goodwin, Alyssa Van Denburg, Sarah K. Murnen, and Linda Smolak, " 'Putting On' Sexiness: A Content Analysis of the Presence of Sexualizing Characteristics in Girls' Clothing," *Sex Roles* 65, no. 1 (May 2011): 1–12, http://web.mit.edu/end_violence/docs/sexualizing-girls-clothing.pdf.

119   Daniel Watterberg, "Online Backlash Grows Against Victoria's Secret Racy Bright Young Things Collection for Teens," *Washington Times,* March 28, 2013, http://www.washingtontimes.com/news/2013/mar/28/online-backlash-grows-against-victorias-secret-rac/.

120   Christina M. Kelly, "One-Third of Tween Clothes are Sexy, Study Finds," Today.com, May 19, 2011, http://www.today.com/id/43081000/ns/today-today_health/t/one-third-tween-clothes-are-sexy-study-finds/#.U_IYGLxdfKk.

121   Goodwin et al, " 'Putting on' Sexiness," 3.

122   Jill, no last name, "Students at Stuyvesant Take Issue with Dress Code," *Feministe,* May 28, 2012, http://www.feministe.us/blog/archives/2012/05/28/students-at-stuyvesant-take-issue-with-dress-code/.

123   "Students Complain About New Dress Code at Stuyvesant," *School-*

Book, May 25, 2012, http://www.wnyc.org/story/302323-students-complain-about-new-dress-code-at-stuyvesant/. Students' comments about the dress code had been compiled by Tiffany Phan and published online in the *Stuyvesant Spectator,* the school's newspaper, on April 27, 2012, with the title "Redress the Dress Code," but that page is no longer active on the *Stuyvesant Spectator*'s website.

124   Jessica Valenti, "Targeting 'Slutty' Students," *The Nation,* June 8, 2012, www.thenation.com/blog/168298/targeting-slutty-students.

125   Ruth La Ferla, "Fit for a First Lady," *New York Times,* December 24, 2013, www.nytimes.com/2013/12/26/fashion/Chirlane-McCray-New-York-City-Bill-de-Blasio-wife-Anni-Kuan.html.

126   Amy Harmon, "Internet Gives Teenage Bullies Weapons to Wound From Afar," *New York Times,* August 26, 2004, www.nytimes.com/2004/08/26/us/internet-gives-teenage-bullies-weapons-to-wound-from-afar.html.

127   Dena Sacco, Rebecca Argudin, James Maguire, and Kelly Tallon, *Sexting: Youth Practices and Legal Implications,* Berkman Center Research Publication No. 2010–8, June 22, 2010, 4–6, http://ssrn.com/abstract=1661343.

128   danah boyd, "Teen Sexting and Its Impact on the Tech Industry" (talk given at the Read Write Web 2WAY Conference, New York, June 13, 2011), www.danah.org/papers/talks/2011/RWW2011.html.

129   J. J. Colao, "In Less Than Two Years, Snapchat Is an $860 Million Company," *Forbes,* June 24, 2013, www.forbes.com/sites/jjcolao/2013/06/24/snapchat-raises-60-million-from-ivp-at-800-million-valuation/.

130   LiJia Gong and Alina Hoffman, "Sexting and Slut-Shaming: Why Prosecution of Teen Self-Sexters Harms Women," *The Georgetown Journal of Gender and the Law* 13, no. 2 (Annual Review 2012): 578.

131   "2012 Sexting Legislation," National Conference of State Legislatures, December 14, 2012, www.ncsl.org/research/telecommunications-and-information-technology/sexting-legislation-2012.aspx.

132   Ibid., 577–589.

133   Ibid., 579.

134   Ibid.

135 Jessica Ringrose, Rosalind Gill, Sonia Livingstone, and Laura Harvey, "A Qualitative Study of Children, Young People and 'Sexting,'" National Society for the Prevention of Cruelty to Children (UK), May 2012, http://www.nspcc.org.uk/Inform/resourcesforprofessionals/sexualabuse/sexting-research_wda89260.html, 54.

136 Lawrence B. Finer and Jesse M. Philbin, "Sexual Initiation, Contraceptive Use, and Pregnancy Among Young Adolescents," *Pediatrics* 131, no. 5 (May 2013): http://pediatrics.aappublications.org/content/early/2013/03/27/peds.2012-3495.full.pdf+html. The authors are affiliated with the Guttmacher Institute.

137 Caroline Heldman and Lisa Wade, "Hook-Up Culture: Setting a New Research Agenda," *Sexuality Research and Social Policy* 7, no. 4 (December 2010): 323.

138 Ibid.

139 Kate Taylor, "Sex on Campus: She Can Play That Game, Too," *New York Times*, July 12, 2013, www.nytimes.com/2013/07/14/fashion/sex-on-campus-she-can-play-that-game-too.html.

140 Anna Latimer, "I Used to Give Out Sex Like Gold Star Stickers (And I'm Glad I Did)," *xoJane* (blog), January 15, 2013, www.xojane.com/sex/i-used-to-give-out-sex-like-gold-star-stickers-and-im-glad-i-did.

141 Zeilinger, *A Little F'd Up*, 213.

142 Ibid., 215.

143 Ibid., 213.

144 Taylor, "Sex on Campus."

145 Rachael D. Robnett and Campbell Leaper, "'Girls Don't Propose! Eew.': A Mixed-Methods Examination of Marriage Tradition Preferences and Benevolent Sexism in Emerging Adults," *Journal of Adolescent Research* 28, no. 1 (January 2013): 96–121.

146 Ibid., 100.

147 Ibid., 113.

148 Ibid., 115.

149 Freitas, *End of Sex*, 44.

150 Taylor, "Sex on Campus."

151 Deborah L. Tolman, *Dilemmas of Desire: Teenage Girls Talk about Sexuality* (Cambridge, MA: Harvard University Press, 2002), 2.

152 Ibid., 3.

153 Ibid., 22.

154 Taylor, "Sex on Campus."

155 Natalie Kitroeff, "In Hookups, Inequality Still Reigns," *New York Times*, November 12, 2013, http://well.blogs.nytimes.com/2013/11/11/women-find-orgasms-elusive-in-hookups/.

156 Ibid.

157 Taylor, "Sex on Campus."

158 Christopher P. Krebs, Christine H. Lindquist, Tara D. Warner, Bonnie S. Fisher, Sandra L. Martin, *The Campus Sexual Assault (CSA) Study* (National Institute of Justice, US Department of Justice, October 2007), www.ncjrs.gov/pdffiles1/nij/grants/221153.pdf.

159 William F. Flack Jr. et al., " 'The Red Zone': Temporal Risk for Unwanted Sex Among College Students," *Journal of Interpersonal Violence* 23, no. 9 (September 2008): 1184.

160 Taylor, "Sex on Campus."

161 Ibid.

162 Freitas, *End of Sex*, 124. She cites as her sources for these statistics Melina M. Bersamin, Deborah A. Fisher, Samantha Walker, Douglas L. Hill, and Joel W. Grube, "Defining Virginity and Abstinence: Adolescents' Interpretations of Sexual Behaviors," *Journal of Adolescent Health* 41, no. 2 (August 2007): 182–88; Jeremy Uecker, Nicole Angotti, and Mark Regnerus, "Going Most of the Way: 'Technical Virginity' Among American Adolescents," *Social Science Research* 37, no. 4 (December 2008): 1200–1215; Laura Duberstein Lindberg, Rachel Jones, and John Santelli, "Noncoital Activities Among Adolescents," *Journal of Adolescent Health* 43, no. 3 (September 2008): 231–38.

163 Milla Impola, "Hey Baby What's Your Number?," *The Daily Texan*, April, 16, 2013, www.dailytexanonline.com/life-and-arts/2013/04/16/hey-baby-whats-your-number.

164 Stephanie A. Sanders and June Machover Reinisch, "Would You Say You 'Had Sex' If . . . ?," *Journal of the American Medical Association* 281, no. 3 (January 20, 1999): 275–277.

165 Steve Landsburg, "Rush to Judgment," *The Big Questions* (blog), March 2, 2012, www.thebigquestions.com/2012/03/02/rush-to-judgment/.

166   "Joel Seligman Statement on Steve Landsburg's Blogs About Rush Limbaugh," Rochester.edu, March 6, 2012, www.rochester.edu/president/memos/2012/landsburg.html.

167   Cecile Richards, "Huckabee's 'Libido' Comment Chilling for Women," CNN.com, January 24, 2014, www.cnn.com/2014/01/24/opinion/richards-huckabee-comment/.

168   Guttmacher Institute, *Fact Sheet: Unintended Pregnancy in the United States*, December 2013, www.guttmacher.org/pubs/FB-Unintended-Pregnancy-US.html.

169   Guttmacher Institute, *State Policies in Brief: An Overview of Abortion Laws*, July 1, 2014, www.guttmacher.org/statecenter/spibs/spib_OAL.pdf.

170   Guttmacher Institute, *An Overview of Abortion in the United States: Slide and Lecture Presentation*, February 2014, www.guttmacher.org/presentations/ab_slides.html.

171   Guttmacher Institute, *Fact Sheet: Induced Abortion in the United States*, July 2014, www.guttmacher.org/pubs/fb_induced_abortion.html.

172   Sarah Smith, "I Didn't Even Know I Was Pregnant!," *Parenting*, March 2006, www.parenting.com/article/didnt-know-i-was-pregnant.

173   Andrea Grimes, "I Was a 'Prolife' Republican . . . Until I Fell in Love," *RH Reality Check* (blog), February 8, 2011, http://rhrealitycheck.org/article/2011/02/08/i-prolife-republicanuntilfell-love/.

174   Guttmacher Institute, *Fact Sheet: Induced Abortion*.

175   Ibid.

176   Andrew Meacham, "Sexting-Related Bullying Cited in Hillsborough Teen's Suicide," *Tampa Bay Times*, November 27, 2009, www.tampabay.com/news/humaninterest/sexting-related-bullying-cited-in-hillsborough-teens-suicide/1054895. All details of Witsell's suicide are from this comprehensive exposé.

177   Erik Eckholm and Katie Zezima, "Documents Detail a Girl's Final Days of Bullying," *New York Times*, April 8, 2010, http://www.nytimes.com/2010/04/09/us/09bully.html.

178   Erik Eckholm and Katie Zezima, "Questions for School On Bullying and a Suicide," *New York Times*, April 1, 2010, http://www.nytimes.com/2010/04/02/us/02bully.html?pagewanted=all.

179   Emily Bazelon, *Sticks and Stones: Defeating the Culture of Bullying*

and Rediscovering the Power of Character and Empathy (New York: Random House, 2013), 171–185.

180 M. L. Hatzenbuehler, "The Social Environment and Suicide Attempts in Lesbian, Gay, and Bisexual Youth," *Pediatrics* 127, no. 5 (May 2011): 896–903.

181 Bianca Bosker, "Jessica Logan Suicide: Parents of Dead Teen Sue School, Friends Over Sexting Harassment," *Huffington Post*, March 18, 2010, www.huffingtonpost.com/2009/12/07/jessica-logan-suicide-par_n_382825.html.

182 Bianca Bosker, "Alexis Pilkington Facebook Horror: Cyber Bullies Harass Teen Even After Suicide," *Huffington Post*, March 24, 2010, www.huffingtonpost.com/2010/03/24/alexis-pilkington-faceboo_n_512482.html.

183 "Rachel Ehmke, 13-Year-Old Minnesota Student, Commits Suicide After Months of Bullying," *Huffington Post*, May 8, 2012 www.huffingtonpost.com/2012/05/08/rachel-ehmke-13-year-old-_n_1501143.html.

184 Paul Elias, "Audrie Pott Suicide: New Girl Blamed in Teen Bullying Death," *Huffington Post*, July 29, 2013, www.huffingtonpost.com/2013/07/28/audrie-pott-suicide_n_3666573.html.

185 Vivian Yee, "On Staten Island, Relentless Bullying Is Blamed for a Teenage Girl's Suicide," *New York Times*, October 25, 2007, www.nytimes.com/2012/10/26/nyregion/suicide-of-staten-island-girl-is-blamed-on-bullying.html.

186 Elizabeth Plank, "In Defence of Amanda Todd," *Huffington Post United Kingdom*, October 15, 2012, www.huffingtonpost.co.uk/elizabeth-plank/in-defense-of-amanda-todd_b_1966479.html.

187 Katie J. M. Baker, "Yet Another Teenage Girl Killed Herself Thanks to Social Media Bullying," *Jezebel*, December 12, 2012, http://jezebel.com/5967905/yet-another-teenage-girl-killed-herself-thanks-to-social-media-slut+shaming.

188 Christine Pelisek, "Rehtaeh Parson's Best Friend Speaks Out," *Daily Beast*, April 27, 2013, www.thedailybeast.com/articles/2013/04/27/rehtaeh-parsons-s-best-friend-speaks-out.html.

189 Ben Fractenberg, "Classmates of Gabrielle Molina, 12-Year-Old Girl Who Committed Suicide, Rally Against Bullying," *Huffington Post*, May 29, 2013, www.huffingtonpost.com/2013/05/29/classmates-

of-gabrielle-molina-12-year-old-girl-who-committed-suicide-rally-against-bullying_n_3352286.html.

190   Heather R. Hlavka, "Normalizing Sexual Violence: Young Women Account for Harassment and Abuse," *Gender & Society* 28, no. 3 (June 2014): 8.

191   Ibid., 10.

192   Ibid., 1.

193   Ariel Levy, "Trial by Twitter," *The New Yorker*, August 5, 2013, www.newyorker.com/magazine/2013/08/05/trial-by-twitter.

194   Michele C. Black et al., *The National Intimate Partner and Sexual Violence Survey: 2010 Summary Report* (Atlanta, GA: Centers for Disease Control and Prevention, November 2011), www.cdc.gov/violenceprevention/pdf/nisvs_executive_summary-a.pdf, 1.

195   Roni Caryn Rabin, "Nearly 1 in 5 Women in U.S. Survey Say They Have Been Sexually Assaulted," *New York Times*, December 15, 2011, www.nytimes.com/2011/12/15/health/nearly-1-in-5-women-in-us-survey-report-sexual-assault.html.

196   Black, *National Intimate Partner and Sexual Violence Survey*, 2.

197   Ibid., 3.

198   Flack et al, "The Red Zone," 1184.

199   William F. Flack Jr. et al., "Risk Factors and Consequences of Unwanted Sex among University Students: Hooking Up, Alcohol, and Stress Response," *Journal of Interpersonal Violence* 22, no. 2 (February 2007): 147.

200   Ibid., 149.

201   Ibid., 153.

202   Ibid., 154.

203   Lisa Wade and Caroline Heldman, "Hooking Up and Opting Out: Negotiating Sex in the First Year of College," in *Sex for Life: From Virginity to Viagra, How Sexuality Changes Throughout Our Lives*, ed. Laura M. Carpenter and John DeLamater, (New York: NYU Press, 2012), 128–45. See pages 137–38.

204   Kimberly A. Lonsway, "Trying to Move the Elephant in the Living Room: Responding to the Challenge of False Rape Reports," *Violence Against Women* 16, no. 12 (December 2010): 1367.

205   James C. McKinley Jr., "Vicious Assault Shakes Texas Town,"

New York Times, March 8, 2011, www.nytimes.com/2011/03/09/us/09assault.html.

206 Paul Vercammen and Kyung Lah, "Prosecutors Weigh Appeal of 30-Day Rape Sentence in Montana," CNN.com, August 30, 2013, www.cnn.com/2013/08/28/justice/montana-teacher-rape-sentence/index.html.

207 Kathryn Abrams, "Sex Wars Redux: Agency and Coercion in Feminist Legal Theory," *Columbia Law Review* 95, no. 2 (March 1995): 306. Thank you to Shira Tarrant, PhD, for referring me to this legal note.

208 David Lisak et al., "False Allegations of Sexual Assault: An Analysis of Ten Tears of Reported Cases," *Violence Against Women* 16, no. 12 (December 2010): 1318.

209 Ibid., 1331.

210 Joanne Belknap, "Rape: Too Hard to Report and Too Easy to Discredit Victims," *Violence Against Women* 16, no. 12 (December 2010): 1335.

211 The White House Council on Women and Girls, *Rape and Sexual Assault: A Renewed Call to Action*, January 21, 2014, www.whitehouse.gov/sites/default/files/docs/sexual_assault_report_1-21-14.pdf.

212 Claire Gordon, "Nonconsensual Sex: How Colleges Rebranded Rape," America.AlJazeera.com, April 17, 2014, http://america.aljazeera.com/watch/shows/america-tonight/articles/2014/4/17/nonconsensual-sexwhenrapeisreworded.html.

213 Jessica Bennett, "The Title IX Complaint Against Yale," *Daily Beast*, April 2, 2011, www.thedailybeast.com/articles/2011/04/02/title-ix-complaint-against-yale-women-allege-a-culture-of-silence-on-campus.html.

214 Stephanie Spangler, *Yale University Report of Complaints of Sexual Misconduct Brought Forward from January 1, 2013 through June 30, 2013* (New Haven, CT: Yale University, July 31, 2013), http://provost.yale.edu/sites/default/files/files/FINAL_Jul2013_Report_Sexual_Misconduct_Complaints_7-31-13.pdf.

215 Margaret Hartmann, "Frat Email Explaining Women are 'Targets,' Not 'Actual People'," *Jezebel*, March 8, 2011, http://jezebel.com/5779905/usc-frat-guys-email-explains-women-are-targets-not-actual-people-like-us-men.

216 Mary Elizabeth Williams, "College Students Cheer Sex Abuse," *Salon*, September 5, 2013, www.salon.com/2013/09/05/college_ students_cheer_sex_abuse/; The Canadian Press, "Saint Mary's University Student Leader Sorry for Sexist Sexual Assault Chant," *Maclean's*, September 5, 2013, www2.macleans.ca/2013/09/05/ saint-marys-university-student-leader-sorry-for-sexist-sexual-assault-chant/.

217 Alex Barnett, open letter to Dartmouth President Phil Hanlon, September 29, 2013, www.dartmouthchange.org/alex-barnett/.

218 Alyssa Keehan, *Student Sexual Assault: Weathering the Perfect Storm* (United Educators, December 2011), www.ue.org/Libraries/Corporate/Student_Sexual_Assault_Weathering_the_Perfect_Storm. sflb.ashx.

219 Jessica Luther, "'We Felt Like We Were Above the Law': How the NCAA Endangers Women," *The Atlantic*, September 26, 2013, www.theatlantic.com/entertainment/archive/2013/09/we-felt-like-we-were-above-the-law-how-the-ncaa-endangers-women/ 280004/.

220 Liza Weisstuch, "Sexism in Rap Sparks Black Magazine to Say, 'Enough!,'" *Christian Science Monitor*, January 12, 2005, www.cs-monitor.com/2005/0112/p11s01-almp.html.

221 Laya Anasu, "Tyga Retained as Yardfest Headliner with Start Time Delayed," *Harvard Crimson*, April 9, 2012, www.thecrimson.com/ article/2013/4/9/tyga-retained-yardfest-concert/.

222 Tanzina Vega and James C. McKinley Jr., "Social Media, Pushing Reebok to Drop a Rapper," *New York Times*, April 13, 2013, www. nytimes.com/2013/04/13/arts/music/reebok-drops-rick-ross-after-social-media-protest.html.

223 White House Council on Women and Girls, *Rape and Sexual Assault*, 14.

224 Jennifer Steinhauer, "Navy Hearing in Rape Case Raises Alarm," *New York Times*, September 20, 2013, www.nytimes.com/2013/ 09/21/us/intrusive-grilling-in-rape-case-raises-alarm-on-military-hearings.html.

225 Alan D. Berkowitz, "Guidelines for Consent in Intimate Relationships," *Campus Safety & Student Development* 3, no. 4, (March/April 2002): 49, www.alanberkowitz.com/articles/consent.pdf.

226   Al Baker, "Sex Charges in Connecticut Are Dissected on the Internet," *New York Times*, March 20, 2013, www.nytimes.com/2013/03/21/nyregion/sexual-assault-charges-in-torrington-conn-are-dissected-in-social-media.html.

227   Vivian Yee, "Statutory Rape, Twitter and a Connecticut Town's Divide," *New York Times*, April 4, 2013, www.nytimes.com/2013/04/05/nyregion/generational-divide-in-torrington-conn-over-sex-assault-case.html.

228   Levy, "Trial by Twitter."

229   Ibid.

230   Ibid.

231   These Twitter comments and more, compiled by David Futrelle, a Chicago blogger, are available at http://wehuntedthemammoth.com/2013/03/18/today-in-rape-culture-more-steubenville-awfullness-on-twitter/.

232   Levy, "Trial by Twitter."

233   Portions of this chapter appeared in my *Huffington Post* article titled "Topless Women at SlutWalk Demand Respect: Is This the Right Tactic?" October 5, 2011, www.huffingtonpost.com/leora-tanenbaum/topless-women-at-slutwalk_b_993361.html.

234   Laura Stampler, "SlutWalk Sweeps the Nation," *Huffington Post*, June 20, 2011, www.huffingtonpost.com/2011/04/20/slutwalk-united-states-city_n_851725.html.

235   See the SlutWalk Toronto website: http://www.slutwalktoronto.com/.

236   "NYPD 'Rape Cops' Lawyer Told Off for Comparing Woman's Privates to 'Snapping Venus Fly Trap,'" *Daily Mail*, April 22, 2011, www.dailymail.co.uk/news/article-1379393/NYPD-rape-cops-lawyer-told-comparing-womans-privates-snapping-Venus-fly-trap.html.

237   Deborah Tuerkheimer, "SlutWalking in the Shadow of the Law," *Minnesota Law Review* 98, no. 4 (2014): 1453–1511.

238   "Surprise Welcome: Topless Protesters Confront Putin in Germany," *Spiegel Online*, April 8, 2011, www.spiegel.de/international/europe/putin-visibly-amused-by-topless-femen-protest-in-germany-a-893128.html.

239   Quoted in Nona Willis Aronowitz and Emma Bee Bernstein,

Girldrive: Criss-Crossing America, Redefining Feminism (Berkeley, CA: Seal, 2009), 44.

240 Adam D. Galinsky et al., "The Reappropriation of Stigmatizing Labels: Implications for Social Identity," *Research on Managing Groups and Teams*, 5 (2003): 221–56; Robin Brontsema, "A Queer Revolution: Reconceptualizing the Debate Over Linguistic Reclamation," *Colorado Research in Linguistics* 17, no. 1 (June 2004), www. colorado.edu/ling/CRIL/Volume17_Issue1/paper_BRONTSEMA. pdf.

241 The complete letter is available on the Black Women's Blueprint website: www.blackwomensblueprint.org/?s=slutwalk&op.x=-927&op.y=-48

242 Aura Bogado, "SlutWalk: A Stroll Through White Supremacy," *To the Curb* (blog), May 13, 2011, http://tothecurb.wordpress. com/2011/05/13/slutwalk-a-stroll-through-white-supremacy/.

243 Crunktastic [Brittney C. Cooper], "I Saw the Sign But Did We Really Need a Sign?: SlutWalk and Racism," *Crunk Feminist Collective*, October 6, 2011, www.crunkfeministcollective.com/2011/10/06/i-saw-the-sign-but-did-we-really-need-a-sign-slutwalk-and-racism/.

244 Ibid.

245 Rodriguez makes the posters available for free as downloads through her website, www.favianna.com. Her statement is available on www. favianna.com.

246 Leora Tanenbaum, *Slut! Growing Up Female with a Bad Reputation* (New York: HarperPerennial, 2000), 113.

247 Judith Butler, *Excitable Speech: A Politics of the Performative* (New York: Routledge, 1997), 2.

248 Ibid., 16–18.

249 Ibid., 100.

250 Randall Kennedy, *Nigger: The Strange Career of a Troublesome Word* (New York: Vintage, 2003), 33–35.

251 Ibid., 39.

252 Ibid., 138.

253 Jabari Asim, *The N Word: Who Can Say It, Who Shouldn't, and Why* (Boston: Houghton Mifflin, 2007), 224–45.

254 Butler, 38.

255 A transcript of Friedman's Boston SlutWalk speech is available on *Feministing* at http://feministing.com/2011/05/09/you-can-call-us-

that-name-but-we-will-not-shut-up/; a video of the speech is available on YouTube at www.youtube.com/watch?v=-oiuXpMQL4E.

256   Levy, "Trial by Twitter."

257   Andrea Peyser, "Subway Jerk Off the Hook," *New York Post*, April 19, 2006, http://nypost.com/2006/04/19/subway-jerk-off-the-hook/.

258   Tracy Connor and Alison Gendar, "Restaurant Boss in Raw-Tipsters. Is He Subway Flasher?," *Daily News*, August 29, 2005, www.nydailynews.com/archives/news/restaurant-boss-raw-tipsters-subway-flasher-article-1.586582.

259   Katie Haegele, "Street Sweepers: Hollaback! and the Global Surge in Antiharassment Activism," *Bitch*, Fall 2011, 34.

260   Figures on the endowments of the wealthiest universities can be found here: www.statisticbrain.com/college-endowment-rankings/.

261   "From Survivor to Victim," *Raped At Tufts University*, http://www.rapedattufts.info/?page_id=96.

262   Michael Winerip, "Stepping Up to Stop Sexual Assault," *New York Times*, February 9, 2014, www.nytimes.com/2014/02/09/education/edlife/stepping-up-to-stop-sexual-assault.html.

263   Ruth Tam, "Activists Applaud White House Effort to Fight Campus Rapes," *Washington Post*, January 25, 2014, www.washingtonpost.com/blogs/she-the-people/wp/2014/01/25/activists-applaud-white-house-effort-to-fight-campus-rapes/; Kayla Webley, "Big Shame on Campus," *Marie Claire*, November 2013, www.marieclaire.com/world-reports/big-shame-on-campus.

264   The petition is available at http://change.org/standwithsurvivors.

265   "Slut Shaming and Why It's Wrong," YouTube video, posted by "Sarah Sloan MacLeod," August 20, 2011, www.youtube.com/watch?v=SXH2K7OC37s.

266   "How Slut Shaming Becomes Victim Shaming," YouTube video, posted by "chescaleigh" [Franchesca Ramsey], December 14, 2012, www.youtube.com/watch?v=1l3h8fzv-BM. A full transcript of the video appears on *Racialicious* at www.racialicious.com/2012/12/19/video-franchesca-ramseys-powerful-how-slut-shaming-becomes-victim-blaming/.

267   "Re: JennaMarbles' 'Slut Edition.,'" YouTube video, posted by "lacigreen" [Laci Green], December 13, 2012, www.youtube.com/watch?v=CCw2MzKjpoo.

268   "Sluts," YouTube video, posted by "haleyghoover" [Hayley G. Hoover], December 13, 2012, www.youtube.com/watch?v=YzB_O_B7-_Y.

269   Alicia W. Stewart, "#IAmJada: When Abuse Becomes a Teen Meme," CNN.com, July 18, 2014, http://www.cnn.com/2014/07/18/living/jada-iamjada-teen-social-media/.

270   Sara Stewart, "'Slut: The Play' Debuts at NYC Fringe Festival This Fall," *New York Post*, August 19, 2013, http://nypost.com/2013/08/19/slut-the-play-debuts-at-nyc-fringe-festival-this-fall/; Sarah Begley, "Gloria Steinem's Favorite New Play," *Daily Beast*, September 27, 2013, www.thedailybeast.com/witw/articles/2013/09/27/gloria-steinem-s-favorite-new-play-tackles-teen-sexual-assault.html.

INDEX

ABOUT THE AUTHOR

Author photograph by Ryan Brown

LEORA TANENBAUM is the author of five books about girls' and women's lives, on topics including the movement of women rising up against sexism in faith communities, competition among women from the boardroom to the delivery room, and the agony of wearing high-heeled shoes. Her book *Slut! Growing Up Female with a Bad Reputation* (HarperPerennial, 2000) is a staple in gender and women's studies and sociology courses on college campuses around the United States. She has been a guest on *Oprah*, *The Today Show*, and National Public Radio.

Tanenbaum is the senior writer and editor for the Planned Parenthood Federation of America and for its advocacy and political branch, the Planned Parenthood Action Fund. She lives in New York City with her two teenage sons. She enjoys reading in print and writing with a pencil . . . though you can follow her on Twitter @LeoraTanenbaum or visit her website at www.leoratanenbaum.com.

BOOKS BY LEORA TANENBAUM
From Harper Perennial

SLUT!
Growing Up Female with a Bad Reputation

Available in Paperback

Girls may be called "sluts" for any number of reasons, including being outsiders, early developers, victims of rape, and targets of others' revenge. An important account of the lives of these young women, and the book that coined the term "slut-bashing," *Slut!* weaves together powerful oral histories of girls and women who finally overcame their sexual labels with a cogent analysis of the underlying problem of sexual stereotyping. Author Leora Tanenbaum herself was labeled a slut in high school. The confessional article she wrote for *Seventeen* about the experience caused a sensation and led her to write this book, opening up debate on the subject of slut-bashing for the first time.

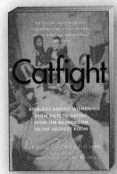

CATFIGHT
Rivalries Among Women—from Diets to Dating, from the Boardroom to the Delivery Room

Available in Paperback

Women often behave toward one another in sneaky, underhanded, ruthlessly competitive ways. *Catfight* is a remarkably researched and insightful foray into the American woman's world of aggression, rivalry, and competition. Tanenbaum draws on real-life examples and the most important studies to date in psychology, human aggression, psychoanalytic theory, and social movements to uncover the pressures that leave women regarding one another as adversaries rather than allies.

I AM NOT A SLUT
Slut-Shaming in the Age of the Internet

Available in Paperback and eBook

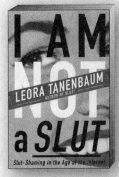

Popular culture encourages young women to express themselves sexually. Yet when they do, they are derided as "sluts." To tackle the contradictory demand of being sexy but not slutty, girls often create an "experienced" identity on social media—even if they're not sexually active—while ironically referring to themselves and their friends as "sluts." But this strategy can become a weapon used against young women in the hands of peers who circulate rumors and innuendo—elevating age-old slut-shaming to deadly levels, with suicide among bullied teenage girls becoming increasingly common. Now, Leora Tanenbaum advances and re-envisions the ground-breaking argument she began with *SLUT!*, sharing new insights and research specifically geared toward the issues of the digital age.

Available wherever books are sold.